1

Shattered Reflections of a Christian
Biases, Burdens, and Blessings

Disclaimer

This book in no way serves as an authority on Christian behavior or a replacement for Biblical principles. These are mere opinions and suggestions to help you to start thinking proactively.

Therefore, should you have conflict in your marriage or family life, please consult a Pastor or Minister of a Bible-based church for guidance.

Additionally, the author wishes to express that the opinions and points are not exhaustive, nor are they final. Also, the author categorically states that her intention is not to malign, hurt or be disrespectful to any person, or to discount that people are walking their own journey and therefore, it is not the author's intent to disrespect anyone's religious belief or relationship with God; nor is the author's intent to disrespect any community or country.

Also, because the author is not a licensed psychologist or an attorney, therefore nothing in this book is to be considered as counseling advice, legal advice or counselor-client, or attorney-client relationship. And, remember that laws and court decisions vary from locality to locality, and are always changing. If you have a legal question, please speak with an attorney for legal advice.

Additionally, please note that the internet is not a reliable source for Biblical principles and teachings and should be used sparingly for research but should not be considered an authority. For Biblical conflicts, teachings, and principles, consult with two or three Biblical clergies in your area.

Copyright Page

Bev Gilliard, LLC
P.O. Box 361969
Decatur, Georgia 30036

Author: Bev Gilliard
Publisher: Bev Gilliard, LLC
Cover Design: Paul Gilliard
ISBN: 9781794186002
Imprint: Independently published
Printed in the United States of America

Table of Contents

Dedication

This book is dedicated to all struggling Christians to helping you grow in your walk with Our Lord and Savior Jesus Christ! If you are seeking renewal, rejuvenation, and self-cleansing of your psychological, emotional, or spiritual being this book is dedicated to you, and to those who are looking for answers, responses, and guidance to commit to a disciplined, self-reflective life.

Though the journey may be gruesome, though you may get weary, this book will hopefully help you to feel safe enough to express your true feelings, feel confident in sharing the intricate stories of your Christian journey, be able to ask questions, and deal with the sufferings and disappointments life deals you from time to time.

By holding on to the promises of God, His covenant with you, that He will never leave you or forsake you and will one day return and take you up to Heaven with Him, you will always have hope.

Bev,
Your Sister in Christ

Acknowledgments

Glory to God, in all things I acknowledge God as Lord and Savior of All. 2 John 1: 1-13 (KJV), "[1] The elder unto the elect lady and her children, whom I love in the truth; and not I only, but also all they that have known the truth; [2] For the truth's sake, which dwelleth in us, and shall be with us forever. [3] Grace be with you, mercy, and peace, from God the Father, and from the Lord Jesus Christ, the Son of the Father, in truth and love. [4] I rejoiced greatly that I found of thy children walking in truth, as we have received a commandment from the Father. [5] And now I beseech thee, lady, not as though I wrote a new commandment unto thee, but that which we had from the beginning, that we love one another. [6] And this is love, that we walk after his commandments. This is the commandment, That, as ye have heard from the beginning, ye should walk in it. [7] For many deceivers are entered into the world, who confess not that Jesus Christ is come in the flesh. This is a deceiver and an antichrist. [8] Look to yourselves, that we lose not those things which we have wrought, but that we receive a full reward. [9] Whosoever transgresseth, and abideth not in the doctrine of Christ, hath not God. He that abideth in the doctrine of Christ, he hath both the Father and the Son. [10] If there come any unto you, and bring not this doctrine, receive him not into your house, neither bid him God speed: [11] For he that biddeth him God speed is partaker of his evil deeds. [12] Having many things to write unto you, I would not write with paper and ink: but I trust to come unto you, and speak face to face, that our joy may be full. [13] The children of thy elect sister greet thee. Amen.

This Biblical scripture is essential in context and relevant to this piece of work. If you use God's word, you must accept all God's words from cover to cover in the Bible without changing one word, without twisting God's word or intent to fit your narratives, and you must not contradict the word of God. 2 John 1:8 -11 is a good wrap up of this analogy.

When you open the word of God, you don't do so because you are good, you are doing so to learn how to be good.

There are some members of society who believes God is a God of love, so when they are being chastised for disobedience and scripture is used to show them "Thus saith the Lord," their go to is that God is loving and Bible verses should not be used to harm. Or in other words, what they are really saying is, "Christians are using Bible verses that are cutting into my soul." But that is precisely what Bible verses do.

Bible verses 'Comforts,' 'Challenge,' 'Change,' 'Condemns,' and 'Chastises' you. And, you can 'Receive' it, 'Respond' to it, 'Repent' because of it, or you can 'Reject' it and suffer the consequences, which is usually death.

The most likely thing to trip up the Christian in their walk with Christ is that they fail to accept the whole truth of God's word. Many professed Christians still want to justify their bad behaviors and disobedience believing that God is a loving God and discounting that God will chastise those He loves they twist God's intention to fit what makes them comfortable, and worst of all, they buckle to the world and compromise in fear of retaliation and retribution. They have no spine when it comes to standing up boldly for God and speaking the truth with conviction.

However, when the clouds open and the Lord returns every person, rich, poor, black, white, brown, weak, strong, will all face Romans 6:23 (KJV), "[23] For the wages of sin is death; but the gift of God is eternal life through Jesus Christ our Lord."

You have the right to choose how you live. We are all sinners, but you can choose to be obedient to the word of God and work each day to turn from your sinful ways, even the ones that haunt you daily!

NOTE: "Any name used to address God is capitalized, regardless of grammar and is a personal preference of the author. Therefore, words pointing to God are written as God, Savior, Lord, Master Potter, Healer, Provider, Him, His, You, or Your, are intentional." Bev Gilliard.

Introduction

Growing up, I can recall sitting on the veranda and watching the birds in flight and wondering how those little wings propel them through the air or how come they do not fall from the sky. I thought, "How amazing is God?"

As I watch the birds, deep in thought, I listened attentively to the tall grass singing as the wind tosses them to and fro, and I saw the butterflies dancing around them trying to find that perfect landing place. Everything working in ideal unison just as God has designed. My loyalty to God was solid, and my version of the gospel was one of love and belonging.

But then I reflected on God, and His infinite goodness towards us, and I analyzed man trying to understand why man, God's beloved and most precious creation, His masterpiece, is but a shattered reflection of a Christian. King David asks in Psalm 8:4-6 King James Version (KJV), "⁴ What is a man, that thou art mindful of him? And the son of man, that thou visitest him? For Thou hast made him a little lower than the angels, and hast crowned him with glory and honor. ⁶ Thou madest him to have dominion over the works of Thy hands; thou hast put all things under his feet:" Here you see how much value God has placed on man. "This is a marvelous thing, that God thinks upon men, and remembers them continually." John Calvin, 1509-1564. God whose glory is so surpassingly great remembers the only creation that disrespects Him, to a lavish man with the highest admiration.

I always stood confident in my relationship with the Lord and my Christian trajectory. I could be laying in my bed, or take part in church activities, and rejoiced in the life I was living. I was serving Jesus Christ no matter where the moment found me and being one that never asked for much, was always satisfied with living the abundant life God promised. But suddenly, I glanced around and found that my youth has faded. I can no longer see the little girl that sat on the veranda and enjoyed the beauty of God's handy work. No longer can I enjoy the simple things in life that once gave me such joy.

Here I am, at the brink of an abyss peering over the edge of my demise, looking death in its face. A lifespan of abuse I had endured has now taken hold of my mind, and freedom seems only a jump away. Life has beaten me down; I am now weary, tired of the fighting and struggling; Tired of being the good Christian to an ungrateful world. Beaten up both physically and emotionally and blinded of anything good that life has to offer. All I now see is the end of my breaking point. My bones ache, my nerves shot, physically and mentally drained. I am weary, worn down, and worn out. Freedom from constant harassment, misuse, abuse, and misery seemed my best possibility and was looking better and better.

Besides God, my Pastor and my husband are the only two people that I felt safe talking to, but both had life happening to them at that moment.

So, I began to agonize of the only two choices that seemed open to me: fundamentalism or agnosticism, and neither alternative was particularly attractive. Feeling antagonistic, I began questioning my relationship with God, though I was not asserting or believing that there is no God, however wondering at that moment if God loves me, where is He right now?

It was ridiculous, I say this without any malice, but growing up, questioning God was inappropriate, and my sitting in the middle of traffic was not the time to be doing so. I realized that part of maturing and growing in Christ, I do not need to be afraid to challenge the uncertainty of agnosticism if it means strengthening my relationship with God. God said, Isaiah 1:18 (KJV), "18 Come now, and let us reason together, saith the LORD: though your sins are as scarlet, they shall be as white as snow; though they are red like crimson, they shall be as wool."

Still, my firm, rigid, and dogmatic faith in God told me it was wrong even to wonder, and its power over my life was swirling around in my head adding more guilt. I heard the words of Thomas Aquinas who wisely noted, "To one who has faith, no explanation is necessary. To one without faith, no explanation is possible." For me, my faith is not just an emotion or notion that I apply when times get rough; faith is an essential element to my life, my being, and my relationship with God. Faith is what helps to get me through my times of darkness, give me strength in times of weakness, and helps to replenish the abundance in my spirit, heart, and mind. Also, faith overrides hopelessness when doubt tries to stifle my belief in God and my vision of greater things. Without faith, I would be nothing.

Therefore, I could not go on questioning the existence of God. Flashes of all the times He has saved me, the evidence of Him dying on the cross and working in my life overwhelmed my soul. I had the evidence all the times God had shown up and shown out for me. Times when I never deserved God's time or attention, He was there for me. Times when I did not ask Him for help, He still showed up. Times when all I deserved was a chastisement, but instead God showed me, love. Times when I was hungry, and He fed me and provided me with abundance. Times when the bill was due, the bank account said zero, but God delayed the payment or miraculously paid the bill. Times when everyone told me, no, but He said, "Not so fast." Times when I should have died, but He said, "No, I am not finished with her, I still need my daughter." Evidence, swirling in my head, tugging at my heart as I rehearsed in my mind what God's presence in my life meant over my lifespan pain.

Then I questioned my reality, that if I, as a creation of God, love God as much as I say I do, why am I not allowing Him to be God in my life right now? Has He not saved me time and time again? What or Who in this life is worth me dying for and disappointing God? What right do I have to end a life that belongs to Him?

Moreover, because I believe in the cross, and the vastness and intricacies of Creation story, my experience is more precious than it was before. The size of my faith in God is now impossible for me to understand. Just knowing that I am fearfully and wonderfully made in God's image, and that Jesus died for my sins, and having God tells me in (Isaiah 55:9, KJV), " [9] For as the heavens are higher than the earth, so are my ways higher than your ways, and my thoughts than your thoughts." All I need to focus on is that God has done more for me than I deserve, more than I will ever be able to comprehend, and more than I will ever be able to thank Him for, therefore, I must live for Him and live to serve Him.

Faced with my current reality that I was stopped in the middle of traffic waiting for someone to hit me, I could feel good and evil tugging at me. It is a causticity of allegorical proportions that as classic sighted as I am, I could no longer see the beauty of the world and was confident a blind man could "see" to describe its beauty.

Momentarily, it seemed like I had no choice but to wait for death to pull me over the edge. Now here I am, waiting for death to come. Without faith, expecting that things would turn out all right no matter what the situation would have made things seem impossible. However, my incredible faith was not to be underestimated. Faith would not allow me to continue to doubt God's love for me or His significance in my life.

Then I concluded, "God loves you despite you; you better call out to God like you did many times before and ask for mercy."

So, I cried out, "Lord save me from myself." I began to talk to God and discussing my issues with honesty and asking Him all sorts of questions I had, some that I knew the response to, some I did not want to know the answer to, and some I just wanted to use to justify how I was feeling.

Suddenly I felt the arms of God wrapped around me, and I can hear God talking to me and telling me how much He loved me. Feeling most likely a stranger in His presence at that moment, I leaned in and laid in His arms to hide from the darkness. Attuned to God and His love for me, my heightened sensitivity toward the spiritual world, and bubbling over with joyousness and a sense of wonderment, I wholeheartedly embraced life once again.

14

God did not brusquely brush my question aside, no, He whispered deep into my soul, the answers to all the questions I had. Then God reminded me of the story of a father who sought deliverance for his son who was unable to speak and had seizures. The man said to Jesus, "If you can do anything, take pity on us and help us." Jesus put it back on the father, and you can see a powerful, joyful faith at work. Jesus said, "If you can." Everything is possible for him who believes." The father only needed to have faith the size of a mustard seed that Jesus could cure his son (Mark 9:17-27). The answers to my question of where God was at that moment began to flood my head and were made crystal clear.

Heartbreakingly, vulnerable, and tearful one minute, joyful and smiling the next, I accepted God was stirring inside me. Being exposed to questioning my relationship with God at one of the most troubling times in my life, only served to strengthen that relationship I have with God, and for that I praise God. I was stunned at my behavior and for allowing myself to think negative thoughts of destruction. There is nothing or no one in this world worth dying for, and at once I felt a sense of peace, and I started to dry the tears from my eyes.

I now know it is okay to examine the fundamentals of my faith, my painful experiences, and my naive view that Christians do not must worry about suicide if they have a strong belief or relationship with God. Also, I came to realize that my biases and burdens can shake my foundations if I do not keep a grip on the hem of Jesus' garment.

Additionally, without a doubt, having faith the size of a mustard seed is genuinely enough to save us in your darkest hours and from the constancy of negativity that overwhelms us, sweeping through your life.

I sighed a sigh of relief for my trepidatiousness about what, if anything, might change once I was gone and started to focus on what I can improve as I continue to live on. I always gage myself as to how much of an asset I must be to Christ because I am such a massive liability, undeserving of His abundant mercies and blessings upon my life.

After much prayer and soul-searching, I realize how much of a mess I was. My whole life was shaken to its core. The months that followed, I repeatedly cried out, "Lord, help me, help me, Lord." It was all that I could manage to muster up, and death kept trying to pull me out of my bed in the middle of the night. The pain in my belly was excruciating; I wanted the agony to end. I continued to pray, and cry, and beg and cry, and the pain, at especially at night, in the moment of silent reflections, the [pain continued to be excruciating.

After much tears and prayers, my faith is strengthened, and my relationship with God became more robust. I realized I love the Lord too much to end a life that He has so graciously given me.

As time passed so did the pain. It became less intense, and soon it stopped. I grew surer of my relationship with God, and that loving Him was enough, despite what the world says, despite who pointed fingers, despite how I was viewed, and despite any abuse. I survived a test, and now I have a testimony to add to the hundreds of proofs of God showing undeserving wretch mercy.

Now, at times I think I am just as Paul, one untimely born, thrust into a world way ahead of my talents, skills, and abilities. Like Paul, I too believed myself to be the chiefest of sinners. But Paul could not have heard of me, that I am worst and yet God refuse to leave me alone and forget about me.

Still, do I dare to compare myself to this apostle in the sinful state I am in? There was just one problem: I no longer felt I could preach the same gospel as Paul. But Yes, I dare to compare myself only in the sense of my being bold to share my faults to honor God, and in understanding my emotional attachment to God while recognizing my weaknesses. That my interactions with people will always leave me feeling unloved and insecure at times and can leave me filled with biases that burden me that I can not sees the blessings God has on my life. Even the simple things like feeling the air on my face that is a blessing I tend to overlook.

Additionally, in the grand scheme of things, God continues to send other people into my life that are safe and helpful.

16

Going forth, instead of making God in my image, I will live my life reflecting the image of God and share His goodness with the world. Because, to get to a place of Christian perfection, you must first reflect and change the things of this world that are preventing you from being in perfect harmony with God.

So, recognizing and accepting we all have biases, and burdens that prevent us from seeing the blessings of a gracious and infinite God, the question is, "Why are you filled with biases, and burdens, that you cannot see your blessings that God bestowed upon you before you were born?" Why are you living such a shattered life, being a mere reflection of the Christian, you ought to be? Hopefully, as you read this book, you can find the answer that clearly shows our biases—at least our preferences partly explain why we as Christians can arrive at different interpretations of the exact teachings of Biblical truth.

Also, while you have your own biases, as a Christian, you will suffer biases in the church from other Christians which closely resembles the traditional bias Christians experience at the hands of non-Christians.

Life happens and is happening. If you were to look at your Christian self in a mirror, you would see more inadequacies than perfection reflecting at you. Many times, this one-way observation keeps you mostly looking at your burdens, and rarely at the blessings.

Also, if you are not attentive to your Christian walk, your faith can stretch to where it snaps and break, it can be challenged to where you question the existence of God, and it can change your relationship in the blink of an eye to where you let go of God, or want to let go of God, but don't.

Additionally, time is no longer drawing nigh; you are living at the end of days and should be prepared, not getting prepared.

Noticeably, everybody is identifying as a Christian. Perhaps because this is a significant distinction that separates us from the world and God is more magnified than He has ever been. However, how many know what it means to identify as a Christian? What sets you apart from the world? Do you know God or only know of God? What is your relationship with God? What preparation are you making to make Heaven your home? What are you doing to overcome your shattered reflection, address your biases, rid yourselves of the unnecessary burdens most of us carry around and learn to focus only on the blessings so you can be in perfect harmony with God and His promises daily?

You must be wary, even suspicious, of anyone who claims to have grasped God's real presence of God intellectually, cognitively, within a mental construct in some simple manner with absolute certainty but does not show they have a personal relationship with God. The heart and soul of the person seem dark. Another caveat is in order here. Genuine, authentic Christian can and should doubt his or her inward, spiritual condition while, at the same time, not question God's love, His forgiveness, and the gift of the Holy Spirit.

Your faith and inward assurance should not be in man; as vital as you may think they are. Claim no real ambivalence toward true doctrine—even as you disposed to admit ambiguity in them. Express no uncertainty within yourself about the God of your salvation, no real doubt as a personal posture or disposition (even when attacks of the enemy come at you about Jesus Christ as your Savior and Lord.

There is significantly more that could be said, and indeed, many more issues that need to be addressed to make this complete.

Therefore, I do not want to leave you with the notion that there are no difficulties or rebuts in this view (as in any viewpoint). However, I do not want you to be swayed by what people think of you, only be influenced by what God thinks of you.

There is shelter, clarity, and healing for whatever your concerns, confusion, and pain are in "Thus saith the Lord." Jesus said in Proverbs 4:7 (KJV), "7 Wisdom is the principal thing; therefore, get wisdom: and with all thy getting get understanding." But you must not only be a hearer, but you must also be a doer. James, the half-brother of Jesus, said James 1: 22-25 (KJV), "22 But be ye doers of the word, and not hearers only, deceiving your own selves. 23 For if any be a hearer of the word and not a doer, he is like unto a man beholding his natural face in a glass:

18

[24] For he beholdeth himself, and goeth his way, and straightway forgetteth what manner of man he was. [25] But whoso looketh into the perfect law of liberty, and continueth therein, he being not a forgetful hearer, but a doer of the work, this man shall be blessed in his deed." It is for this reason; I like honest, harsh, pragmatic words with Biblical proof that cut to the heart of the matter and being guided by 1 Corinthians 14:37 (KJV), "[37] If any man think himself to be a prophet, or spiritual, let him acknowledge that the things that I write unto you are the commandments of the Lord." Because, while you were yet a sinner, Jesus died but we are still burdened, and He has supplied everything in His word to set us free and give us a life of health, wealth, happiness, and joy. Christians need to be bold with tough skins for the worst of times yet to come, or you risk being shaken from God. So, please excuse my unusual frankness in these words as I attempt to address issues of the human condition that is plaguing us all and the potential risk we all face of missing out on Heaven if our behaviors and relationship are not in alignment with the Word of God and the things of God.

The Problem of Bias

The greatest insult to Christ is to believe that your sins are still not forgiven. That is why I am an active evangelist of the truth that your entire lifetime of sins has been paid for because that is what His sufferings have done for us. He took the fullness of the punishment so that you can enjoy the fullness of forgiveness. You are entirely forgiven of an entire lifetime of sins!

Purportedly, Christianity that is bias based can incite unrest, influence repentance, or propagate fear, defame character, and does not lead followers willingly from sin, and is therefore not of God. Only God's faithful followers have the momentum to live a life of example for His people——to come out of the world and overcome sin. Also, obedient Christians teach the way to obey God's laws or develop His holy, righteous character and refrain from judging others.

You are all familiar with your tendency to be more tolerant of your moral failings than the moral failings of others. When you do something wrong, you rationalize your behavior. However, when someone else does something wrong, you condemn them. You have a hard time being objective when you have a stake in the outcome. Even when you are trying to be as exact as possible, if you are already on a particular "side," this can hinder your ability to view the situation objectively. This is a dangerous road; many terrible injustices are rationalized in the name of "God's kingdom." Jesus Christ is still all over the gospel, and power without accountability is dangerous. Therefore, it is important to be impartial. Isaiah 57:15 (KJV), "15 For thus saith the high and lofty One that inhabiteth eternity, whose name is Holy; I dwell in the high and holy place, with him also that is of a contrite and humble spirit, to revive the spirit of the humble, and to revive the heart of the contrite ones".

However, because the unconscious nature of bias generally occurs outside of your awareness, it can make it especially difficult to recognize and correct through your conscious efforts in evaluating your morality which leads you to overestimate your objectivity. You tend to evaluate yourselves favorably as being less biased and more ethical than others.

The problem is, this bias also extends to family members and friends of your in-group and those close to us. You assess your in-group more positively, and you are likelier to excuse unethical behavior by an in-group member. You judge other people instead of having God use us as His vessel to excuse the same behavior committed by someone outside the group.

However, hypothetically speaking, when you are influenced by bias in a case you do not have much hope when you have a real interest at stake. Bias doesn't just affect your final decisions; it can permeate your whole judgment, and you will find yourself having a hard time being objective about a range of judgments and in a variety of contexts.

Also, the effects of bias can continue beyond your initial evaluations. When another person's morally questionable behavior benefits you, you give it your stamp of approval and discount what God says.

However, you must seek the truth, to be fair, and honest in your dealings, and to carry out justice for all parties.

Similarly, it is in the broader interest of the Christian community people should not view your actions as trying to sweep things under the rug, this does real damage, not only to your church but to the entire Christian community. Enough said!

Despite any bias you may have, the most damaging and divisive thing in the church and that is a dangerous slope is a disbelief that God exists; And, to do so comes with "dire consequences!"

The Atheist Mindset

The atheist mindsets are a general set of beliefs that the existence of God, or any diety for that matter, is faust.

Understand, atheism is not a religion or part of any denomination or any religious belief, only a held lack of knowledge about the existence of God; Their mindset is unconvinced that God is the Creator, Lord, and King and they refuse to search for the truth about God's existence. Psalms 10:4 (KJV)The wicked, through the pride of his countenance, will not seek [after God]: God [is] not in all his thoughts. John 3:15, 18-21 (KJV), "15 That whosoever believeth in him should not perish, but have eternal life. 18 He that believeth on him is not condemned: but he that believeth not is condemned already because he hath not believed in the name of the only begotten Son of God. 19 And this is the condemnation, that light is come into the world, and men loved darkness rather than light because their deeds were evil. 20 For every one that doeth evil hateth the light, neither cometh to the light, lest his deeds should be reproved. 21 But he that doeth truth cometh to the light, that his deeds may be made manifest, that they are wrought in God."

Also, their morality and belief system is arbitrary under the word of God. Malachi 3: (KJV), "13 Your words have been stout against me, saith the LORD. Yet ye say, What have we spoken so much against thee? 14 Ye have said, It is vain to serve God: and what profit is it that we have kept his ordinance, and that we have walked mournfully before the LORD of hosts? 15 And now we call the proud happy; yea, they that work wickedness are set up; yea, they that tempt God are even delivered. 16 Then they that feared the LORD spake often one to another: and the LORD hearkened, and heard it, and a book of remembrance was written before him for them that feared the LORD, and that thought upon his name. 17 And they shall be mine, saith the LORD of hosts, in that day when I make up my jewels; and I will spare them, as a man spareth his own son that serveth him. [18] Then shall ye return, and discern between the righteous and the wicked, between him that serveth God and him that serveth him not."

Atheism - that large and consistent immoral theory could not exist without reference to a belief in God. They do need God as the source for all morality, value, or order in the universe; because philosophy and science are capable of doing that. Also, Jeremiah 1:5 (KJV), " 5 Before I formed thee in the belly I knew thee, and before thou camest forth out of the womb I sanctified thee, and I ordained thee a prophet unto the nations."

Still, many atheists believe in the writings of Friedrich Wilhelm Nietzsche, an atheist who was mentally ill. They believed that Nietzsche didn't mean that there was a God who had actually died, instead of that the idea of one had, and the idea of a universe that was governed by physical laws and not by divine providence was now his reality; very contradictory in itself. For those who is believed Nietzsche did not believe in God, where is the explanation for Nietzsche being affected by the death of God? Nietzsche did not see God's death as something good. Nietzsche felt that without a God, Western Europe's fundamental belief system was in jeopardy, as he penned in Twilight of the Idols (Indie Books), "When one gives up the Christian faith, one pulls the right to Christian morality out from under one's feet. This morality is by no means self-evident. Christianity is a system, a whole view of things thought out together. By breaking one main concept out of it, the faith in God, one breaks the whole." 1 Corinthians 7:15 (KJV), "But if the unbelieving depart, let him depart. A brother or a sister is not under bondage in such [cases]: but God hath called us to peace."

This increasing secularization of thought in the West led the philosopher to realize that not only was God dead but that human beings had killed him with their scientific revolution, their desire to better understand the world.

As stated, atheists are people, described in 2 Corinthians 4:4 (KJV). "[4] In whom the god of this world hath blinded the minds of them which believe not, lest the light of the glorious gospel of Christ, who is the image of God, should shine unto them."

Many atheists think God is nonexistent, a humanmade construct or a myth. They reject the notion of the existence of God or any sort of deity, higher power but still refusing to acknowledge that God is the beginning and the end, and they discount the Bible; they cannot comprehend or wrap their mind around the fact that God exists, that God is real, and they have misconstrued ways of viewing their own existence in the world totally discounting God and saying, "There is no God". But God calls them fools because according to Psalm 14:1 (KJV), "[1] The fool hath said in his heart; there is no God. They are corrupt; they have done abominable works; there is none that doeth good." Still, there are some who claim to be atheists and are searching for truth. Exodus 3:14 (KJV), "[14] And God said unto Moses, I Am That I Am: and he said, Thus shalt thou say unto the children of Israel, I Am hath sent me unto you." The best and most contextually suitable option for this Biblical verse in this context is that God does not need an explanation of "Who He Is." You just need to believe that He is and that He will do as He says.

The questioning of God's existence starts in the 'finite' mind of people who try to explain an 'infinite' God. But God instructed you in Proverbs 3:5-6 (KJV), "[5] Trust in the LORD with all thine heart; and lean not unto thine own understanding. [6] In all thy ways acknowledge him, and he shall direct thy paths."

Additionally, the atheist mindset is complicated, and there is a conundrum about the atheist mind. While they don't believe in the existence of deities, some atheists believe with absolute certainty that there is some universal spirit and they think about the meaning and purpose of life.

Examine their ways closely, and you will find most atheists behave in a manner likened to someone identifying as a Christian, but Psalms 14:1 (KJV) (To the chief Musician, [A Psalm] of David.) The fool hath said in his heart, [There is] no God. They are corrupt; they have done abominable works, [there is] none that doeth good.

You can further understand the mindset of the atheist if you examine Psalm 14:4 (KJV), "[4] Have all the workers of iniquity no knowledge? who eat up my people as they eat bread and call not upon the LORD." Here you can see God saying they lack knowledge and fail to call upon Him, to turn to Him for guidance.

Therefore, in just looking at Psalm 14:1, 4 (KJV) you see that the mindset of an atheist is that of a fool who had a purpose in his heart that there is no God because they lack knowledge and do not call upon God. And in Psalm 53 (KJV), "[1] The fool hath said in his heart, There is no God. Corrupt are they and have done abominable iniquity: there is none that doeth good. [2] God looked down from heaven upon the children of men, to see if any did understand, that did seek God. [3] Every one of them is gone back: they are altogether become filthy; there is none that doeth good, no, not one. [4] Have the workers of iniquity no knowledge? Who eat up my people as they eat bread: they have not called upon God. [5] There were they in great fear, where no fear was: for God hath scattered the bones of him that encampeth against thee: thou hast put them to shame because God hath despised them. [6] Oh that the salvation of Israel was come out of Zion! When God bringeth back the captivity of his people, Jacob shall rejoice, and Israel shall be glad."

Additionally, some atheist is combative, and their motivation is not always a sincere desire to get an answer. Psalm 53 (KJV) further elaborates that the mindset of an atheist is corrupt, sinful, filthy, and again, lacking knowledge. Furthermore, they are fearful when they do not need to be afraid. Psalm 53: 1- 6 (KJV), "[1] The fool hath said in his heart, There is no God. Corrupt are they, and have done abominable iniquity: there is none that doeth good. [2] God looked down from heaven upon the children of men, to see if there were any that did understand, that did seek God. [3] Every one of them is gone back: they are altogether become filthy; there is none that doeth good, no, not one. [4] Have the workers of iniquity no knowledge? who eat up my people as they eat bread: they have not called upon God. [5] There were they in great fear, where no fear was: for God hath scattered the bones of him that

26

encampeth against thee: thou hast put them to shame, because God hath despised them. ⁶Oh that the salvation of Israel were come out of Zion! When God bringeth back the captivity of his people, Jacob shall rejoice, and Israel shall be glad."

Moreover, even when their questions may seem legitimate, their intent may not be pure. They may want to argue about God and will engage a believer with questions, even legitimate questions, to test the believer's knowledge and faith with no sincere desire to learn about God.

Someone told the story of an atheist who was engaged in a public debate with a Christian about the existence of God. To emphasize a point and take a firm stance that there is no God, the atheist wrote on a blackboard: "God is nowhere." In rebuttal, the Christian went up to the blackboard and split the last word so that the statement then read, "God is now here."

Turning away from God and His word will mean risking despair or a meaninglessness life. What could the point of life be without a God and without hope? Revelation 21:8 (KJV)

⁸But the fearful, and unbelieving, and the abominable, and murderers, and whoremongers, and sorcerers, and idolaters, and all liars, shall have their part in the lake which burneth with fire and brimstone: which is the second death."

The critical thing to remember is to never engage in a debate about God. Also, never waver in your beliefs about God and His plan for salvation; respond to questions with, "Thus saith the Lord," and add a personal response or testimony about what God has done or continue to do in your life. Following that response is most effective.

More significantly, do not forget you have the Bible and the Word of God that clears up any confusion you may have about God's truth and the mindset of an atheist. You can never go wrong with Biblical truth because God truths never change. Psalm 14:1 (KJV), "¹The fool hath said in his heart, there is no God. They are corrupt; they have done abominable works; there is none that doeth good."

Additionally, there are those in the science field that believes there is no God. Scientology members have atheists notions about God whether they admit it or not because they do not believe in God and are trying to use science to explain away God's existence and the things of God.

However, Scientologists will never explain away the God of Isaac and Abraham, the God Who flung the stars in the sky and light the earth by day with the sun and let the moon and the stars rule the night. The God who can count the sands on the earth and the has numbered the stars.

So, while Scientologists dispute creation story and believe Science can explain away everything in the Bible including the existence of God, they are yet to explain where dirt comes from, The same dirt (dust) discussed in Genesis that God used to create man. Study Scientology close enough, and you will find that no matter how hard they try they cannot explain the simple things of nature like the air you breathe.

The underlining culprit that is pulling God's people apart from God and into this lie of Scientology is the devil. And, he is luring many Scientologist leaders with money and greed. But God warned the chumps that have fallen into this pit that the fool and their money will soon part. Proverbs 21:20 (KJV), "20 There is treasure to be desired and oil in the dwelling of the wise; but a foolish man spendeth it up."

Also, they lack real knowledge. But God's truth is available to anyone who wants to open their heart and mind to learn of God. God said in 2 Corinthians 4:3-4 (KJV), "3 But if our gospel be hid, it is hid to them that are lost: 4 In whom the god of this world hath blinded the minds of them which believe not, lest the light of the glorious gospel of Christ, who is the image of God, should shine unto them."

Understand, their seeming lack of knowledge is not because they do not know God exists, it because the devil has warped their minds like the serpent did to Eve in the garden. But anyone choosing to follow Satan blindly and do not seek after God is playing the fool, God is talking to you in Romans 1:18-23 (KJV), "18 For the wrath of God is revealed from heaven against all ungodliness and unrighteousness of

28

men, who hold the truth in unrighteousness; ¹⁹ Because that which may be known of God is manifest in them; for God hath shewed it unto them. ²⁰ For the invisible things of him from the creation of the world are clearly seen, being understood by the things that are made, even his eternal power and Godhead; so that they are without excuse: ²¹ Because that, when they knew God, they glorified him not as God, neither were thankful; but became vain in their imaginations, and their foolish heart was darkened. ²² Professing themselves to be wise, they became fools, ²³ And changed the glory of the incorruptible God into an image made like to corruptible man, and to birds, and four-footed beasts, and creeping things." And, in Romans 2:15 (KJV), "¹⁵ Which shew the work of the law written in their hearts, their conscience also bearing witness, and their thoughts the mean while accusing or else excusing one another;)."

As you can see, taken together, Romans 1:18-23 and Romans 2:15, states that everyone has an inherent knowledge and a God-given moral compass of God's existence and God is known to them from creation. Biblically speaking then, from before they were born. Therefore, a self-proclaim atheist is very aware of God's existence but has purpose in his/her heart not to believe in God, not to accept God, and not to follow God.

Additionally, many people attend church who are still with an atheists mindset. They lack faith in God, they lack faith in God's abilities, in God's promises, and shows little to no respect for the things of God, including referencing God on His Sabbath day. This may well explain why some people in the church are so bitter, harsh, unmerciful, and possess the wrong attitudes in the church from those who cannot see Gods blessings on their life.

Be mindful how you engage with an aethist. 1 Corinthians 10:27(KJV), "²⁷ If any of them that believe not bid you [to a feast], and ye be disposed to go; whatsoever is set before you, eat, asking no question for conscience sake." However, your faith and trust in God come by being around those of like minds, your faith community. Proverbs

13:20 (KJV), "²⁰ He that walketh with wise men shall be wise: but a companion of fools shall be destroyed."

In God's time, every man, including professed atheist will come to know God. Therefore, "If you either reject or show as a nonbeliever, you're still going to know who God is. Revelation 1:7 (KJV), "⁷ Behold, he cometh with clouds; and every eye shall see him, and they also which pierced him: and all kindreds of the earth shall wail because of him. Even so, Amen."

Finally, stated in 1 Peter 5:8 (KJV), "⁸ Be sober, be vigilant; because your adversary the devil, as a roaring lion, walketh about, seeking whom he may devour:" Pray that God draws you nearer to the cross. Jesus gave His life for you at Calvary because He knows your worth. And, because Jesus thought you were worth saving, He sacrificed His life for you. Jesus did not have to do it, but He loves you so much that's why He did it. This is the best love you will ever know. By His stripes, you are healed. Therefore, if God gives you breath, you still have hope.

Acts 2:38 (KJV), "³⁸ Then Peter said unto them, Repent, and be baptized every one of you in the name of Jesus Christ for the remission of sins, and ye shall receive the gift of the Holy Ghost. However, according to Romans 6:23 (KJV), "²³ For the wages of sin [is] death; but the gift of God [is] eternal life through Jesus Christ our Lord."

Therefore, apply James 4:7 (KJV), "⁷ Submit yourselves therefore to God. Resist the devil, and he will flee from you." By doing so, you are assured in John 8:32 (KJV), "³² And ye shall know the truth, and the truth shall make you free." Finally, Pray Psalms 119:12-16 (KJV), "¹² Blessed art thou, O LORD: teach me thy statutes. ¹³ With my lips have I declared all the judgments of thy mouth. ¹⁴ I have rejoiced in the way of thy testimonies, as much as in all riches.¹⁵ I will meditate in thy precepts, and have respect unto thy ways.¹⁶ I will delight myself in thy statutes: I will not forget thy word."

Doubting God

Isaiah 54:5 (KJV), "⁵ For thy Maker is thine husband; the LORD of hosts is his name; and thy Redeemer the Holy One of Israel; The God of the whole earth shall he be called."

Daniel 10:5-6 (KJV), "¹⁸ Then there came again and touched me one like the appearance of a man, and he strengthened me, ¹⁹ And said, O man greatly beloved, fear not: peace be unto thee, be strong, yea, be strong. And when he had spoken unto me, I was strengthened, and said, Let my lord speaks; for thou hast strengthened me." Galatians 6:7 (KJV), "Be not deceived; God is not mocked: for whatsoever a man soweth, that shall he also reap."

For some Christians, especially those who feel unsupported by the church, doubt and despair it replacing their once happy attitude about going to church. 1 John 4:16 (KJV), "¹⁶ And we have known and believed the love that God hath to us. God is love, and he that dwelleth in love dwelleth in God, and God in him." Their fire is out and replaced with anxiety and reaction instead of Christian response. Those who do not stay in their Bible and connected to God will lose their way. Millennials are particularly vulnerable due to this trend.

Hebrews 3 describes how the children of Israel were not allowed to enter the promised land because they doubted God's Word. However, instead of saying "They shall not enter My promised land," God called the promised land "My rest." Hebrews 3:11(KJV), "¹¹ So I sware in my wrath, They shall not enter into my rest." This means that what the natural land was to the children of Israel in the Old Testament, God's grace and rest are to the believer under the new covenant. That is your inheritance today. God wants to bring you out of lack and into the land of abundance! He wants to bring you out of sickness into robust health! And this promised land is the place of His rest.

Many of us worry about many things in this world, bills, family, relationship, money, size of your homes, latest model car, who is prettier, who wears the best clothing, who is smarter, on and on we are troubled by the very things that God tells us He owns and not to worry about. And, the very thing God tells to fear, guess what? We do not fear! Hebrews 4:1(KJV), "Let us, therefore, fear, lest, a promise being left us of entering into his rest, any of you should seem to come short of it." God's rest in the scripture is Heaven. So that is what God wants you to fear, missing out on Heaven.

Down here on earth, the church is a place where transformation should be taking place in your life, and your relationship in God is strengthening. A place where Christians, and non-Christian visitors, and those who believe, can see the transformative, healing power of Jesus at work.

However, the church is ever-shrinking because many millennials have no Christian traditions. Also, many secular millennials, which includes some who grew up in the church and knew of God, don't value church and are beginning to toot up their noses at their parent's religious affiliation, questioning the importance of God, and joining online discussion groups that refute God's existence or the importance of church attendance and worship.

The church will continue to shrink in attendance because millennials, many whom are currently not taking part in any organized religion, choose to when they have children of their own, and will have nothing to pass down to their children. And, their children of when grown up, will have nothing to very little to do with God or His plan of salvation. Therefore, the next generation will be walking further away from the truth and drifting further away from God.

Moreover, some professed Christians doubt the existence of God, especially when dealing with trauma and grief. And not all Christian behave in a Christlike manner.

At the heart of every single one of your battle, your doubts, and your fears that you face every day is your real enemy, the devil who prowls around like a roaring lion seeking to devour you. Listen to what the Bible says in 1 Peter 5:8 (KJV), "⁸Be sober, be vigilant; because your adversary the devil, as a roaring lion, walketh about, seeking whom he may devour," He will stop at nothing to gain new ground. He and his forces have quoted God's words since the beginning of time, twisting it, trying their best to manipulate the truth, their main goal only to deceive and lead astray. However, God who loves you and gave His son to die for you, will not tolerate doubt. God promises in Jude 5 (KJV), "⁵I will, therefore, put you in remembrance, though ye once knew this, how that the Lord, having saved the people out of the land of Egypt, afterward destroyed them that believed not.

You have to go to Isaiah 40:28 (KJV), "Hast thou not known? hast thou not heard, [that] the everlasting God, the LORD, the Creator of the ends of the earth, fainteth not, neither is weary? [there is] no searching of His understanding." Like many Christians, you have doubts which reverberate in your soul. From time to time your faith is shaken. Hebrews 11:1 (KJV), "Now faith is the substance of things hoped for, the evidence of things not seen."

Remember even Jesus called out:" My God, My God why hast thou forsaken me!" Jesus' cry to His Father was not one of despair because He was not giving up on His Father and He was not letting go of Him. Even though Jesus was crying out, Jesus still acknowledged the very existence and authority of God and found peace in His name.

Your doubts sometimes stem from your biases, burdens and even when your blessings are not given to you at your desired time.

However, God's goal was not for His glory but for your spiritual inheritance. God's grace was not to set you free from sin but to make you productive. The abundant life He offered was not eternal, it was now and everlasting. You gain a life of prosperity when you live the gospel.

Also, when you see the hurt in the world and see the pain, hunger, and suffering in the world, and you see the good and evil in man, there too can your doubt be multiplied.

On top of that, throughout the centuries He endures countless criticisms from both inside and outside His church.

Additionally, even in your sinfulness, when you are at your worst, God still ensures you are abundantly blessed. He stands beside you waiting for you to yell out for Him as you fall — what a merciful God. The Bible conveys to us in 2 Peter 3:9 (KJV), "9 The Lord is not slack concerning his promise, as some men count slackness; but is longsuffering to us-ward, not willing that any should perish, but that all should come to repentance."

Therefore, when you doubt, and your faith is shaken, you can find comfort in reading God's word, especially the story of Jesus dying on the cross just for you. Read John 3:16 (KJV, "16 For God so loved the world, that he gave his only begotten Son, that whosoever believeth in him should not perish, but have everlasting life." This verse alone should bring you peace amid doubt and fear.

Prayerfully, Jesus offers grace and mercy. To the woman caught in adultery, Jesus offered mercy John 8:1-11 (KJV), "1 Jesus went unto the Mount of Olive. 2 And early in the morning he came again into the temple, and all the people came unto him, and he sat down and taught them. 3 And the scribes and Pharisees brought unto him a woman taken in adultery; and when they had set her in the midst, 4 They say unto him, Master, this woman was taken in adultery, in the very act. 5 Now Moses in the law commanded us, that such should be stoned: but what sayest thou? 6 This they said, tempting him, that they might have to accuse him. But Jesus stooped down, and with his finger wrote on the ground, as though he heard them not. 7 So when they continued asking him, he lifted up himself, and said unto them, He that is without sin among you, let him first cast a stone at her. 8 And again he stooped down and wrote on the ground. 9 And they which heard it, being convicted by their own conscience, went out one by one, beginning at the eldest, even unto the last: and Jesus was left alone, and the woman standing in the midst. 10 When Jesus had lifted up himself and saw none but the woman, he said unto her, Woman, where are those thine accusers? hath no man condemned thee? [11] She said, No man, Lord. And Jesus said unto her, Neither do I condemn thee: go, and sin no more". Jesus set boundaries and showed grace.

Likewise, fellowshipping and surrounding yourself with other believers, just worshipping, praying, and giving thanks can draw you closer to God. When doubts begin to stir about your motives for believing or loving God, with the "right" amount of faith and praise, you will feel closer to God and alleviate any doubts you have of His goodness and mercy. There is power in praise and in acknowledging God's power and authority.

Also, God supplies comfort in His word. In Luke 21:9 (KJV), "[9] But when ye shall hear of wars and commotions, be not terrified: for these things must first come to pass; but the end is not by and by."

From time to time, you will still be asking the same question, "Does Jesus loves me?" However, the response is not limited to yes or no, but instead to a deep soul searching and response to, "How much do I love Jesus?" For times of doubts and feelings of despair remember that Jesus, your example, experienced a sense of separation from God, His Father, but showed us that even when you have a cross to bear, and you feel separated from Him, you must still acknowledge God, His infinite power and His authority over your life, surrender your hearts and hold on.

Philippians 4:6-9 (KJV), "[6] Be careful about nothing, but in everything by prayer and supplication with thanksgiving let your requests be made known unto God. [7] And the peace of God, which passeth all understanding, shall keep your hearts and minds through Christ Jesus. [8] Finally, brethren, whatsoever things are true, whatsoever things are honest, whatsoever things are just, whatsoever things are pure, whatsoever things are lovely, whatsoever things are of good report; if there be any virtue, and if there be any praise, think on these things. [9] Those things, which ye have both learned, and received, and heard, and seen in me, do: and the God of peace shall be with you."

Psalm. 139:7-12 (KJV), "Psalm 139:7-12 (KJV), "[7] Whither shall I go from thy spirit? or whither shall I flee from thy presence? [8] If I ascend up into heaven, thou art there: if I make my bed in hell, behold, thou art there. [9] If I take the wings of the morning and dwell in the uttermost parts of the sea; [10] Even there shall thy hand lead me, and thy right hand shall hold me. [11] If I say, Surely the darkness shall cover me; even the night shall be light about me. [12] Yea, the darkness hideth not from thee; but the night shineth as the day: the darkness and the light are both alike to thee."

Every promise God has made to you, God will fulfill because God does not lie. All you need to do is hold tight and have faith the size of a mustard seed.

God's Authority

Revelation 19:16 (KJV), "^{16} And he hath on his vesture and on his thigh a name written, KING OF KINGS, AND LORD OF LORDS." You may have heard people say that "God's Word is our authority, but perhaps you do not fully understand what it means. Romans 13:1 (KJV), "^{1}Let every soul be subject unto the higher powers. For there is no power but of God: the powers that be are ordained of God." And, 2 Timothy 3:16 (KJV), "^{16} All scripture is given by inspiration of God and is profitable for doctrine, for reproof, for correction, for instruction in righteousness."

Also, God is the Creator of all things and including the Creator of man. No man is greater than his Creator. Adam did not question God's authority when God was giving him some authority over God's creation, and we should not question God's authority either.

God is the ultimate authority simply because He is "the LORD, and there is no other." It is He who created everything, including mankind. God is the Father of mankind, and as such, He has authority over us.

Revelation 1:8 (KJV), "^{8} I am Alpha and Omega, the beginning and the ending, saith the Lord, which is, and which was, and which is to come, the Almighty." The Bible is God's authority. Nothing can change it or replace it, you cannot make it anything other than what it is, and God warns woe unto anyone who changes one word. Like God, you can take or leave it; you have free will.

Understand this: Whatever God tells you to do, be obedient and do it because guaranteed, it is for your own good. Also, when God gives you something to do; God is not expecting you to do it in your own strength, God will fully equip you! God will give you the strength, the resources, and the guidance when you pray for help in Jesus' name.

Read and reread through the Bible from cover to cover so you will be able to exegete the scriptures in ways that make sense. At the back of the

Bible, you will discover that God won and that there are many who overcame.

The serpent questioned God's authority back in the Garden of Eden and deceived Eve (Read Genesis 3:1–6). Then Adam disobeyed and ate the fruit (Read Genesis 3:6), despite what God had told him (Read Genesis 2:17). By Adam ignoring God's authority and doing what God forbid him not to do, the consequences were him and Eve being thrown out the Garden of Eden, and consequently, sin entered the world, and each of us is born into sin and shapen in iniquity and with a rebellious nature.

However, because God is our authority in every area, we need to make sure that we know what His Word says and strive to make it our authority in every area of life. We need to recognize when the beliefs and philosophies of men are contrary to God's Word (Read Colossians 2:8; and Ephesians 4:14), bring "every thought into captivity to the obedience of Christ," (Read 2 Corinthians 10:5), and respond by "speaking the truth in love" (Read Ephesians 4:15) to a world that has tried to deny the authority of the Father.

The Bible feed, revives, and replenish your soul and bring you through all types of adversity, so get acquainted with the text of Scripture and become absorbed in them. Many people today, unfortunately, do not give God thanks for the things they achieved or have. They believe that everything they have or that they are is by their own doing, their hard work. Like Satan, they doubt God's authority. For Satan, his problem began with him saying "I will." When Satan said, "I will," Satan turned from hearing God's voice and began to seek his own will. To put another will over God's is to say that His will is not perfect. The lust to sin dwells in human nature. In other words, it is contaminated and motivated by the sinful tendencies that dwell in all people because of the fall into sin and disobedience in the garden of Eden. (What is a sin?) God calls Himself by name, saying, "I AM." (Exodus 3:14) He does not give this name to anyone else. The one who wants to be something in himself is therefore in conflict with God and is expelled.

2 Corinthians 10:8 (KJV), "⁸ For though I should boast somewhat more of our authority, which the Lord hath given us for edification, and not for your destruction, I should not be ashamed:" By God's grace and mercy, meditating day and night, take heed to the biblical texts - God's words, in context, less you will go astray. Romans 13:1(KJV), "Let every soul be subject unto the higher powers. For there is no power but of God: the powers that be are ordained of God."

1 Corinthians 15:24 (KJV), "²⁴ Then cometh the end, when he shall have delivered up the kingdom to God, even the Father; when he shall have put down all rule and all authority and power." Matthew 28:18 (KJV), "And Jesus came and spake unto them, saying, All power is given unto me in heaven and in the earth."

Trusting God

John 1:1-3 (KJV), "In the beginning was the Word, and the Word was with God, and the Word was God. ²The same was at the beginning with God. ³All things were made by him, and without him was not anything made that was made."

God's truth and the truth about God gives believers the assurance, strength, guidance, protection, and comfort for each day that we can trust in Him. Once you come into the presence of God, He picks you up, clean you up and use you. What is more incredible is that God does everything to hold on to you and will never discard you.

Still many believers trust their spouse, family members, and friends more than they trust God. They will believe everything these people tell them but not what the Word of God says. But it is not what people think about us; it is what God thinks about you. However, they even trust the lies advertisers tell them when it comes to their finances, and how they can get rich quick but will not trust God, the Giver, and supplier of all their needs.

Putting your hopes in man only to have them hurt you to the core, versus trusting God that loves you so much He made the greatest sacrifice for you. There is no one that would ever give up their lousy brat of a child, let alone their perfect child in whom they are well pleased, to let you live – it just would not happen – but God did (See John 3:16-18).

Our greatest privilege is to come to know God, trust Him and enjoy God's presence. John 15:5 (KJV), "⁵I am the vine, ye are the branches: He that abideth in me, and I in him, the same bringeth forth much fruit: for without me ye can do nothing."

God seals you as His one of His children and dwells in you through the Holy Spirit. Romans 8:11 (KJV), "¹¹But if the Spirit of him that raised up Jesus from the dead dwell in you, he that raised up Christ from the dead shall also quicken your mortal bodies by his Spirit that dwelleth in you. This does not mean you can live ungodly because the Holy Spirit convicts you and guide you into all truth. Galatians 5:22-23 (KJV), " [22] But the fruit of the Spirit is love, joy, peace, longsuffering, gentleness, goodness, faith, [23] Meekness, temperance: against such, there is no law."

Additionally, sometimes you may feel you can do it on your own. Too scared to trust God, too proud to ask for help, you got it. But this mindset just keeps you stagnant in your mess and does not allow you to open your heart and trust God. At times this lack of trust stems from the fact that you put God in this little box with limited abilities. You think your problem is too massive that God cannot handle it, so you limit a limitless God by what we perceive Him to be in our limited minds. So thinketh, so shall it be. Romans 12:2 (KJV), "[2] And be not conformed to this world: but be ye transformed by the renewing of your mind, that ye may prove what is that good, and acceptable, and perfect, will of God."

Additionally, You feel you have just been asking and asking God for favors. Proverbs 3:5 (KJV), "Trust in the LORD with all thine heart, and lean not unto thine own understanding." God never slumbers or sleep and is on call 24/7/365 days per year, ready to listen when you call upon Him. When you humble yourself like little children and cry out if you must, "God, I cannot make it on my own, I need You, and I depend on You to see me through, that is all God needs to start working wonders in your life. When you get to the end of your rope, and you do not know what to do, hang on in faith and trust God to fix your problems for you. When you do not understand why certain things are happening in your life, trust God to bring you into full understanding. When life has shaken you to the core, and all your foundations are crumbling, trust God to step right in on time and provide the crutch you need to hold you upright. Just trust God and believe and wait. Lean not to your own understanding; you do not have the capacity to imagine all that God is or all that God can do.

Also, you are blessed with the treasures of God's love, and amazing grace found in His words. The Bible is instructions for how to live and is packed full of God's goodness and promises of blessings. John 14:26

(KJV), "²⁶ But the Comforter, which is the Holy Ghost, whom the Father will send in my name, he shall teach you all things, and bring all things to your remembrance, whatsoever I have said unto you." Sadly, people go to church, hear what they want to hear, and many leave the same way they came. They usually end feeling lost or unsure of their relationship with God because they never took the time to spend time with God reading His word.

God has opened many avenues for you to build a relationship with Him. You have His word, but you also have a prayer. Prayer is your fastest connection to God. Many times, people pray when things are going wrong in their life instead of staying connected to God through prayer. Soon, their situation becomes so desperate that they feel like God abandon them as opposed to blaming themselves for failing to build a relationship with God. God invites His children to bring their request to Him. You do not have to fear because God already has given you His permission. Philippians 4:6-7 (KJV), "⁶ Be careful for nothing, but in everything by prayer and supplication with thanksgiving let your requests be made known unto God. ⁷ And the peace of God, which passeth all understanding, shall keep your hearts and minds through Christ Jesus."

All God asks in return is that you put Him first in your life and not be afraid. He wants you to put your confidence and trust in Him, all the time, in everything. Psalms 56:3-4 (KJV), "³ What time I am afraid, I will trust in thee. ⁴ In God I will praise his word, in God I have put my trust; I will not fear what flesh can do unto me." Jeremiah 29:11 (KJV), "¹¹ For I know the thoughts that I think toward you, saith the LORD, thoughts of peace, and not of evil, to give you an expected end." We do not have to be afraid to love and trust God. Because according to the word of God in 1 John 4:18 (KJV), "¹⁸ There is no fear in love; but perfect love casteth out fear: because fear hath torment. He that feareth is not made perfect in love." All God asks is that we be obedient to His commandments Proverbs 3:1-35 (KJV), "¹ My son, forget not my law; but let thine heart keep my commandments: ² For length of days, and long life, and peace, shall they add to thee. ³ Let not mercy and truth forsake thee: bind them about thy neck; write them upon the table of thine heart: ⁴ So shalt thou find favor and good understanding in the sight of God and man. ⁵ Trust in the LORD with all thine heart; and lean not unto thine own understanding. ⁶ In all thy ways acknowledge him, and he shall direct thy paths. ⁷ Be not wise in thine own eyes: fear the LORD and depart from evil. ⁸ It shall be health to thy navel, and marrow to thy bones. ⁹ Honor the LORD with thy substance, and with the firstfruits of all thine increase: ¹⁰ So shall thy barns be filled with plenty, and thy presses shall burst out with new wine. ¹¹ My son, despise not the chastening of the LORD; neither be weary of his correction: ¹² For whom the LORD loveth he correcteth; even as a father the son in whom he delighteth. ¹³ Happy is the man that findeth wisdom, and the man that getteth understanding. ¹⁴ For the merchandise of it is better than the merchandise of silver, and the gain thereof than fine gold. ¹⁵ She is more precious than rubies: and all the things thou canst desire are not to be compared unto her. ¹⁶ Length of days is in her right hand, and in her left-hand riches and honor. ¹⁷ Her ways are ways of pleasantness, and all her paths are peace. ¹⁸ She is a tree of life to them that lay hold upon her: and happy is every one that retaineth her. ¹⁹ The LORD by wisdom hath founded the earth; by understanding hath he established the heavens. ²⁰ By his knowledge, the depths are broken up, and the clouds drop down the dew. ²¹ My son, let not them depart from thine eyes: keep sound wisdom and discretion: ²² So shall they be life unto thy soul, and grace to thy neck. ²³ Then shalt thou walk in thy way safely, and thy foot shall not stumble. ²⁴ When thou liest down, thou shalt not be afraid: yea, thou shalt lie down, and thy sleep shall be sweet. ²⁵ Be not afraid of sudden fear, neither of the desolation of the wicked, when it cometh. ²⁶ For the LORD shall be thy confidence and shall keep thy foot from being taken. ²⁷ Withhold not good from them to whom it is due when it is in the power of thine hand to do it. ²⁸ Say not unto thy neighbor, Go, and come again, and tomorrow I will give; when thou hast it by thee. ²⁹ Devise not evil against thy neighbor, seeing he dwelleth securely by thee. ³⁰ Strive not with a man without cause, if he has done thee no harm. [31] Envy thou not the oppressor and choose none of his ways.

[32] For the froward is an abomination to the LORD: but his secret is with the righteous. [33] The curse of the LORD is in the house of the wicked: but he blesseth the habitation of the just. [34] Surely, he scorneth the scorners: but he giveth grace unto the lowly. [35] The wise shall inherit glory: but shame shall be the promotion of fools." Keep God's law; write them in thine heart, and He will give you the desires of our heart. Mark 11:24 - Therefore I say unto you, What things soever ye desire, when ye pray, believe that ye receive [them], and ye shall have [them].

As you spend time reading your Bible, meditating on Scripture, and you develop a healthy prayer life, you will find that your relationship with God will grow and soon your dependence on Him and trust in Him will grow. Psalms 37:5 (KJV), "Commit thy way unto the LORD; also trust in him, and he shall bring [it] to pass." Psalms 31:14-15 (KJV), "14 But I trusted in thee, O Lord: I said, Thou art my God. 15 My times are in thy hand: deliver me from the hand of mine enemies, and from them that persecute me." Amen!

The Color of Jesus

Questions about the color of Jesus has been around for a very long time. God expected our curiosity and has supplied enough information to settle the curiosity that burns inside us about the color of His Son, how He looks, His color. Race and religion are two things people can get very passionate about. Combine them, and you have a recipe for some severe disagreements based on deeply-held personal beliefs and feelings. John 7:24 (KJV), "24 Judge not according to the appearance, but judge righteous judgment."

People have always tried to fit The Holy Trinity into a box that makes them comfortable. However, God said in His words, "I am that I am." And God is described in John 4:24 (KJV). "24 God is a Spirit: and they that worship him must worship him in spirit and in truth." Additionally, 1 John 1:5 (KJV), "5 This then is the message which we have heard of him, and declare unto you, that God is light, and in him is no darkness at all."

So, what is the color is Jesus? Is Jesus black, yellow, blue, red, or white? Depending on whom you asked, to black people Jesus is black, to Caucasian people, Jesus is Caucasian, and so forth.

Truthfully, God does not care about color, and He made us in His own image. People confuse "In His own image and likeness" to mean we look like God. No, God is All and All Things to each person. He does not include any inequality for His creation. Genesis 1:27(KJV), "27 So God created man in his [own] image, in the image of God created he him; male and female created he them." God made us look like He wants us to look for His purpose and His glory.

Psalm 104 (KJV) reads, Bless the LORD, O my soul. "1 O LORD my God, thou art very great; thou art clothed with honour and majesty. 2 Who coverest thyself with light as with a garment: who stretchest out the heavens like a curtain: 3 Who layeth the beams of his chambers in the waters: who maketh the clouds his chariot: who walketh upon the wings of the wind:"

The closest description of Jesus was on the Mount of Transfiguration found in Matthew 17: 1-2 (KJV), "¹ And after six days Jesus taketh Peter, James, and John, his brother, and bringeth them up into a high mountain apart, ² And was transfigured before them: and his face did shine as the sun, and his raiment was white as the light." And the description for God is found in The Book of Revelation 1:14-15 (KJV) which reads, "¹⁴ His head and his hairs were white like wool, as white as snow; and his eyes were as a flame of fire; ¹⁵ And his feet like unto fine brass, as if they burned in a furnace; and his voice as the sound of many waters." And, Daniel 10:5-6 (KJV), "⁵ Then I lifted up mine eyes, and looked, and behold a certain man clothed in linen, whose loins were girded with fine gold of Uphaz: ⁶ His body also was like the beryl, and his face as the appearance of lightning, and his eyes as lamps of fire, and his arms and his feet like in colour to polished brass, and the voice of his words like the voice of a multitude."

Some people insist that these verses, especially the last one, prove that Jesus was black, but other people disagree, saying that this is a description of Jesus in his Heavenly form, and does not tell us anything about what he looked like while he was living on earth.

Bottom line, John 4:2 (KJV), "² God is a Spirit: and they that worship him must worship him in spirit and in truth." John 4:2 is talking about Spirit as God's nature - He is not a physical being. There is no room for physical features, characteristics, or traits in His creating. Also, 1 John 1:5 (KJV), "⁵ This then is the message which we have heard of him, and declare unto you, that God is light, and in him is no darkness at all." God is "Light." God does not equate to us in terms of race, color, or creed. The Psalmist says it best in Psalms 104:1-2 (KJV), "₁ Bless the Lord, O my soul. O Lord my God, thou art very great; thou art clothed with honor and majesty. ₂ Who coverest thyself with light as with a garment: who stretchest out the heavens like a curtain." As children of God, we are also clothed with this light of "honor and majesty."

Also, God is incorporeal -- without body or physical form -- he does not have the identifying characteristics of a human being. I also knew that God is the creator of all. He can only create His likeness, which is always good in quality. He cannot create something that is unlike Himself or outside His intelligence. As God's children, we can show evidence of His likeness only in terms of perfection. Therefore, we are also incorporeal, or spiritual.

God's Love for His creation is abundant, unchanging, always at hand. His people are varied and unique in innumerable ways, but they all come from Him, the one God.

They fell before Him and gave away their crowns to the One Who is Worthy to be crowned. This is the response of a loving, grateful heart to a loving, forgiving, and glorious God! These elders have no pride and are not seeking glory. Now they really understand who deserves the glory. None of them are hanging on to their crowns. They give them away.

We as His children can never be categorized as superior or inferior to one another. Instead, we each express glory and beauty. These are reflected in all of us. Good qualities, such as love, joy, satisfaction, and peace, come from His perfect being, and our identity as His children involves the expression of these qualities. There are no whites and blacks before God. All colors are one, and that is the color of servitude to God. Scent and color are not necessary. The heart is important. If the heart is pure, white, or black or any color individually God's majesty, honor, makes no difference.

God does not look at colors; He looks at the hearts 1 Samuel 16:7 (KJV), "7 But the Lord said unto Samuel, Look not on his countenance, or on the height of his stature; because I have refused him: for the Lord seeth not as man seeth; for man looketh on the outward appearance, but the Lord looketh on the heart."

Here we reach a realm where all colors merge into one—the "color of servitude to God." If we overlook outward differences, serve God and worship God with a pure heart, we fulfill the purpose of creation. In this sense, we submerge ourselves in the color of God.

In the interim, it does not matter what color Jesus is. What matters is that you strive to make it into this number. Revelation 7:9 (KJV), "9 After this I beheld, and, lo, a great multitude, which no man could number, of all nations, and kindreds, and people, and tongues, stood before the throne, and before the Lamb, clothed with white robes, and palms in their hands."

Burdened by the Cross

Jesus is entirely God (John 1:1–3, 14), but He came to earth as Man. The Bible says in Philippians 2:8 (KJV), "being found in fashion as a man, He humbled Himself, and became obedient unto death, even the death of the cross." Jesus left Heaven and came to earth, took on the form of a man, to fulfill the plan of salvation. He surrendered His divine privileges and powers in heaven and became a man with all the attributes of any other human being, including the same feelings of every other human being.

Jesus goes to Garden of Gethsemane, and He prayed to say, "42 Saying, Father if thou be willing, remove this cup from me: nevertheless, not my will, but thine, be done." Luke 22:42 (KJV). Jesus knew Judas Iscariot, was the traitor who will betray Him but He lived out the plan of Salvation nonetheless out of love for us. (Read Luke 6).

God in His infinite mercy and love does not want any of us to suffer; That is why He gave us Jesus. The Bible doesn't say, "For God so loved the world, He gave you a bunch of sweet-smelling roses." No, it said in John 3:16-17 (KJV), " 16 For God so loved the world, that he gave his only begotten Son, that whosoever believeth in him should not perish, but have everlasting life. 17 For God sent not his Son into the world to condemn the world; but that the world through him might be saved."

While man can never appreciate the entire horrific story of the cross or will ever be able to fully comprehend the level of excruciating pain Jesus experience by having all the sins of the world put upon Him, He hung in disgrace, on that cross for your sins.

You cannot escape the historical question, "Did Jesus die on the cross and did the resurrection happen or not?" Scholars are quick to note, "If it happened, it happened," so much for your dogmas." Others want irrefutable proof that the body of a non-resurrected Jesus has been found and cannot accept the Biblical story as true. They need the literal facts of the resurrection for "truth" cannot stand without, in this case, the physical "facts."

However, for the true believer, the cross is not fiction, nor is it a mere symbol; The burden of the cross is inseparably connected with following Jesus. But Jesus' blood was spilled.

Also, the cross is evidence of God's love for His children and proof of Jesus' suffering and servitude. Your Cross in return is proof of the love He expects from us in return. However, do you "get it" —can you quantify, capture, and described the mystery of the cross.

Additionally, there are two distinct ways the cross impacts a Christian: One, joyfully when you see the death of Christ upon the cross as a revelation of God's love for humanity. When you understand the depth of His love that He sacrificed His only Begotten Son, so you might live. The other, somberly, the cross beckons and compels us to hang your head in shame and reverence when you understand the suffering, pain, and brokenness Jesus had to suffer to bear your sins. When He looked into His Father's eyes, and imagine a son hurt, bleeding, tears flowing, looks up to his father who is looking on and he asks His Father, "Matthew 27:45-50 (KJV), "[45] Now from the sixth hour there was darkness over all the land unto the ninth hour. [46] And about the ninth hour, Jesus cried with a loud voice, saying, Eli, Eli, lama sabachthani? That is to say, My God, my God, why hast thou forsaken me? [47] Some of them that stood there, when they heard that, said, This man calleth for Elias. [48] And straightway one of them ran, and took a sponge, and filled it with vinegar, and put it on a reed, and gave him to drink. [49] The rest said, Let be, let us see whether Elias will come to save him. [50] Jesus, when he had cried again with a loud voice, yielded up the ghost." Mercy!

Oh, how marvelous it is that Jesus freely went to Calvary to set the whole world free from sin. So, here you have a Son hanging in pain on a cross, a crown of thorns on His head, nails in his hands and feet, and the wounds from the stripes on His back and the spears that was plunged deep in His side, bleeding, capable of changing His mind at any time, capable of destroying the world with a wink or a whisper, but choosing to hang in shame and being mocked and tortured by the very people He was trying to save.

Ironically, Peter shows himself to be quite lacking in the stability and integrity one expects, often completely misunderstanding Jesus, and denying Jesus three times. But despite Peter's failings, Jesus continues to trust Peter to fulfill His purpose of going to the cross. (Read John 21).

The cross was a burden for Christ because it was a lonely and painful time for Him; He was being betrayed by the people He should have been able to trust the most, His disciples, that journeyed with Him, and preached with Him. Luke 23:38-42 (KJV), "[38] And a superscription also was written over him in letters of Greek, and Latin, and Hebrew, THIS IS THE KING OF THE JEWS. [39] And one of the malefactors which were hanged railed on him, saying, If thou be Christ, save thyself and us. [40] But the other answering rebuked him, saying, Dost, not thou fear God, seeing thou art in the same condemnation? [41] And we indeed justly; for we receive the due reward of our deeds: but this man hath done nothing amiss. [42] And he said unto Jesus, Lord, remember me when thou comest into thy kingdom."

Also, the very people Jesus helped, the blind that He made see, the lame that He made walked, the five thousand that Jesus fed, those He baptized, and even the good Samaritan was nowhere to be found.

Additionally, there Jesus hanged, suspended on the cross between Heaven and earth, alone, separated from his earthly parents. He looks down and sees a woman who is broken and crying for her son hanging helplessly on a Cross for crimes that He had not done, her innocent baby, but He only sees a soul in need of Savior.

More significantly, when He turned His eyes and fixed it towards Heaven, and he looked to His Heavenly Father, Whose face is now turned away from Him because He must chastise His Son for the sin of man, at that moment both the spiritual and physical pain was intense. Being "forsaken" by His loving father and left to die, bearing the sins of an ungrateful world, was harsh when Jesus understood how much His Father love Him only to now be separated from God when He needed

Him most. Up to that time, Jesus had never been separated from His Father. The reason He could do all kinds of miracles when He walked the earth was that His Father was with Him. (John 5:17, 19 (KJV), "[17] But Jesus answered them, My Father worketh hitherto, and I work.[18] Therefore the Jews sought the more to kill him, because he not only had broken the Sabbath but said also that God was his Father, making himself equal with God. [19] Then answered Jesus and said unto them, Verily, verily, I say unto you, The Son can do nothing of himself, but what he seeth the Father do: for what things soever he doeth, these also doeth the Son likewise."

He came as Man and suffered as Man. The blood, sweat, and tears were real. The pain was real. The death was real. Every time He mentioned the Father, He found strength and comfort. So here is the emotional suffering and sadness of a man in pain as he was left to hang on the cross by himself. He could not seek help from Heaven. But there is spiritual suffering here which we sometimes do not see. Not only was Jesus suffering in those moments, but God, His father, was suffering as well. As Jesus' Father, you can imagine how much God must have wept for His son. Imagine your father standing there looking on as you get beaten, whipped and the skin ripped off your body, thorns placed on your head, and you are being humiliated and mocked and unable to help you.

But look at this, even though Jesus was sinless, faultless, and Holy and He willingly went to the cross, God who cannot lie, Whose nature and words are just, and never changes, had no choice but to turn away from His Son out of shame because of the sins that now consumes His son. A perfect Christ could not go to the cross, that would mean that man has no hope of being save when faultless. No, it was an imperfect Christ whose imperfection was because He was consumed by the sin of man that went to the cross. 2 Corinthians 5:21 (KJV), "[21] For he hath made him to be sin for us, who knew no sin; that we might be made the righteousness of God in him." It was only then that Jesus could have suffered and died for our sins. (Note: A Perfect Jesus went to Heaven because sinners cannot enter Heaven).

Matthew 27:46 (KJV), "[46] And about the ninth hour Jesus cried with a loud voice, saying, Eli, Eli, lama sabachthani? that is to say, My God, my God, why hast thou forsaken me?" He is now separated from His Father, Who loved Him beyond measure, Who could have said, "Son You do not have to do this," but instead, God, His Father, must now turn His back on Jesus, His Son, at a time when Jesus needed His Father the most.

Understand, Jesus suffered on the cross, but God suffered as well as having to watch His Perfect Son endure such a horrific death for an ungrateful people that He created with His own hands. John 19:34 (KJV), "[34] But one of the soldiers with a spear pierced his side and forthwith came there out blood and water." Jesus's suffering was horrific and God, even though powerful, He felt helpless and broken. Still, God was consumed with love and pride for His Son.

Imagine the tears that God shed and how grieved the Holy Spirit was. The Bible tells us in Genesis 6:3 (KJV), "And the LORD said, My spirit shall not always strive with man, for that he also is flesh: yet his days shall be a hundred and twenty years." But as grieved as the Holy Spirit was, neither of The Holy Trinity, God the Father, Son and Holy Spirit, turned away from man or we all would have perished, and there would not be a salvation story.

No, God turned away from Jesus out of love for His Son and because of His love for us. As Jesus' Father, God could not watch His Son suffer and not destroy the world to save His Son. Habakkuk 1:13 (KJV), "[13] Thou art of purer eyes than to behold evil, and canst not look on iniquity: wherefore lookest thou upon them that deal treacherously, and holdest thy tongue when the wicked devoureth the man that is more righteous than he?"

Therefore, God had no choice but to look away from His Son to remain faithful to the plan of salvation, and to the sacrifice, He chose to make for mankind. John 3:16-17 (KJV), "[16] For God so loved the world, that he gave his only begotten Son, that whosoever believeth in him should not perish, but have everlasting life. [17] For God sent not his Son into the world to condemn the world; but that the world through him might be saved."

Still, even though God's heart was broken at that moment, He was the proudest Father. Jesus' willingly made the greatest sacrifice of mankind, and it was a sweet-smelling savor to Him. Ephesians 5:2 (KJV), "[2] And walk in love, as Christ also hath loved us, and hath given himself for us an offering and a sacrifice to God for a sweet-smelling savor." And the love between Father and Son was clearer when Jesus said in John 10:17-18 (KJV), "[17] Therefore doth my Father love me, because I lay down my life, that I might take it again. [18] No man taketh it from me, but I lay it down of myself. I have the power to lay it down, and I have the power to take it again. This commandment have I received of my Father."

So, God looks on with a bittersweet love at His son Who is battered, bruised, broken and bleeding for an ungrateful people. Imagine your child crying out in pain; could you just look away and ignore their pleas for help? Well, that is what God had to do when He saw His baby Jesus, Who was born in that lowly manger, hanging on that Old Rugged Cross that is now an emblem of suffering and shame, and forever a promise to man and a burden for man. Jesus, the Perfect Servant, decided in the Garden of Gethsemane that He would pay the price for our sins. And, God because of His love for us, looked away and allowed His Son to go to the cross for our assurance of salvation.

Moreover, scripture declares the cross to be the outward, man's shame, that God had to humble Himself to watch and allow a man to torment and kill His Son in shame; A Son that is worth more than the entire world to Him. Picture, you are giving up a trillion dollars for an "I owe you note." And the cross is an inbound link through Christ to eternity with God.

The cross was the object of God's wrath against sin as well as the object of man's accumulated hatred and malice. For this reason, The Cross of Jesus is a burden for sinners and has many different meanings

56

to the sinner. For who could endure the cross, and perhaps bear to suffer wrongfully, were it not for Jesus' sake or to follow Christ? The cross was not the occasion for mere stoic indifferent. Jesus's scars will forever serve as a reminder to man of His time upon the Cross to save us from our sins and as a sign of His love for us to give us a second opportunity to make Heaven our home.

The story of the cross is your stronghold for when your doubt becomes shaken. The Cross also serves as a reminder to Satan and to us of how far God is willing to go for His children. Satan is embroiled in deadly warfare against God for the saints of God, He lost to God and got kicked out of Heaven, He tempted Crist and lost at the Cross, and God warns us in 1 Peter 5:8 (KJV), "8 Be sober, be vigilant; because your adversary the devil, as a roaring lion, walketh about, seeking whom he may devour." Indeed, you cannot expect to find roaring lions amongst sheep together peacefully unless the roaring lion has some treacherous motive? Same with the devil. He is not walking amongst God's sheep to love on us, no, his motive is to devour you.

Bearing the cross after Christ was a precious privilege of the early disciples, and still exists for us to avail ourselves. Philippians 2:5-11 (KJV), "5 Let this mind be in you, which was also in Christ Jesus: 6 Who, being in the form of God, thought it not robbery to be equal with God: 7 But made himself of no reputation, and took upon him the form of a servant, and was made in the likeness of men: 8 And being found in fashion as a man, he humbled himself, and became obedient unto death, even the death of the cross. 9 Wherefore God also hath highly exalted him, and given him a name which is above every name: 10 That at the name of Jesus every knee should bow, of things in heaven, and things in earth, and things under the earth; 11 And that every tongue should confess that Jesus Christ is Lord, to the glory of God the Father".

God forewarns of the tremendous opposition you will encounter, not only from those who oppose the principles of the church but opposition from those inside the church, and from the powers that be — presidents, kings, and governors Revelations 6:12 (KJV), "12 For we wrestle not against flesh and blood, but against principalities, against powers, against the rulers of the darkness of this world, against spiritual wickedness in high places." The hardest to bear will be the opposition you will face your kindred — fathers, mothers, and children. Moreover, if in the world you have affliction, in Him you have peace John 16:33 (KJV), "33 These things I have spoken unto you, that in me ye might have peace. In the world ye shall have tribulation: but be of good cheer; I have overcome the world." Cling to the Cross because Satan is going to lose - in the end, God wins!

And for us because of the choice Jesus made to die upon the cross, we experience the joy of God's love, grace, and mercy. Numbers 6:25 (KJV), "25 The LORD makes his face shine upon thee and be gracious unto thee." Alan Jackson's song, "The Old Rugged Cross" capture the essence of the Cross. His song says, On a hill far away stood an old rugged cross the emblem of suffering and shame, and I love that old cross where the dearest and best for a world of lost sinners was slain."

There is something great about being at the feet of Jesus at the bottom of the Cross. Especially when you are under a load of burdens, and you come into knowledge. Wonderful things happen at the cross as the burdens of your heart roll away to happen, if not at once, ultimately. following Christ, John 14:27 (KJV), "27 Peace I leave with you, my peace I give unto you: not as the world giveth, give I unto you. Let not your heart be troubled, neither let it be afraid". Matthew 11:28-30 (KJV), "28 Come unto me, all ye that labor and are heavy laden, and I will give you rest. 29 Take my yoke upon you and learn of me; for I am meek and lowly in heart: and ye shall find rest unto your souls. 30 For my yoke is easy, and my burden is light".

On this account alone believers are bidden even to rejoice in tribulation. 1 Peter 4: 13-16 (KJV), "13 But rejoice, inasmuch as ye are partakers of Christ's sufferings; that, when his glory shall be revealed, ye may be glad also with exceeding joy. 14 If ye be reproached for the name of Christ, happy are ye; for the spirit of glory and of God resteth upon you: on their part, he is evil spoken of, but on your part, he is glorified.

¹⁵ But let none of you suffer as a murderer, or as a thief, or as an evildoer, or as a busybody in other men's matters. ¹⁶ Yet if any man suffers as a Christian, let him not be ashamed; but let him glorify God on this behalf."

Therefore, enduring persecutions and tribulations with patience and faith for the kingdom of God's sake, "2 Thessalonians 1:4-5 (KJV), "⁴ So that you yourselves glory in you in the churches of God for your patience and faith in all your persecutions and tribulations that ye endure: ⁵ Which is a manifest token of the righteous judgment of God, that ye may be counted worthy of the kingdom of God, for which ye also suffer".

Ephesians 2:8 (KJV), "⁸ For by grace are ye saved through faith; and that not of yourselves: it is the gift of God".

The point is not a relationship but discipleship. Moreover, it is insisted that suffering for Christ's sake is a prime characteristic of a faithful follower of your Lord. To evade the cross is to forfeit the title of a worthy witness in the world for the Lord Jesus, just as much as to display patient fortitude under fiery trials for the name of Christ is to proclaim the unswerving loyalty which marks one worthy of the devotion he professes to his Master.

Today's Christian does not seem to think much on the Cross or of Heaven. They cannot envision getting to go there or seeing the beauty of what God promises. The cross of Christ is reduced to an empty sign or modified to suit the conventional notions of a self-indulgent and complacent Christendom. The purpose of Christ death on the cross is to atone for your sins and give us an opportunity to make Heaven your home. However, if you cannot glory in the thought, then what is the purpose of Jesus' suffering on the cross?

Christians ought to pay attention to the stern callings of God. He plainly and solemnly calls for the uncompromising disowning of even the very closest of earthly ties, anything that would interfere with faithful discipleship to Himself. Matthew 10:37 (KJV), "He that loveth father or mother more than me is not worthy of me: and he that loveth son or daughter more than me is not worthy of me." Moreover, this is immediately followed by the weighty warning to all mere triflers whose devotion would be stilled by the first appearance of suffering for the truth's sake. Matthew 10:38 (KJV) says, "³⁸ And he that taketh not his cross, and followeth after me, is not worthy of me." You're worth, my worth, your worth was proven at the Cross when Jesus lovingly died for you to prove how worthy you are to Him. Your burden now lies in your responsibility to show that you are worthy of His sacrifice by living a life of testimony that honors God.

Moreover, to thrive on making Heaven your home where you will live eternally with God and join the Angels as they sing Holy, Holy, Holy to worship and praise Him.

Colossians 3:13 reminds us, "bearing with one another and, if one has a complaint against another, forgiving each other; as the Lord has forgiven you, so you also must forgive."

Ephesians 4:32 also command us, "Be kind to one another, tenderhearted, forgiving one another, as God in Christ forgave you." You can forgive because God has already forgiven us and has freed us from the emotional baggage, hurt and damage that relational dysfunction can bring. You can look to God to heal us where bitterness will fail to fulfill us.

God will test your allegiance, and your worthiness will be manifested. The power of that old rugged cross offers assurance that one day Jesus will return and take you up to glory with Him forever. Galatians 6:14 (KJV), "¹⁴ But God forbid that I should glory, save in the cross of your Lord Jesus Christ, by whom the world is crucified unto me, and I unto the world". Being crucified on the cross, Christ redeemed us, Galatians 3:13 (KJV), "¹³ Christ hath redeemed us from the curse of the law, being made a curse for us: for it is written, Cursed is every one that hangeth on a tree." Jesus freely invites anyone to come to Him. The condition of coming to Christ was only to have a need, bodily or spiritual: John 7:37 (KJV), "³⁷ In the last day, that great day of the feast, Jesus stood and cried, saying, If any man thirst, let him come unto me, and drink". But Jesus carefully warns everyone who wants to follow Him of the burden of the cross; Luke 9:23 (KJV), "²³ And he said to them all, If any man will come after me, let him deny himself, and take up his cross daily, and follow me." And He gives us the assurance of eternal salvation, John 6:37 (KJV), "³⁷ All that the Father giveth me shall come to me; and him that cometh to me I will in no wise cast out."

Moreover, if in the world you have affliction, in Him you have peace John 16:33 (KJV), "³³ These things I have spoken unto you, that in me ye might have peace. In the world ye shall have tribulation: but be of good cheer; I have overcome the world."

When probation closes, and fate deals out its hand on the matter, those who follow Christ and remained faithful, enduring to the end shall glorify Christ. 2 Thessalonians 1:10 (KJV), "¹⁰ When he shall come to be glorified in his saints and to be admired in all them that believe (because your testimony among you was believed) in that day". Though joy is by no means confined to a future day: even now you glory in tribulations Romans 5:3 (KJV), "³ And not only so, but your glory in tribulations also: knowing that tribulation worketh patience". Amen.

Burdened By The Commandments

Romans 7:1 (KJV), "[1] Know ye not, brethren, (for I speak to them that know the law,) how that the law hath dominion over a man as long as he liveth?"

The Ten Commandments are glorious. It is comprised of what you should and should not do regarding loving God and loving man and points you away from sin. The problem has never been the Ten Commandments or God's perfect law. The burden of the Ten Commandments has always been imperfect man's inability to keep God's perfect law.

Proverbs 4 (KJV), "[1] Hear, ye children, the instruction of a father, and attend to know to understand. [2] For I give you good doctrine, forsake ye, not my law. [3] For I was my father's son, tender and only beloved in the sight of my mother. [4] He taught me also, and said unto me, Let thine heart retain my words: keep my commandments, and live."

The Ten Commandments and was in place and existed from the time of Creation and before God made the man, to ensure God's people would not be living in total disobedience before God gave them to Moses on Mount Sinai. Let us look at Genesis 2:1-3 (KJV), "[1] Thus the heavens and the earth were finished, and all the host of them. [2] And on the seventh day God ended his work which he had made, and he rested on the seventh day from all his work which he had made. [3] And God blessed the seventh day and sanctified it: because that in it he had rested from all his work which God created and made." Genesis 2:5, 7 (KJV), "[5] And every plant of the field before it was in the earth, and every herb of the field before it grew: for the LORD God had not caused it to rain upon the earth, and there was not a man to till the ground. [7] And the LORD God formed man of the dust of the ground and breathed into his nostrils the breath of life, and man became a living soul.

Adam was placed in the Garden amid a finished work. Everything was prepared for him. God had created the trees, animals, birds, fishes, and He had rested on the seventh day and hallowed it before He decided to form man, and way before God gave the commandments to Moses on Mount Sinai, in Genesis 16 - before the Commandments were written on tablets of stone. The devil convinced Adam by way of Eve that he needed to do something to qualify for all the things with which he was already blessed. The devil gave him a false narrative and Adam believed the devil, ate the fruit and cursed to a life of sorrow. Genesis 3:1–6 (KJV), "[1] Now the serpent was more subtle than any beast of the field which the LORD God had made. And he said unto the woman, Yea, hath God said, Ye, shall not eat of every tree of the garden? [2] And the woman said unto the serpent; We may eat of the fruit of the trees of the garden: [3] But of the fruit of the tree which is in the midst of the garden, God hath said, Ye shall not eat of it, neither shall ye touch it, lest ye die. [4] And the serpent said unto the woman, Ye shall not surely die: [5] For God doth know that in the day ye eat thereof, then your eyes shall be opened, and ye shall be as gods, knowing good and evil. [6] And when the woman saw that the tree was good for food and that it was pleasant to the eyes, and a tree to be desired to make one wise, she took of the fruit thereof, and did eat, and gave also unto her husband with her; and he did eat."

The truth is God highly regarded Adam, and he was blessed and wanted for nothing! Genesis 3:22-23 (KJV), "[22] And the LORD God said, Behold, the man is become as one of us, to know good and evil: and now, lest he put forth his hand, and take also of the tree of life, and eat, and live forever: [23] Therefore the LORD God sent him forth from the garden of Eden, to till the ground from whence he was taken." Now he is cursed. Well, God said, Genesis 3:19 (KJV), "[19] In the sweat of thy face shalt thou eat bread, till thou return unto the ground; for out of it wast thou taken for dust thou art, and unto dust shalt thou return."

Adultery was covered in Genesis 39:9 (KJV), "[9] There is none greater in this house than I; neither hath he kept back anything from me but thee, because of thou art his wife: how then can I do this great wickedness and sin against God?"

Look at what the Bible says in Exodus 20:3-17 (KJV), "3 Thou shalt have no other gods before me. ⁴Thou shalt not make unto thee any graven image or any likeness of anything that is in heaven above, or that is in the earth beneath, or that is in the water under the earth. ⁵Thou shalt not bow down thyself to them, nor serve them: for I the LORD thy God am a jealous God, visiting the iniquity of the fathers upon the children unto the third and fourth generation of them that hate me; ⁶And shewing mercy unto thousands of them that love me and keep my commandments. ⁷Thou shalt not take the name of the LORD thy God in vain; for the LORD will not hold him guiltless that taketh his name in vain. ⁸Remember the sabbath day, to keep it holy. ⁹Six days shalt thou labour, and do all thy work: ¹⁰But the seventh day is the sabbath of the LORD thy God: in it thou shalt not do any work, thou, nor thy son, nor thy daughter, thy manservant, nor thy maidservant, nor thy cattle, nor thy stranger that is within thy gates: ¹¹For in six days the LORD made heaven and earth, the sea, and all that in them is, and rested the seventh day: wherefore the LORD blessed the sabbath day and hallowed it. ¹²Honor thy father and thy mother: that thy days may be long upon the land which the LORD thy God giveth thee. ¹³Thou shalt not kill. ¹⁴Thou shalt not commit adultery. ¹⁵Thou shalt not steal. ¹⁶Thou shalt not bear false witness against thy neighbor. ¹⁷Thou shalt not covet thy neighbor's house, thou shalt not covet thy neighbor's wife, nor his manservant, nor his maidservant, nor his ox, nor his ass, nor anything that is thy neighbor's." And then God sealed His commands in Leviticus 22:31(KJV), "³¹Therefore shall ye keep my commandments, and do them: I am the Lord."

The law condemns, look deeply, you find that Adam was fearful. Genesis 3:10 (KJV), "¹⁰And he said, I heard thy voice in the garden, and I was afraid because I was naked, and I hid myself." Adam was afraid, the deeper root of stress is fear. But before he was fearful. Adam felt condemned because he partook of the tree of the knowledge of good and evil. The tree of good and evil is a picture of the law which gives us knowledge of right and wrong and points us away from sin. Romans 3:20 (KJV), "²⁰ Therefore by the deeds of the law there shall no flesh be justified in his sight: for by the law is the knowledge of sin."

Also, the first commandment Biblically documented that God gave to man, Adam, and Eve, would seem to be the Sabbath Day commandment. However, in Mark 12:28-29 (KJV), "²⁸ And one of the scribes came, and having heard them reasoning together, and perceiving that he had answered them well, asked him, Which is the first commandment of all? ²⁹ And Jesus answered him, The first of all the commandments is, Hear, O Israel; The Lord, our God, is one Lord:" This is relevant because you know God's words never changes, and here you see how important it is not to take a single Bible verse and let it be the basis for your entire conclusion on anything in the Bible. (Reference also Exodus 16:26-28, 30). Additionally, when Cain killed Able, God asked Cain, Genesis 4:10-11 (KJV), "¹⁰ And he said, What hast thou done? the voice of thy brother's blood crieth unto me from the ground. ¹¹ And now art thou cursed from the earth, which hath opened her mouth to receive thy brother's blood from thy hand;" God would not have to hold Cain accountable for murder if Cain did not know it was wrong and Cain would not have hidden his brother's body after killing him if Cain did not know it was against the will of God that, "Thou shall not kill." Cain knew that murdering his brother was a sin.

The same with honoring your parents. The sad story of Jacob and his mother Rebecca deceiving Isaac to get the birthright of his brother Joseph shows us that before the giving of the ten commandments on Mount Sinai.

Also, Genesis 35 shows us that idolatry was a sin way before the commandments were giving on Mount Sinai. And Genesis 39:7-10: (KJV), "⁷ And it came to pass after these things, that his master's wife cast her eyes upon Joseph; and she said, Lie with me. ⁸ But he refused and said unto his master's wife, Behold, my master wotteth not what is with me in the house, and he hath committed all that he hath to my hand;

⁹ There is none greater in this house than I; neither hath he kept back anything from me but thee, because thou art his wife: how then can I do this great wickedness, and sin against God? ¹⁰ And it came to pass, as she spoke to Joseph day by day, that he hearkened not unto her, to lie by her, or to be with her." Here we see Potiphar, an officer of Pharaoh, captain of the guard, an Egyptian, wife tempting Joseph with adultery, but Joseph knew better and asked her in verse 9, "…how then can I do this great wickedness and sin against God?" And then he flees. (Read Genesis 39 and interesting story). Now, remember, all these are happening before the ten commandments were given to Moses on Mount Sinai.

Significantly, at the time the Commandments were written, the people feared God, Exodus 20:18-21 (KJV), "¹⁸ And all the people saw the thunderings, and the lightning, and the noise of the trumpet, and the mountain smoking: and when the people saw it, they removed and stood afar off. ¹⁹ And they said unto Moses, Speak thou with us, and we will hear: but let not God speak with us, lest we die. ²⁰ And Moses said unto the people, Fear not: for God is come to prove you, and that his fear may be before your faces, that ye sin not. ²¹ And the people stood afar off, and Moses drew near unto the thick darkness where God was."

Contrary to popular beliefs, God did not give the law for a man to live by or to make man holy. God communed with Moses Exodus 34:28 (KJV), "²⁸ And he was there with the Lord forty days and forty nights; he did neither eat bread nor drink water. And He wrote upon the tables the words of the covenant, the ten commandments. The ten commandments are God's moral laws that keep us out of trouble. God gave the law so that we know we are sinners in need of a Savior. When we are obedient, the laws point us away from sin, our disobedience of the commandments, then, points us towards sin. Sin is anything that goes against God's will and His laws. To transgress or disobey God's commandments, His laws, is to commit sin.

Today, the Ten Commandments seems to be under attack and disrespected. Revelation 12:17 (KJV), "¹⁷ And the dragon was wroth with the woman and went to make war with the remnant of her seed, which keeps the commandments of God, and have the testimony of Jesus Christ."

Many people are puffed up with their own greatness and want to justify their bad behavior and lawlessness, so they claim that God did away with His commandments. This lie of the devil has affected every aspect of humanity. So, God is asking you in Romans 6:15 (KJV), "15 What then? shall we sin, because we are not under the law, but under grace? God forbids." The Bible makes God position very clear when Jesus said, "Matthew 5:17-20 (KJV), "17 Think not that I am come to destroy the law or the prophets: I am not come to destroy, but to fulfill. 18 For verily I say unto you, Till heaven and earth pass, one jot or one tittle shall in no wise pass from the law, till all be fulfilled. 19 Whosoever, therefore, shall break one of these least commandments, and shall teach men so, he shall be called the least in the kingdom of heaven: but whosoever shall do and teach them, the same shall be called great in the kingdom of heaven. 20 For I say unto you, "That except your righteousness shall exceed the righteousness of the scribes and Pharisees, ye shall in no case enter into the kingdom of heaven."

Like God has a plan for mankind to have us to live with Him in heaven, Satan too has him a plan for mankind to have us burn with him in hell. God knows the beginning and the end warns us 1 Peter 5:8 (KJV), "8 Be sober, be vigilant; because your adversary the devil, as a roaring lion, walketh about, seeking whom he may devour:" Also, God reminded us we know we are His. 1 John 5:19 (KJV), "19 And we know that we are of God, and the whole world lieth in wickedness." Two thousand years have passed, and nothing has changed. Indeed, Satan's has not changed. He still wants to prove he is more significant than God and He wants to draw everyone away from God and under his power. Until the end of time, Satan will continue to whisper his lies into the ear of disbelievers and Christians who are choosing sin over righteousness. Satan is encouraging pride and doubt to cause a division between the people of God, just as he did with the Angels while he was in heaven.

And, Satan is working overtime to ensure he deceives anyone who is willing to disobey God's commandments, with the idea that God did away with His commandments and that their human abilities preclude any need for God. The devil is smarter than many psychiatrists, psychologists, and even many believers. He does not deal with the peripherals and the superficial. Do you know what his first name is? It is not "thief" or "murderer," even though he steals and murders. His first name is Satan, which is Hebrew for "prosecutor at law" or "accuser."

Do you know what the role of a prosecutor is in the court of law? He is there to prosecute you and condemn you. He never talks about your good points. He will bring up all the dirty laundry and relentlessly accuse you till you feel condemned.

So, the devil's name tells us that he goes straight to the root of your problems. He does not come to you and say, "Let your business slide" or "Neglect your children." On the contrary, he comes to say things like, "How can you let the business slide?" or "Call yourself a Christian! Call yourself a good father. You're a lousy father!" He accuses you till you feel condemned. And he uses the law, which is holy, right and just, to condemn you. That is why condemnation—the root cause of all your problems—is so subtle. That is why condemnation usually goes undetected.

However, John 13:34-35 (KJV), "34 A new commandment I give unto you, That ye love one another; as I have loved you, that ye also love one another. 35 By this shall all men know that ye are my disciples if ye have love one to another." God's absolute goodness, wisdom, and love must never be brought into question.

Therefore, you must never be biased against the word of God and His Ten Commandments. The Cross and God's commandments are the foundation upon which the covenant between God and man is built. Deuteronomy 4:13 (KJV), "13 And he declared unto you his covenant, which he commanded you to perform, even ten commandments; and he wrote them upon two tables of stone." Accordingly, 1 John 2:3-6 (KJV), "3 And hereby we do know that we know him if we keep his commandments. [4] He that saith, I know Him, and keepeth not His commandments, is a liar, and the truth is not in him. [5] But whoso keepeth His word, in him verily is the love of God perfected: hereby know we that we are in Him. [6] He that saith He abideth in him ought himself also so to walk, even as He walked."

Solomon, the wisest man on earth, made it clear that the commandment is for everyone and if we all kept the commandment, there would be no problems in the world. However, it is quite amazing how many of the commandments are broken regularly basis, even by Christians. Everyone would worship God on the Seventh-day; there would be no adultery, crowded prisons, crooked politicians, liars, and cheaters.

If you examine the commandments closely, they cover a broad spectrum of what God is expecting from each one of us and yet if obeyed, will save man from all the ills in the world.

Still, people want to do away with ten commandments so they can be lawless. Jeremiah 17:9 (KJV), "[9] The heart is deceitful above all things, and desperately wicked: who can know it?" Of course, the man that wants several wives definitely want the ten commandments done away with, so does the person who does not want a law that says do not covet, those who want what their neighbor has do not want a law forbidding them to steal and so on.

Therefore, their intent about doing away with the commandments must be to make the devil happy because he is the only one that would win if that happens. Thank God it will never happen.

Instead, of wasting your time with wishful thinking, why not change your heart and live Godly. Repeatedly you may have promised to obey God and fail. You cannot do it by yourself. You need to put on the whole armor of God and Hebrews 8: allow God to write it in your heart.

When you break the commandments, you do not only break God's law; you break His heart. And when you break one, God said you break them all. James 2:10 (KJV), " [10] For whosoever shall keep the whole law, and yet offend in one point, he is guilty of all."

Is Grace A License To Sin?

Hebrews 10:26 (KJV), "For if we sin wilfully after that, we have received the knowledge of the truth, there remaineth no more sacrifice for sins." This Bible verse alone makes it clear that "grace is not a license to sin." But let us go on. Daniel 12:2 (KJV), "2 And many of them that sleep in the dust of the earth shall awake, some to everlasting life, and some to shame and everlasting contempt.

Unfortunately, we have all sinned against God because to break the law of God is to sin 1 John 3:4 (KJV), "4 Whosoever committeth sin transgresseth also the law: for sin is the transgression of the law." Romans 3:23 (KJV), "23 For all have sinned, and come short of the glory of God;" so we all deserve to be judged by God according to the Law. The Bible tells us that the wages of sin is death Romans 6:23 (KJV), "23 For the wages of sin is death; but the gift of God is eternal life through Jesus Christ our Lord" and separation from him Isaiah 59:2 (KJV)."2 So, we are all under the righteous judgment of God.

We are sinners, by nature children of wrath; Ephesians 2:3 (KJV), "3 Among whom also we all had our conversation in times past in the lusts of our flesh, fulfilling the desires of the flesh and of the mind; and were by nature the children of wrath, even as others."

Continuously, people abuse the truth of God's grace and inaccurately presents false teachings as pure grace, and telling people that they are always covered under God's grace - giving people a license to sin.

However, grace is not a license to sin and is a distortion to the restoration of God's truth. God said in Genesis 6:3,5 (KJV), "3 And the Lord said, My spirit shall not always strive with man, for that he also is flesh: yet his days shall be a hundred and twenty years. 5 And God saw that the wickedness of man was great in the earth and that every imagination of the thoughts of his heart was only evil continually."

There are many controversies, inaccuracies, and counterfeits to God's truths throughout history. People have been misapplying God's word and twisting God's word to fit their needs.

Does God's grace give us a license to sin? Scripturally, and obviously, the answer is no. On the contrary, Romans 6:14 tells us that God's grace is the power over sin. It is also unfortunate that a small number misrepresent the truth of God's amazing grace, using "grace" as an excuse for living a licentious lifestyle that is in clear violation of God's Word. As with any truth from God, there will be a minority who are abusing grace unashamedly. Clearly, they misunderstand the purpose for which God's has bestowed His amazing grace upon us. When confronted about his or her adulterous relationship, the response usually is, "Well, I'm under grace, so you can't condemn me." As if they are entitled and it is expected no matter. Or the person has shown no desire to stop a lifestyle of sin and defends himself or herself by saying, "God's grace covers me." There is a significant problem with their matter of fact attitude. None of us know when probation will close for us. They are playing with their salvation if nothing else.

Still, how do you address this problem without backing away from God's grace? What do you say to those who use grace as a license to sin? Are these people genuinely living under grace in the first place? Here is an illustration of how God's grace works.

Scenario 1: First, you committed a crime, and you got caught. The police catch you go to court, and you are found guilty, so you go to jail; That is justice. You got what you deserved.

Scenario 2 you committed a crime, and you got caught. The police catch you go to court and you are found guilty, but the judge sets you free. That is mercy. God intervened, so you did not get what you deserved.

Scenario 3: Third, you committed a crime, and you got caught. The police catch you go to court and you are found guilty, the judge not only sets you free but the judge also wipes it from the records. That is both God's mercy and grace at work. Not only did you not have to answer for your crime and get what you deserve under (man's justice), God also covered and pardoned you under (mercy), and God restored you by wiping it from your record (grace). So, man's justice, we get what we deserve. In mercy, God covers you and bless so you don't get what you deserve, or you get less than you deserve. In grace, God covers you and bless you with what you do not deserve and may choose to restore you and give you a fresh start or leave you better positioned than you were.

Grace is God's unmerited favor against sin. So, to be saved by grace means you are getting what you do not deserve from God. The judgment due to you because of your sin against God, for which you do not deserve forgiveness: 1 Corinthians 6:9-10 (KJV), "⁹ Know ye not that the unrighteous shall not inherit the kingdom of God? Be not deceived: neither fornicators, nor idolaters, nor adulterers, nor effeminate, nor abusers of themselves with mankind, ¹⁰ Nor thieves, nor covetous, nor drunkards, nor revilers, nor extortioners, shall inherit the kingdom of God." The sins that will befall you may be received unmerited forgiveness. And in addition, you will get what you do not deserve, death, and you will get more than you deserve, the opportunity to live with God in Eternity and being in God's presence.

God gives this to you through Jesus' blood and the Cross. You do not deserve to go to heaven, but God's grace through Jesus will get many undeserving people in, but there is no guarantee who will get into Heaven. If Heaven was sure to everyone, then there is no need for the ten commandments, and there was no need for Jesus to shed His blood.

However, by Jesus shedding His blood, God will grant some of us sinful worms grace, but that is what God intended His Grace to be used for while we know better and can do better. God said in Luke 12:48 (KJV), "⁴⁸ But he that knew not, and did commit things worthy of stripes, shall be beaten with few stripes. For unto whomsoever much is given, of him shall be much required: and to whom men have committed much, of him they will ask the more."

Let us be clear; anyone is living in sin is not living under grace; they are living on borrowed time. If a man tells you, he is leaving his wife for his secretary, and he tells you he is under "grace," tell him that he is not under grace but under deception and he has no business under there!

Believe only in the authority of God's Word, not what man says, not even your preacher if he cannot show you Biblical proof. 1 John 4:1 (KJV), "1 Beloved, believe not every spirit, but try the spirits whether they are of God: because many false prophets are gone out into the world." If people are genuine in sharing Biblical truth, then they can produce the Bible verse. living under grace, he would not be dominated by such a sin. A person living under grace is not consumed with committing sin or want to continue living in sin! How can he or she be when God's word and authority clearly state in Romans 6:14 (KJV), "14 For sin shall not have dominion over you: for ye are not under the law, but under grace"? A revelation of grace will never produce a licentious lifestyle. And no one living in sin can legitimately use grace as an excuse to justify sin, because it is antithetical to God's Holy Scriptures.

God's grace is sufficient but makes no mistake, the interpretations and insinuations and innuendos that people can sin as they have a mind because they are under grace is a lie of Satan to deceive man and keep them behaving lawlessly. There will always be a small number of people who are abusing grace, stirring controversy with false grace teachings, and living in ways that do not glorify the Lord. But what should our response be? Should we shy away from preaching and teaching the pure grace of God because of the controversies and abuses? Certainly not. I exhort you today, with the words of Titus, to "Speak these things, exhort, and rebuke with all authority. Let no one despise you."

However, if you hear of any teachings that tell you it is all right to sin, to live without any regard for the Lord, and that there are no consequences to sin, because you are under grace, flee from that teaching. Get away from them as far as you can. Because on the contrary, grace sets a sinner free from a desire to sin. Chains break, burdens are rolled away, and all sorts of sinful lifestyles and addictions, broken marriages, and destroyed relationships are miraculously and permanently restored to the glory of God. Grace brings you into oneness with God.

Also, true grace teaches that believers in Christ are called to live holy, blameless, and above reproach. It teaches that sin always produces destructive consequences and that it is only through the power of the gospel of Jesus Christ that one can be set free from the dominion of sin. Study Titus 2:11–15 (KJV), "[11] For the grace of God that bringeth salvation hath appeared to all men, [12] Teaching us that, denying ungodliness and worldly lusts, we should live soberly, righteously, and godly, in this present world; [13] Looking for that blessed hope, and the glorious appearing of the great God and our Saviour Jesus Christ; [14] Who gave himself for us, that he might redeem us from all iniquity, and purify unto himself a peculiar people, zealous of good works. [15] These things speak, and exhort, and rebuke with all authority. Let no man despise thee."

Genuine grace is not a license to sin; it is the power to live above the dominion of sin. Genuine grace does not compromise God's holy standards and condone sin; it is the answer that gives people the power to live great lives zealous for good works.

Therefore, it is essential that we do not draw our conclusions about God's grace based on the few who abuse it but study God's Word for ourselves to understand what the original, unadulterated gospel of grace indeed is. Do not allow anyone to put doubts in your heart and corrupt your mind about hearing and receiving God's grace. If you do, you will be allowing them to rob you of the treasure of the true gospel laid out in God's Word and of its power to set you free from a cycle of sin and defeat.

Instead, seek counseling from Clergy who are true to the Living Word of God and to whom God has entrusted with the gospel. Colossians 2:8 (KJV), "Beware lest any man spoils you through philosophy and vain deceit, after the tradition of men, after the rudiments of the world, and not after Christ." Study the word of God for yourself and lean not to your own understanding. As the Apostle Paul instructed Timothy, his young protégé in 2 Tim. 2:1(KJV), "Thou, therefore, my son, be strong in the grace that is in Christ Jesus. 2, Tim. 2:15 (KJV), "[15]Study to shew thyself approved unto God, a workman that needeth not to be ashamed, rightly dividing the word of truth." For this reason, it is important to discount the inaccuracies surrounding God's grace and the false teachings that have grown prevalent and has led many astray and leading many more.

The Word of God says in no uncertain terms that the grace of God teaches us to deny ungodliness and live godly lives. People may use the word grace freely, calling themselves "grace preachers" with "grace ministries" or "grace churches." But we need to be discerning. Just because they use the word grace does not mean they are accurately or genuinely standing for the gospel of grace. Test everything! Be sure that their position against sin is clear, as sin is destructive and brings with it a whole host of damaging consequences. Jesus warns in Matthew 7: (KJV), " [21]Not every one that saith unto me, Lord, Lord, shall enter into the kingdom of heaven; but he that doeth the will of my Father which is in heaven.[22] Many will say to me in that day, Lord, Lord, have we not prophesied in thy name? and in thy name have cast out devils? and in thy name done many wonderful works? [23] And then will I profess unto them, I never knew you: depart from me, ye that work iniquity." Meaning there will be preachers telling you lies. Therefore, watch out for false grace teachings that contradict Scripture.

This is most unfortunate because all across the world people are hearing this lie and the devil is busy helping them spread it. Meanwhile, God's Holy words and revealing plan of salvation is not being taught. God's revelation and good news that is changes lives and draw people into an intimate relationship with Jesus are being challenged. But, do not dismay. God has His appointed shepherds over our flocks, preaching and teaching that is careful to offer authentic Scriptural proof of "Thus saith the Lord."

Thankfully, God's mercies and grace are everlasting and available to those who believe and put their trust in God. His genuine work of grace is working both in His church and in Saints. In other words, do not back away from preaching the grace of God. In fact, we should be doubling down on our preaching of the whole gospel that teaches all to "[deny] ungodliness and worldly lust" and to "live soberly, righteously, and godly in the present age." The more pure grace is preached, the more false grace teachings will be stamped out.

Equally significant, true grace doesn't disregard morals of ten commandments. There have been many inaccurate explanations about the Ten Commandments in false grace teachings. Be clear that true grace teaches that the Ten Commandments are holy, just, and right. True grace teaching upholds the moral excellencies, values, and virtues espoused by the Ten Commandments. The Ten Commandments are so perfect in its standard and so unbending in its holy requirements that Galatians 3:11 states that no man can be justified by the law in the sight of God. Justification before God can only come by faith in Christ.

Since the time Jesus departed this earth, 2000 plus years, not a single man has obeyed the Ten Commandments perfectly and be justified. Listen carefully, under grace, when you experience the love of our God, you will not desire to sin! Under true grace, you want to live holy, not happy because grace is a love relationship with God that produces true holiness! As Apostle Paul boldly proclaimed, Roman 13:10 (KJV), "[10] Love worketh no ill to his neighbor: therefore love is the fulfilling of the law." When the love of Jesus is in us, we cannot help but fulfill the law. When your heart is overflowing with the goodness of God's grace, you fall deeper and deeper in love with Him, and it is so natural that a loving-kindness exudes your spirit, you lose the desire to commit sin.

Being firmly rooted and proved in the grace of God you have the power to love because God first loved you. 1 John 4:19 (KJV), "[19] We love him because he first loved us."

The fact is that when God's people are under grace, not only do they fulfill the letter of the law, but they also exceed it or go the extra mile. The law commands us not to commit adultery, and there are people who can fulfill just the letter of the law and not commit adultery outwardly.

However, inwardly, they have no love for their spouses. Grace changes all that. Grace does not just deal with the surface; it goes deeper and teaches a man to love his wife as Christ loved the church.

In the same way, the law can command us not to covet, but it has no ability to make us cheerful givers. Again, God's grace goes beyond the superficial to inwardly transform our covetous hearts into hearts that are loving, compassionate, and generous. Remember the story of a rich man named Zacchaeus, which was the chief among the publicans in Luke 19? Luke 19: 5-7 (KJV), "And Jesus entered and passed through Jericho. [2] And, behold, there was a man named Zacchaeus, which was the chief among the publicans, and he was rich. [3] And he sought to see Jesus who he was; and could not for the press, because he was little of stature. [4] And he ran before and climbed up into a Sycamore tree to see him: for he was to pass that way. [5] And when Jesus came to the place, he looked up, and saw him, and said unto him, Zacchaeus, make haste, and come down; for today I must abide at thy house. [6] And he made haste, and came down, and received him joyfully. [7] And when they saw it, they all murmured, saying, That he was gone to be guest with a man that is a sinner. [8] And Zacchaeus stood, and said unto the Lord: Behold, Lord, the half of my goods I give to the poor; and if I have taken anything from any man by false accusation, I restore him fourfold. [9] And Jesus said unto him, This day is salvation come to this house, forsomuch as he also is a son of Abraham.

[10] For the Son of man is come to seek and to save that which was lost. (Read the full story in Luke 19) Here you see an unworthy publican (tax collector), accused by a Pharisee and called out for his unworthiness, but Jesus calls to Him, and now he is under grace by being allowed to receive Jesus into his home. He humbly asks God for mercy, but Jesus gives him both mercy and grace. Jesus is not sitting down with him and going over the commandments.

Instead, God made it known that is why Jesus came, to save sinners. And because this tax collector felt privileged to be in his presence, and the love and grace of Jesus touched his heart, the once-covetous and corrupt tax collector Luke 19:8 (KJV), "⁸ And Zacchaeus stood, and said unto the Lord: Behold, Lord, the half of my goods I give to the poor; and if I have taken anything from any man by false accusation, I restore him fourfold." Under grace, he no longer desires to sin and covet.

In contrast, the rich young ruler in Luke 18 came to our Lord Jesus boasting that he had kept all the commandments. This young man was expecting Jesus to compliment him on his law keeping and was feeling confident of himself. But notice what Jesus said to him. Instead of complimenting him, Luke 18:22 (KJV), " . You see, every time we boast in our ability to be justified by the law, our Lord will point out an area we lack in. He told the young man to sell all that he had, give it to the poor, and follow Him. Jesus was giving him the very first commandment, "You shall have no other gods before Me," (not even money) and look at what happened. The young ruler walked away sorrowful. He was not even able to give away one dollar! I believe the Holy Spirit placed these two stories side by side in Luke 18 and 19 to show us what boasting in the law produces and what the power of the Lord's unconditional grace produces in people's lives.

God's grace is not against God's perfect and glorious law of the Ten Commandments. In fact, Apostle Paul says, "For I delight in the law of God according to the inward man" (Romans 7:22). However, he goes on to say, "But I see another law in my members, warring against the law of my mind, and bringing me into captivity to the law of sin which is in my members" (Romans 7:23). Can you see it? The law of God is holy, just, and good, but it has no power to make you holy, just, and good. Hear what Paul says in Romans 7:7–8, 12–14

Paul taught that when you combine God's perfect law with the flesh (the sin principle), the result is unholiness, a life that is dominated by sin, condemnation, and death. In man's flesh dwells no good thing and if we are in this mortal body, the sin principle in our flesh will continue to be stirred. But praise is to our Lord Jesus Christ; this does not have to end in misery and hopelessness. Because of what Jesus has done on the cross, we can have the veil of the law removed, so that we can behold

Jesus face-to-face and be gloriously transformed: (Read 2 Corinthians 3:11, 14, 18)

It is clear from God's Word that the law stirs up our sinful nature, whereas grace produces true holiness. Holiness is all about becoming more and more like Jesus, and it comes about when the veil of the law is removed. When the veil is removed, we see our beautiful Savior face-to-face, and His glorious grace transforms us from glory to glory. The glorious gospel of grace always produces great lives. As we behold Jesus, we will grow from glory to glory and shine as a testament of the Lord's goodness and moral excellencies.

Grace does not mean automatic salvation for all . When our Lord Jesus died at Calvary, He took all of humanity's sins with one sacrifice of Himself at the cross. He took the judgment, punishment, and condemnation for every sin upon Himself. That is the value of the one Man, Jesus. He is an overpayment for all our sins. However, that does this mean everyone is automatically forgiven and saved under grace. Of course not! While your sin was paid for at Calvary, you must make a personal decision to die to self, come into submission with Christ, ask for forgiveness of your sins and thrive to sin no more, and give your life to God through baptism.

To conclude, to fully understand the grace of God, it is essential we understand the difference between law and grace. John 1:17 tells us, "[17] For the law was given by Moses, but grace and truth came by Jesus Christ." (Don't take this out of context, the ten commandments are the laws authorized and written by God and given to Moses to deliver to man, this is the best explanation for those trying to understand). The law was given through a servant; grace and truth came through the Son. The law instructs man on how to live pleasing unto God, and grace reveals the nature, character, and love of God. God waits with loving arms open and ready to forgive. Still, it is necessary that you do not make faulty assumptions about God's grace and mercy because while God is merciful, and, the unrepented soul and those who insist in believing that there is no God, will not go unnoticed.

Burdened by The Sabbath

There can be no doubt that Christ, His disciples, and Sabbath Keepers kept Saturday, the seventh-day Sabbath. Yet, today, most Christians are professing Sunday is the Sabbath, the first day of the week. However, no Biblically versed believer or student of the Scriptures will ever deny that God instituted the Sabbath at creation, before He formed man from the dust, and before He gave it to Moses on Mount of Olive, and God designated the seventh day to be kept holy. Genesis 2:2–3 (KJV), "²And on the seventh day God ended his work which he had made; and he rested on the seventh day from all his work which he had made. ³And God blessed the seventh day, and sanctified it: because that in it he had rested from all his work which God created and made." It was later codified as the Fourth Commandment found in Exodus 20:8-11 (KJV), "⁸Remember the Sabbath day, to keep it holy. ⁹Six days shalt thou labour, and do all thy work: ¹⁰But the seventh day is the sabbath of the LORD thy God: in it thou shalt not do any work, thou, nor thy son, nor thy daughter, thy manservant, nor thy maidservant, nor thy cattle, nor thy stranger that is within thy gates: ¹¹For in six days the LORD made heaven and earth, the sea, and all that in them is, and rested the seventh day: wherefore the LORD blessed the sabbath day and hallowed it."

God set aside the Sabbath day, one day out of seven days, just for us to commune with Him. The Word of God makes it expressly clear that Sabbath observance is a distinctive sign or "mark" between God and His people. You show your love for God, by taking time out to worship Him and come into His presence and spend time with Him. God also uses this time to fellowship with us and show us His love. That is the point of Sabbath day worship and why you should keep the day holy.

In the Bible, on Sunday Jesus' Resurrection took place. (See Matthew 28:1-7, Mark 16:1-8, Luke 24:1-8, and John 20:1-18.) Jesus died on a

Friday and rose on a Sunday. Even in His death Jesus "remembered" the Sabbath Day and kept it Holy.

So, who Changed the Sabbath from Saturday to Sunday? There is absolutely no Biblical text stating that God, Jesus, or the apostles changed the Sabbath to Sunday—not one text, not one word, not even a hint or suggestion. If there were, those chapters and verses would be loudly heralded by Sabbath opposers. Had Paul or any other apostle taught a change from Sabbath to Sunday, the first day of the week, an absolute firestorm of protest would have arisen from conservative Jewish Christians. The Pharisees and scribes would have insisted that Paul or any other person even suggesting such a thing be stoned to death for the sin of Sabbath-breaking. This would have been a much larger issue than the controversy over circumcision!

The Christians during the apostolic era, from about 35 to 100 A.D., kept Sabbath on the designated seventh day of the week. For the first 300 years of Christian history, when the Roman emperors regarded themselves as gods, Christianity became an "illegal religion," and God's people were scattered abroad Acts 8:1 (KJV), "[1] And Saul was consenting unto his death. And at that time there was a great persecution against the church which was at Jerusalem; and they were all scattered abroad throughout the regions of Judaea and Samaria, except the apostles." Judaism, however, was regarded at that time as "legal," as long as they obeyed Roman laws. Thus, during the apostolic era, Christians found it convenient to let the Roman authorities think of them as Jews, which gained them legitimacy with the Roman government. However, when the Jews rebelled against Rome, the Romans put down their rebellion by destroying Jerusalem in A.D. 70 and again in A.D. 135.

Obviously, the Roman government's suppression of the Jews made it increasingly uncomfortable for Christians to be thought of as Jewish. At that time, Sunday was the rest day of the Roman Empire, whose religion was Mithraism, a form of sun worship. Since Sabbath observance is visible to others, some Christians in the early second century sought to distance themselves from Judaism by observing a different day, thus "blending in" to the society around them.

Yet today, most of the professing Christian world keeps Sunday, the first day of the week, calling it the Sabbath. The New Testament plainly shows we are to continue keeping the commandments (Mathew 5:17–18; 19:17; 28:20)—all ten of them. The self-righteous Pharisees had already falsely accused Christ of breaking the Sabbath because He violated the added man-made rules and traditions they placed upon the Sabbath (Mark 2:24). The total absence of any such controversy over a change in the day of worship is one of the best evidence showing the apostles and other New Testament Christians did not change the day.

On the contrary, Paul and his traveling companions kept many Sabbaths long after the resurrection of Jesus Christ. Read of them in your own Bible in Acts 13:14, 27, 42–44; 15:21; 16:13; 17:2; and 18:4. Acts 13:42–44 is especially significant in that Paul and Barnabas, when speaking at a Jewish synagogue, were invited to speak the next Sabbath again. This would have been Paul's golden opportunity to tell the people to meet with him the next day rather than waiting a whole week for the Sabbath. But, "on the next Sabbath, almost the whole city [Jews and Gentiles alike] gathered to hear the word of the Lord."

The Sunday law was officially confirmed by the Roman Papacy. The Council of Laodicea in A.D. 364 decreed, "Christians shall not Judaize and be idle on Saturday but shall work on that day; but the Lord's day they shall especially honor, and, as being Christians, shall if possible, do no work on that day. If, however, they are found Judaizing, they shall be shut out from Christ" (Strand, op. cit., citing Charles J. Hefele, A History of the Councils of the Church, 2 [Edinburgh, 1876] 316).

Cardinal Gibbons, in Faith of Our Fathers, 92nd ed., p. 89, freely admits, "You may read the Bible from Genesis to Revelation, and you will not find a single line authorizing the sanctification of Sunday. The Scriptures enforce the religious observance of Saturday, a day which we [the Catholic Church] never sanctify."

Again, "The Catholic Church, ... by virtue of her divine mission, changed the day from Saturday to Sunday" (The Catholic Mirror, the official publication of James Cardinal Gibbons, Sept. 23, 1893).

"Protestants do not realize that by observing Sunday, they accept the authority of the spokesperson of the Church, the Pope" (Our Sunday Visitor, February 5, 1950). "Of course the Catholic Church claims that the change [Saturday Sabbath to Sunday] was her act... And the act is a mark of her ecclesiastical authority in religious things" (H.F. Thomas, Chancellor of Cardinal Gibbons).

"Sunday is our mark of authority... the church is above the Bible, and this transference of Sabbath observance is proof of that fact" (Catholic Record of London, Ontario Sept 1, 1923). What a shocking admission! However, the Bible, the one and only true authority, The Living Word of God, says in Matthew 15:9 (KJV), "[9] But in vain they do worship me, teaching for doctrines the commandments of men." And again in Mark 7:7 (KJV), "[7] Howbeit in vain do they worship me, teaching for doctrines the commandments of men." God does not accept your Sunday worship as His Sabbath day although God says He has sheep in Sunday churches and He will, in His time, bring them out. John 10:16 (KJV), "[16] And other sheep I have, which are not of this fold: them also I must bring, and they shall hear my voice, and there shall be one fold, and one shepherd." Where, then, do men get the "authority" to change the Fourth Commandment by substituting Sunday for the original Sabbath Christ and the apostles kept?

Also, the popes of Rome may speak as if they are God but are not. Biblically Rome is the Beast (Devil) which many shall follow and be a loss. We see prophecy coming to pass when we read Daniel 7:25 (KJV), "[25] And he shall speak great words against the most High, and shall wear out the saints of the most High, and think to change times and laws: and they shall be given into his hand until a time and times and the dividing of time."

The Papacy has assumed many infallibilities which belong only to God. The Papacy has changed the time; they managed to convince many people how to pray and be forgiven for their sins and profess to forgive them of their sins, which belongs only to God for only God can forgive anyone of their sins. They priest want to be called "father" when God clearly instructs in Matthew 23:9 (KJV), "⁹And call no man your father upon the earth: for one is your Father, which is in heaven." They profess to open and shut heaven and convince people their loved one is trapped in limbo when the Bible does not teach this hogwash anywhere and instead teach that your loved ones are asleep until Jesus return (Read the section, "What happens when you die?"). Entry into Heaven will be determined by God and belongs only to God.

Also, the Papacy profess to be higher than all the kings of the earth, which the only One with any such authority is God who Revelation 19:16 (KJV), "¹⁶And he hath on his vesture and on his thigh a name written, KING OF KINGS, AND LORD OF LORDS." And in, 1 Timothy 6:15 (KJV), "¹⁵Which in his times he shall shew, who is the blessed and only Potentate, the King of kings, and Lord of lords," therefore such title belongs only to God. God also warned in Revelation 17:14 (KJV), "¹⁴These shall make war with the Lamb, and the Lamb shall overcome them: for he is Lord of lords, and King of kings: and they that are with him are called and chosen, and faithful." And they blaspheme and go against the laws of God when they decide and make indulgences for sin. This is the worst of all blasphemies!

Additionally, Daniel 4 says they "shall wear out the saints" by wars, crusades, massacres, inquisitions, and persecutions of all kinds. What in this way have they not done against all those who have protested against their innovations, and refused to submit to their idolatrous worship? For example, the exterminating crusades published against the Waldenses and Albigenses, the Smithfield fires in England, and God and man against this persecuting, ruthless, and impure Church.

And they "think to change times and laws" Appointing fasts and feasts; canonizing persons whom he chooses to call saints; granting pardons and indulgences for sins; instituting new modes of worship utterly unknown to the Christian Church; new articles of faith; new rules of practice; and reversing, with pleasure, the laws both of God and man.-–Dodd" (Emphasis his; Clarke's Commentary on the Bible, Volume IV, p. 594).

During the Sabbath day, all working is to cease so you can work on building a deeper relationship with God, and do so without worrying about bills, personal problems and all the trivial things of this world. The Sabbath day is time for singing and shouting and blessing the Lord. How glorious God feels when His saints take the time out to come and be with Him.

Additionally, Christians have a responsibility to share the Sabbath with others and bring people into the presence of God. But how can you fulfill your duty when you cannot even drag yourself out of bed to arrive at church on time. And if you are purposeful to do so a few times out the year, how many times are you rushing the Pastor to hurry up with the sermon because you have places to go, people to see, and money to make?

Still, most of you go about Sabbath worship in such a canonical way that you run people away from the church. You have all sorts of biases about the Sabbath and Christianity, like no dancing, jewelry, makeup, some churches do not even want you to clap or say Amen and Halleluiah.

Also, some members will quickly point out what is proper, inappropriate, and destructive behaviors to visitors. This is why you must keep your eyes fixed on God – don't gaze on Him, don't glance at Him, keep your focus fixed on Him. Isaiah 8:20 (KJV), "[20] To the law and to the testimony: if they speak not according to this word, it is because there is no light in them."

Again, there is no Biblical proof that the Seventh-day, Saturday, was changed to Sunday, to keep Sunday holy. There is no such law in the Bible, and it goes against the Nature of God who changes not, and do not lie.

God gave His fourth commandment found in Exodus 20:8-11. It is a matter of Biblical and secular history that God never changed His holy Sabbath or transferred its solemnity to Sunday. The Sunday law is a law of the Catholic Church alone and is not Biblically based. The Catholic Church says, by my divine power I abolish the Sabbath day and command you to keep holy the first day of the week. And lo! The entire civilized world bows down in reverent obedience to the command of the Holy Catholic Church" (Thomas Enright, CSSR, President, Redemptorist College [Roman Catholic], Kansas City, MO, Feb. 18, 1884). Their other lies include that "The Pope has the power to change times, to abrogate laws, and to dispense with all things, even the precepts of Christ. The Pope has the authority and has often exercised it, to dispense with the command of Christ" (Decretal, de Tranlatic Episcop). What will you believe? Whom will you follow? The God of your Bible—or the traditions of men?

With that cleared up that God never changes His Sabbath day and it remains forever unchanged as the Seventh-day which is Saturday, what are the burdens that this day is causing many. Potential members and visitors are chased away before they confirm a commitment to visit. Sabbath keepers are not to force people into truth; that is not what God wants from any of us. You are to allow people to come into truth through sharing God in love and allow God to work in them bringing them into a full understanding and then on their own they will surrender and accept God out of love. Romans 14:5 (KJV), "5 One man esteemeth one day above another: another esteemeth every day alike. Let every man be fully persuaded in his own mind." Understand though, do not, do not, do not, misinterpret this verse to mean you can continue to worship God's Sabbath on a day you choose, it must be on the seventh day. What God is saying here is His proof that He gives you free will. In other words, people can share Biblical truth with you, show you the Biblical proof but God does not desire that the person force or persuade you to make a change. God wants you to make the changes in your life to be obedient to His commandments and to surrender to His will out of love.

For believers and practicing Sabbath keepers, some reason facilitating meetings on the Sabbath Day to discuss, for example, the upcoming church picnic, or raising money for a new HVAC system is more convenient than coming back on Sunday to handle church business. Of course, the general consensus agrees that these meetings must be held on the Sabbath because no one is willing to give God another day out of their week to attend meetings about His necessary work.

Also, besides having had no problem holding meetings, you engage in ungodly conversations and gossip on the Sabbath that disrespect the sanctity of the House of God and His Holy day. Plus, there is housework to be done, laundry needs to be washed, and those who have jobs must get ready for action the next day. Meetings on Sundays will not do; it cuts into the week ahead preparation. So, oh no! That is asking far too much.

Meanwhile, you condemn those who do good for others the Sabbath. However, Jesus speaking in Luke 6: 1- 10 (KJV), "And it came to pass on the second Sabbath after the first, that he went through the corn fields; and his disciples plucked the ears of corn, and did eat, rubbing them in their hands. ² And certain of the Pharisees said unto them, Why do ye that which is not lawful to do on the sabbath days? ³ And Jesus answering them said, Have ye not read so much as this, what David did, when himself was an hungered, and they which were with him; ⁴ How he went into the house of God, and did take and eat the shewbread, and gave also to them that were with him; which it is not lawful to eat but for the priests alone? ⁵ And he said unto them, That the Son of man is Lord also of the Sabbath. ⁶ And it came to pass also on another sabbath, that he entered into the synagogue and taught: and there was a man whose right hand was withered. ⁷ And the scribes and Pharisees watched him, whether he would heal on the sabbath day; that they might find an accusation against him. ⁸ But he knew their thoughts, and said to the man which had the withered hand, Rise up, and stand forth in the midst. And he arose and stood forth. [9] Then said Jesus unto them, I will ask you one thing; Is it lawful on the sabbath days to do good, or to do evil? to save life, or to destroy it? [10] And looking round about upon them all, he said unto the man, Stretch forth thy hand. And he did so: and his hand was restored whole as the other." This by no means an excuse to violate God's commandment but to be mindful when we are dogmatic about it. God did good deeds on the Sabbath, healing the sick and feeding others, not catching sales and worrying about how to enhance self or what is most convenient for self. There is a difference.

Some of us go as far as to set aside Sabbath worship to catch the right sales and fun stuff that is, unfortunately, happening on the Sabbath. This is a sure sign that you are not on fire for the Lord because if you were, no sales could pull you away from going to church and offering praise for the Lord. But when you have been in the secret place of the highest, and you have been touched by the Lord or grab hold of Jesus' garment you will know the only savings you want is Jesus saving you from your sin. Halleluiah!

All these Sabbath distractions and burdens are designs of the Devil. However, Christians ought to "Remember" the Sabbath Day to keep it Holy. If you read the 10 Commandments, you will notice that it is the only day God asks us to remember. God calls us never to forget to worship on that one day, His Holy Sabbath Day. A time He set aside to commune with us personally. For Sunday worshippers, most of you are doing it out of your own convenience because you know Saturday is the Seventh day and therefore the Sabbath. Those who have not come into the truth as to which day is the Sabbath, God's Sabbath is the Seventh Day, Saturday, the day God made Holy and commanded everyone to "Remember to keep it Holy." For those who argue the Sabbath was done away with when we came under grace, God's words are the same yesterday, today and tomorrow.

In conclusion, you now have the truth that the Sabbath day is the seventh day, which is Saturday, not the first day Sunday. You have

God's words found in Exodus 20:8-11 as proof. And, you have the Living Word of God, rebuke in Matthew 15:9 (KJV), "[9] But in vain they do worship me, teaching for doctrines the commandments of men." And again in Mark 7:7 (KJV), "[7] Howbeit in vain do they worship me, teaching for doctrines the commandments of men."

Understand, if you continue to choose to worship on Sunday as a sign of keeping the Sabbath you may as well choose any day Monday to Friday that is convenient when Sunday won't do, because none of it will make a difference if you are not obedient to the commandment that says Remember the Sabbath Day to keep it Holy (Reference Exodus 20:8-11). And let us not forget, when you break one commandment you are guilty of breaking all ten. May God have mercy on you!

Leadership Bias

How many of us genuinely like your Pastors and ministry leaders? Moreover, by like: you genuinely support their ministry, respect them as appointed leaders, refrain from gossiping about them, and is understanding when they say no? Alternatively, are you bias against your Pastor?

How many people do you know who make fun of their Pastor? Romans 13:4 (KJV), "⁴ For he is the minister of God to thee for good. But if thou do that which is evil, be afraid; for he beareth not the sword in vain: for he is the minister of God, a revenger to [execute] wrath upon him that doeth evil."

In 2 Kings chapter 2, a massive demonstration of young men assembled for the purpose of sarcastically taunting and insulting and mocking Elisha a prophet of God, and they met their death. 2 Kings 2:22-25 (KJV), "²² So the waters were healed unto this day, according to the saying of Elisha which he spake. ²³ And he went up from thence unto Bethel: and as he was going up there came forth little children out of the city, and mocked him, and said unto him, Go up, thou bald head; go up thou bald head. ²⁴ And he turned back, and looked on them, and cursed them in the name of the LORD. And there came forth two she bears out of the wood, and tare forty and two children of them."

The Lord's punishment was the mauling of forty-two of them by two female bears. The penalty of death was based on the seriousness of the crime; their ridicule of Elisha which was indirect ridicule of God. This judgment was God's warning to all who would scorn the prophets of the Lord.

While you may be disgruntled about the Pastor assigned to your church; maybe because he does not look like you or talk like you, or maybe he is too fat, or too skinny. He does not preach as good as the Pastor before him; His sermons are boring. He does not call you enough, or worst yet, he is only at church 300 days out of the year. You complain, and complain, and complain, the Pastor cannot do anything to satisfy you or measure up to your expectation; your Leadership bias is an indirect bias and dissatisfaction with God because His Pastors, prophets, is God in them.

Sometimes, in helping others, you become tired, stressed, or burned out. Usually, problems begin to surface with over-dependence on the pastor of the church who has a variety of responsibilities to nourish and guide the entire flock.

Many people do not consider their Pastors well-being. However, if you stop to ask your Pastor, "How are you doing?" And, you allow him to speak, and you truly listen, your Pastor will tell you how worn out, and burnout he is.

Pastors are dealing with far more stress and pressures than their congregation knows. Some stress caused by members who test and bait them with questions to make him look foolish to destroy their ministry, just like they did to Jesus; Read Matthew 21:23-27 (KJV), and Matthew 22:15-22 (KJV).

Many Pastors experience overwhelm because of they are too passive, or too humble to check unruly congregants. Soon, they become resentful, angry, bitter, and begin to lose the joy of ministry they once love. Soon, they become broken, and in their brokenness, they struggle to stay motivated and to keep control

Additionally, Pastors have their family tugging at them. However, feeling entitled, congregants use their relationship with the Pastor to pull him away from ministering at some crucial times which may add to the stress. They fail to realize that the Pastor holds the entire congregation in his or her heart from those they consider the least to the most self-identified privileged. While the pastor cares about every member, the pastor's priorities are not tied up in the elite, or largest tithe returner, no, his priorities are for that which He was called, to minister to God's people, their spiritual well-being and the church's community engagement.

Your Pastors must set limits and take time out for self-care, to relax, and balance their ministry life and their family life in such a way it does not affect their health, and sleep, especially when the demands get overwhelming. Pastors must withdraw from the crowds and retreat alone or with friends and turn off their phone and block all avenues of communication for one day. Jesus withdrew from the crowds, Luke 5:15-16 (KJV), "15 But so much the more went there a fame abroad of Him: and great multitudes came together to hear, and to be healed by him of their infirmities. 16 Moreover, he withdrew himself into the wilderness, and prayed." It is imperative that you allow your Pastors to enjoy quiet moments, the church can go on with or without him for a moment; it will go on if he is dead. Do not always be in a hurry, tempted to be everything to everyone, addressing members, sometimes mocking demands, cynicism, and inappropriate agenda and manipulation that you become paralyzed with fear of failure.

Chose not to force things, and instead trust God's will and purpose for your life. Like Jesus, speak the truth in love to those whom you find challenging. It may mean that you ask, "What do you want me to do for you?" Jesus asked the two blind men who called out to him in Matthew 29:32 (KJV), "32 And Jesus stood still, and called them, and said, "What will ye that I shall do unto you?" They needed to ask for what they needed, and they needed to trust Jesus. Read Matthew 20:29-34.

Other times, it may require that you take extreme measures. Let us not forget that Jesus used a whip to clear out the temple of the vendors and money changers who were taking advantage of the poor and turning God's house into a gambling den. (Matthew 21:12-17, John 2:12-16).

Also, some members will wear you out, but you must let them help themselves. Many expect the Pastor to fix their problem(s). When a certain man was there, which had an infirmity thirty and eight years wanted someone to put him in the pool Jesus challenged him, "Rise, take up thy bed, and walk." Read John 5:1-14 (KJV). It was up to him to be motivated and to take responsibility for himself. Likewise, Pastors, at times, must make members do for themselves.

Also, with setting boundaries, it is essential to set priorities: "No servant can serve two masters. Either he will hate the one and love the other, or he will be devoted to the one and despise the other" (Luke 16:13). John 5:44 (KJV), "44 How can ye believe, which receive honor one of another, and seek not the honor that cometh from God only?" Obey God, not man: Matthew 21:28-31 (KJV), "28 But what think ye? A certain man had two sons; and he came to the first, and said, Son, go work today in my vineyard. 29 He answered and said, I will not: but afterward he repented, and went. 30 And he came to the second and said likewise. And he answered and said, I go, sir: and went not. 31 Whether of them, twain did the will of his father? They say unto him, The first. Jesus saith unto them, Verily I say unto you, That the publicans and the harlots go into the kingdom of God before you."

A minister occupies a prominent place in his community. He is the teacher of the young and the counselor of the old. He handles the preservation of good morals by both. His example, whether good or bad, is in no small extent followed. His mode of life is the subject of discussion on the street corner and in other places. He is separated from the world by his public ordination, and carries with him always, whether in or out of the pulpit, superior obligations to exhibit, throughout his entire department, the purity of the religion which he professes to teach.

Christians are targeted for torture, slavery, and death due solely to their religious identity. Moreover, some Christians lack cohesion, and, a considerable number of Christian does not seem as worried over the challenges to come.

Many Christians are apathetic about the end of time, as much as they are with the discontentment about their role(s) in the church.

They seem to have a resolve not to make the same mistake they did in underestimating their congregation's dissatisfaction on issues of their governance, position, and leadership than they are about winning souls for God.

Nevertheless, little do they are too troubled or doubt the outcomes of the church elections; they believe their popularity will help them to win, and that is all that matter, position, title, with no real work, no plans for soul winning.

Truth is essential to Christian faith; It is that intellectual, cognitive truth, about God, the glimpses, visions, even knowledge adequately understood as justified belief about God.

Therefore, you must separate yourself from people who are seeking applause and be willing to make changes to your walk. Be must be purposeful if you are to be successful; Therefore, it is essential that you think about the relationship you have or want with God, not with your friends in the church. Be purposeful about what you want your life to reflect and be resolute and unswerving in the way you live.

From time to time some of us consider rebaptism, while an individual choice, and a start, rebaptism does no good if you revert to old behaviors; instead, you may be making a mockery of God to your brothers and sisters in the church.

Pastors must always consider the satisfaction and belonging of their members at church and the situational pressures you may face when you must check unruly members.

However, Pastors must also believe it is okay to set boundaries and do so because limits are essential to your relationship with God, for your peace of mind, and to keep your sanity. You are no earthly good without boundaries. Sometimes this means confronting unruly members.

Sure, confronting is never easy, but neither is being faced.
However, you have two choices, confront the person, or remain silent? If you want the bad behavior to stop, and you want to feel better, and become better, you have to do something, and sometimes it will mean taking drastic measures and being firm with a combative people to being passive with someone, who perhaps, do not realize their behavior is

unwelcoming. Pastors, in every situation, should not feel an obligation to speak up and confront biased statements, sometimes it is best to take some cases to God in prayer and leave it at the feet of Jesus.

In other words, some actions are not worth fighting, so pick and choose your battles wisely and leave the rest to the mercy of God.

Also, throughout the time it has been proven that a person cannot please everyone, so why bother. Church members will always find something wrong with leadership and be ready to point their finger of blame and shame at them.

However, despite disgruntled members, Pastors must set effective boundaries and practice self-care. Without it, you see Pastors completing suicide, suffering from anxiety and depression, some are dealing with personal insecurities and hidden problems, that ministry gets overwhelming, and soon they want to quit and walk away from their calling.

Still, members behave with reckless disregard and selfish desires about only their needs. The Pastor is paid to be at your beckoning call. Wrong! God's servant is not meant to be your footstool and should not be treated with such disrespect and disdain.

Pastors, it's not "selfish" to set boundaries and practice self-care in your ministry. You owe it to yourself if you will be an effective leader and do the will of God.

Members get right with God, support your Pastors to your fullest ability and stop complaining. Think on Proverbs 13:3 (KJV), "³ He that keepeth his mouth keepeth his life: but he that openeth wide his lips shall have destruction." And, Proverbs 3:27 (KJV), "²⁷ Withhold not good from them to whom it is due when it is in the power of thine hand to do it."

Wolves In Sheep's Clothing

Matthew 7:16 (KJV), "¹⁶ Ye shall know them by their fruits. Do men gather grapes of thorns or figs of thistles?" Throughout the Church's 2,000-year history, there is much confusion over the "men of the cloth" who claim to represent God or should be ministers! But do they? Many claims God is leading them through some sentimental "feeling" in their hearts. In most cases, they will attend Bible colleges and seminaries, where they are drilled to accept their school's beliefs. Upon graduating, they present with these dubious credentials, having been thoroughly trained to twist Scripture to legitimize their own doctrines.

Many times, the wolf disguised in sheep's clothing knows God's Word better than we thought, crafting, and twisting it so much, we might even find ourselves feeling confused over what truth is anymore.

So how can we see through their deception to protect ourselves? 2 Thessalonians 2:9 (KJV), "[Even him], whose coming is after the working of Satan with all power and signs and lying wonders." God's Word is clear; it says they will be known by their fruits. Not by how much money they have. Not by how many followers they have. Not by how many books they have written or the great things they have done. What fruit will know them exists in their lives. Is there love, joy, peace, patience, kindness, goodness, gentleness, faithfulness, and self-control? Are they sharing the gospel of Christ, and pointing others to the forgiveness and freedom that He alone can bring? What do they say about who Jesus is? What do they believe about the authority of God's Word?

We may have to look more closely than what is on the outside. 2 Corinthians 11:14-15 (KJV), "¹⁴ And no marvel; for Satan himself is transformed into an angel of light. ¹⁵ Therefore it is no great thing if his ministers also be transformed as the ministers of righteousness; whose end shall be according to their works."

The world often views "success" and popularity differently than how God sees. What is at heart? Eventually, the truth of who they are will be brought into the light. 1 Corinthians 4:5 (KJV), "⁵ Therefore judge nothing before the time, until the Lord come, who both will bring to light the hidden things of darkness and will make manifest the counsels of the hearts: and then shall every man have praise of God."

Selecting men to become God's ministers takes careful deliberation over a long period of time. The ministers that claim to be call and are seeking gifts, and to shower with love, and develop a relationship with people, their ministry is a facade.

Christ's disciples did not choose themselves or run political campaigns to advance their promotion or choice. God chose the disciples. Ordaining a minister that springs from self-vanity, lust, greed, and pride, are, at best, extraordinarily complicated and capable of deception—even self-deception. The best way to spot what is "fake," by understanding first what is "real." To expose the false lies of the enemy is to know the Truth of the One voice which matters most. Know the real, and you will know what is false.

In addition, all other scriptural qualifications must be met. Philippians 2:7-9 (KJV), "⁷ But made himself of no reputation, and took upon him the form of a servant, and was made in the likeness of men: ⁸ And being found in fashion as a man, he humbled himself, and became obedient unto death, even the death of the cross. ⁹ Wherefore God also hath highly exalted him, and given him a name which is above every name."

Additionally, church leadership is delegated into positions—ranks— of authority and responsibility: Ephesians 4:11 (KJV), "¹¹ And he gave some, apostles; and some, prophets; and some, evangelists; and some, Pastors and teachers".

Why? Ephesians 4:12-13 (KJV),"¹² For the perfecting of the saints, for the work of the ministry, for the edifying of the body of Christ: ¹³ Till you all come in the unity of the faith, and of the knowledge of the Son of

God, unto a perfect man, unto the measure of the stature of the fulness of Christ."

God leads His ministers; He makes clear to them whom to choose by examining a man's fruits, in addition to other biblical guidelines. Acts 20:28 (KJV), "28 Keep watch over yourselves and all the flock of which the Holy Spirit has made you overseers. Be shepherds of the church of God,[a] which he bought with his own blood." You can trust God's word to be true and rely on Him for guiding us.

For this reason, loyal ministers are not to be elected by popularity or for their feel-good preaching style and do not volunteer or run clique campaigns to somehow "land" a ministerial position.

However, recently, churches have been carelessly and casually ordained men as liberal ministers for the wrong reasons and against the word of God. Matthew 15:9 (KJV), "9 But in vain they do worship me, teaching for doctrines the commandments of men." Some of these untrained "ministerial appointments" are placed in charge of God's people and given free rein to teach and instruct God's flock. Matthew 15:13 - But he answered and said, Every plant, which my heavenly Father hath not planted, shall be rooted up," because they should never have been ordained in the first place.

Many pastors present themselves as having supernatural powers Matthew 24:23-25 (KJV), "23 Then if any man shall say unto you, Lo, here is Christ, or there; believe it not. 24 For there shall arise false Christs, and false prophets, and shall shew great signs and wonders; insomuch that, if it were possible, they should deceive the very elect. 25 Behold, I have told you before." Many are making a mockery of the gospel pretending that they can solve health or spiritual problems—or outright deception of healings taking place. 2 Peter 3:15-16 (KJV), "15 And account that the longsuffering of our Lord is salvation; even as our beloved brother Paul also according to the wisdom given unto him hath written unto you; 16 As also in all his epistles, speaking in them of these things; in which are some things hard to be understood, which they that are unlearned and unstable wrest, as they also do the other scriptures, unto their own destruction."

Then there are some with no formal training just a silver tongue. Many Christians are left scratching their head and questioning their faith as they ponder whether the source of power in these churches is of God, yet many are following these fake ministers who are focused on church growth for more incentives and income. Too many of these fake pastors, ministering comes with an ulterior motive to get rich quickly.   Also, they are entering the ministry and looking for a consuming hobby, adoration, or social tradition. The problem is it is difficult to single out and keep these opportunists out of pulpits. The phenomenon is dangerous and criminal. Unfortunately, religious freedom protections prevent church leadership from stopping such pastors from being locked up for their criminal behavior, unless their activities are proven to be criminal. Matthew 7:15-20 (KJV), "[15] Beware of false prophets, which come to you in sheep's clothing, but inwardly they are ravening wolves. [16] Ye shall know them by their fruits. Do men gather grapes of thorns or figs of thistles? [17] Even so, every good tree bringeth forth good fruit, but a corrupt tree bringeth forth evil fruit. [18] A good tree cannot bring forth evil fruit; neither can a corrupt tree bring forth good fruit. [19] Every tree that bringeth not forth good fruit is hewn down and cast into the fire. [20] Wherefore by their fruits, ye shall know them."

These "wolves in sheep's clothing" have infiltrated God's Church, many on television reaching millions of people with their false ministries. God warns in Matthew 7:15 (KJV), "[15] Beware of false prophets, which come to you in sheep's clothing, but inwardly they are ravening wolves." With time, God warns that Acts 20:29 (KJV), "[29] For I know this, that after my departing shall grievous wolves enter in among you, not sparing the flock." You can see why precautions are necessary for selecting ministers who claim to have received God's calling. The worst thing that could happen to such men (and those under them) would be to give them too much authority and power. Sooner or later, they would become virtual dictators.

In selecting men to become elders, Paul gave Timothy detailed guidelines: 1 Timothy 3:2(KJV), "A bishop then must be blameless, the husband of one wife, vigilant, sober, of good behavior, given to hospitality, apt to teach." A man's fruits are not produced overnight and must be evaluated and need careful deliberation. He must have a long track record of faithful service to God.

Paul wrote that some attributes that would disqualify a man from being a minister include a man must, 1 Timothy 3:6 (KJV), "[6] Not a novice, lest being lifted up with pride he falls into the condemnation of the devil."

The apostle Paul was so zealous that he even persecuted and imprisoned Christians, bringing many of them to their deaths. Paul admittedly stated in Acts 22:4 (KJV), "[4] And I persecuted this way unto the death, binding and delivering into prisons both men and women". He was so compelling and, as a result, respected that the high priest and council of elders of Judea gave him the authority to act on their behalf.

"Knowing this...scoffers will come in the last days with scoffing, following their own sinful desires." 2 Pet. 3:3

Stand firm on Christ the Solid Rock. John 8:32 (KJV), "[32] And ye shall know the truth, and the truth shall make you free." Pray for a spirit of discernment about your leaders. John 16:13 (KJV), "[13] Howbeit when He, the Spirit of truth, is come, He will guide you into all truth: for He shall not speak of Himself; but whatsoever He shall hear, that shall He speak: and He will shew you things to come." Amen! Glory be to God!

Women as Ministers

In Genesis 1 and Genesis 2, God gave both man and woman stewardship of the earth. Also, Luke 8:1-3 Women were with Jesus as He preached the gospel: Luke 8:1-3 (KJV), "[1] And it came to pass afterward, that he went throughout every city and village, preaching and shewing the glad tidings of the kingdom of God: and the twelve were with him, [2] And certain women, which had been healed of evil spirits and infirmities, Mary called Magdalene, out of whom went seven devils, [3] And Joanna the wife of Chuza Herod's steward, and Susanna, and many others, which ministered unto him of their substance.

As a woman, your feelings of insecurity trying to maneuver and be accepted in a man's world is heightened. These feelings could be connected to your passion about ministry, or perhaps because a man, who has little training, can serve and comfort others while you, an educated and certified woman by an accredited institution, goes unnoticed or gets skipped over, it happens.

Your feelings are further diminished when everyone applauds you for your great sermons and pities you for what they considered is unfair but does nothing to speak out about the sexual harassment they feel is happening. Or, they applauded you for being great, but your achievements are met with silence, and little to nothing is said from the pulpit, but your male counterpart is hailed for his accomplishments.

Sexual harassment in the church can have serious implications not only for how you treat women but also for what roles you allow or encourage them to play in the church. Sexual harassment says women as less competent, even those more qualified than some of the men in leadership, and negatively affects women's performance and makes them less likely to want to direct.

So, what if you are the woman who feels called by God to ministry. You feel gifted in your calling as a Pastor, but now you feel the pain of sexual harassment?

Don't be disheartened; God has spoken and sets the standards for the role of women in the church. God forbids women from becoming ministers in His Church and has long ago determined that men be the leaders in their families and in the Church. Paul admonished in 1 Corinthians 14:34 (KJV), "[34] Let your women keep silence in the churches: for it is not permitted unto them to speak; but they are commanded to be under obedience as also saith the law."

Truthfully, when the man is absent, or he fails to assume his God-given responsibilities as a leader in his family, women must fill those roles, which is not what God intended for the family structure.

In such cases, women "carry the burden"—all the responsibility for the family care and children upbringing - out of necessity.

However, in the Church, that is not the case. Christ said, "Matthew 16:18 (KJV), "[18] And I say also unto thee, That thou art Peter, and upon this rock, I will build my church, and the gates of hell shall not prevail against it."

God is not a God that can lie, and He is not the author of confusion. God leads and guides us into all truths through His words.

Therefore, for those who question the church's position on women pastoral leadership as being bias or sexist against women, this is an issue to take up with God. Patriarchy has nothing to do with it. Instead, those who are stirring trouble and doing the devils bidding is either misinterpreting Scripture knowingly or unknowingly, or placing the laws of man above the laws of God, and that includes any disgruntled women intending to be ministers in God's church when God forbids it. At the heart of the battle, we face every day, is a real enemy who prowls around seeking someone to devour. 1 Peter 5:8 (KJV), "[8] Be sober, be vigilant; because of your adversary the devil, as a roaring lion, walketh about, seeking whom he may devour," He will stop at nothing to gain new ground.

104

Admittedly God-gifted men with a vision and He gifted women. Still, God has assigned women with their role in the church, and He is not expecting women to lead even when they feel called. There is a difference between field evangelism and preaching from the pulpit. Additionally, "1 Timothy 2:12 (KJV), " [12] But I suffer not a woman to teach, nor to usurp authority over the man, but to be in silence."

Jesus expects women to do the will of God and to evangelize out in the field and be fishers of men as they did when they followed Him.

Let us look at Matthew 12: 46-50 (KJV) with a focus on verse 50. Matthew 12: 46-50 (KJV). " [46] While he yet talked to the people, behold, his mother and his brethren stood without, desiring to speak with him. [47] Then one said unto him, Behold, thy mother and thy brethren stand without, desiring to speak with thee. [48] But he answered and said unto him that told him, Who is my mother? And who are my brethren? [49] And he stretched forth his hand toward his disciples, and said, Behold my mother and my brethren! [50] For whosoever shall do the will of my Father which is in heaven, the same is my brother, and sister, and mother." Jesus never said the same is a minister, preacher, bishop, or elder in The Church of God.

The women disciples were out with Jesus as He preached and taught about God but in the role of evangelist spreading the word of God. All women are free to do so today, and there is no church preventing them from doing so.

Also, when Jesus called to His Disciples, Luke 23:49 (KJV), " [49] And all his acquaintance, and the women that followed Him from Galilee, stood afar off, beholding these things." Luke 5:11 (KJV), " [11] And when they had brought their ships to land, they forsook all, and followed him." These women went of their own accord but nowhere in the Bible did they take leadership. They served as helpers in the ministry which is what Jesus calls each of us to do, to be fishers of men. That is what the women were doing with Jesus, fishing for souls.

Sure, women who desire to be Pastors in the church feels, it is natural that they may feel disappointed, hurt or even upset. However, it is also essential to think reflectively and prayerfully and to choose your inner-response wisely. If you prayerfully consider the word of God, first, you would have to admit that God does not change and His word is everlasting, and second, If God says it, then that must settle it for all believers.

Clearly, what is happening is that the Devil is trying to cause division by infiltration the church with laws of man and issues of the world. The devil is using people who are willingly pushing women's rights stereotype agenda and prejudice ideas and trying to dispute the words of God. You serve a perfect God who does not make a mistake. However, it is man's law that is trying to change God's commands and label "Thus saith the Lord," as sexist. God allows women to serve in many capacities within the church including as deaconesses.

Nobody is saying that a thriving church is an inclusive church which asks for input from women. However, thus saith the Lord supersedes any laws of man which has no place in the church. The only "ism" Christians need to listen to, and push is God's "ism," and God says, 1 Timothy 2:11-14 (KJV), "[11] Let the woman learn in silence with all subjection. [12] But I suffer not a woman to teach, nor to usurp authority over the man, but to be in silence. [13] For Adam was first formed, then Eve. [14] And Adam was not deceived, but the woman being deceived was in the transgression."

Also, churches recognize the Biblical role of women in the church and know that women can supply tremendous insights into trends in the church in general. Pastors who care deeply about issues such as abuse, rely on women to share their insights and knows it is essential to include women's voices and their perspective and experiences related to the church because their opinions may differ from men, and their contributions and different input brings unique opportunities that will prove helpful as you move toward the development and implementation phases.

Even if you do not believe that it is God who regulated His Church and the role of women in it, you cannot argue with God's word; That is final.

Ministry is hard enough without the world, many are non-church going, not-committed, unbelievers, and nonchristian, bringing man's sexist charges into God's church. Christianity is warfare, and the devil will try to infiltrate the church from wherever he can. II Corinthians 1:24 (KJV) says, "[24] Not for that we have dominion over your faith but are helpers of your joy: for by faith ye stand."

I Peter 3:1-4 shows a beautiful aspect of such humble submission: "1 Peter 3:1-4 (KJV), "[1] Likewise, ye wives, be in subjection to your own husbands; that, if any obey not the word, they also may without the word be won by the conversation of the wives; [2] While they behold your chaste conversation coupled with fear. [3] Whose adorning let it not be that outward adorning of plaiting the hair, and of wearing of gold, or of putting on of apparel; [4] But let it be the hidden man of the heart, in that which is not corruptible, even the ornament of a meek and quiet spirit, which is in the sight of God of great price."

The church should not be placed in a position to excuse sexual harassment away. However, you have every right to reason with God Isaiah 1:18 (KJV), "Come now, and let us reason together, saith the LORD: though your sins be as scarlet, they shall be as white as snow; though they be red like crimson, they shall be as wool," and with leaders in the church, to even experience hurt because of your strong desire to serve God. However you must search deep within your soul and in the Bible for God's truth, and then live God's truth.

For women who desire to be pastors or serve it ministry in a leadership position, consider what you want to do and talk with someone equipped to guide you or to discuss the church's position on roles of women in the church. Read Luke 14:28-32 (KJV), "[28] For which of you, intending to build a tower, sitteth not down first, and counteth the cost, whether he have [sufficient] to finish [it]? [29] Lest haply, after he hath laid the foundation, and is not able to finish [it], all that behold [it] begin to mock him, [30] Saying, This man began to build and was not able to finish. [31] Or what king, going to make war against another king, sitteth not down first, and consulteth whether he be able with ten thousand to meet him that cometh against him with twenty thousand? [32] Or else, while the other is yet a great way off, he sendeth an ambassage and desireth conditions of peace?"

These truths are not meant to be discouraging or to stir anger, James 3:17 (KJV), "But the wisdom that is from above is first pure, then peaceable, gentle, [and] easy to be intreated, full of mercy and good fruits, without partiality, and without hypocrisy."

Finally, 1 Peter 3:15 (KJV), "But sanctify the Lord God in your hearts: and [be] ready always to [give] an answer to every man that asketh you a reason of the hope that is in you with meekness and fear." We are all supposed to be about saving souls. Do not be caught up in a church position or placement. Just be an effective fisherwoman wherever you are and keep yourself accessible and available to God so God can use you and move you at will.

Hope this helps—if you still have concerns, have someone with actionable insights to pray with you and help you bring order to this complicated situation.

The Church and Technology

As the church grows, new believers are coming in and posing questions that challenge their Christian foundation, leaving many unprepared to defend "their truth." Some are using technology while the preacher preaches to see if He is telling a lie. Now, nothing is wrong with technology, it has its place, even in the church. How, when and why we are using it is the problem

Encountering highly intelligent people who are not afraid to object to their point of view, some Christian become defensive and go out their way to isolate the new believer who are using technology to challenge them. However, you do not need to fear with the Bible ready to answer any questions they may have. Anything that cannot be answered by the Bible is not worth engaging in because it becomes a situation of the Word versus the World. This is not to say you cannot listen respectfully, but remember, everything written on the internet is not true and it is not an authority on "This saith the Lord," your Bible is.

Truth is a relative concept, dependent on one's point of view, cultural narrative, and their walk with Christ, which is not determined by how long the person have been in the church, just where they are in their relationship with God, and what they are choosing to believe.

Therefore Christians neither debate or argue God or the things of God. In such matters you pray for a spirit of discernment, and let the unbeliever be.

What is most troubling about technology is that Christians who are born and raise in the church are drifting further and further away from the confines of the church, especially in these days of smartphones, internet service, and identifying as the religiously unaffiliated call "Nones?"

"Nones," are growing significantly and are making church going irrelevant at a startling pace. They are not particular to associate with any religion or committing to a set of beliefs; this is quickly becoming a thing of the past. But God said in Hebrews 10:25 (KJV), "25 Not forsaking the assembling of yourselves together, as the manner of some is; but exhorting one another: and so much the more, as ye see the day approaching."

Even to some church-going Christians, church-going is rapidly becoming redundant mundane experience, and like the atheist mindset, they are slowly becoming influenced by science and technology. This trend started when Satan convinced Christians to replace the Bible in their hands with technology. God sent Jesus, His Son, to save people from their sin and open a better way for humanity to follow. There are those who have surrendered their own will to follow God's perfect will. Yet, God must keep His hands outstretched to prevent Satan from carrying out his plans altogether. Together these faithful souls form the Church, the entire body of Christians. The Bible makes it clear that the true church of Christ is made up of all those who deny themselves, take up their cross, and follow Him. (Ephesians 2:19-22).

Also, Christians with their Bible in their hands are a thorn in Satan's side. He knows he must work overtime to bring doubt, pride, division, or whatever he can to turn Christians hearts from God. He knows he must work overtime to bring doubt, pride, division, or whatever he can to turn Christians hearts from God.

Additionally, the Bible is a rebuke for the devil, a reminder of God's authority and power. When a Bible wielding believer hold his or her Bible inhis or her hands, the devil trembles. But with technology replacing the Bible, which seems too heavy, too bulky, too inconvenient, don't seem as cool as the iPad, tablet, smartphone or laptop computer, the devil feels assured and embolden that he can win at distracting and separating Christians from the word of God. People are even impressed to print out their Bible text on paper ang go up to the pulpit and read as oppose to standing before the congregation with their Bible in their hands. You can almost see the sorrow on God's face with tears rolling down His cheeks. He gives so much to you and you can't give a little to Him that cost you nothing.

If you are one who has chosen to use technology over your Bible, slowly but surely, Satan will separate you from God. How? Glad you asked.

In church, instead of focusing on Biblical verses, and following along with the Scripture being read, how many time do you checking your emails, text messages, Facebook, Twitter, Instagram, and all the other media distractions, things you otherwise would not be doing with your Bible in your hand? Let us agree you said once, well, once is too much when the entire Sabbath belongs to the Lord, (Review Exodus 20:8-11). That quick glance you gave to social media was time stolen from God and handed over to the devil; you just made Satan's day. You disagree that a quick glance at your technology does not mean Satan has a hold of you. Perhaps, but Satan is willing to go as slow as he needs if he can chip away at your relationship with God until Satan totally separates you from God and wins your soul; that is how he works. Think this is a lie, check the Clergy in your church upfront on Sabbath. Even the Clergy has replaced their Swords and is reading the Scripture from tablets and smartphones. Some merely to perpetrate to be in the now, and not even realizing they are conforming to the world and Satan have them drifting from the Word and the covenant they made with God. There is an argument to be made for this because let us say there is a nonbelieving visitor who dropped in. That visitor wants to know more about God, but everybody on the pulpit has tablets, smartphones, or pieces of paper they are reading from, nobody has a Bible, how much of an impact do you think are you having on that person versus if they saw everyone with their Bible in their hands? This is clergy inviting the world into the church to please creature instead of the creator. This is clergy worrying about the pleasing of man to ensure they are viewed as relevant instead of staying true to what God needs and allowing God to be God.

Additionally, 4 in 10 millennial Christians fact-check sermon claims on Google, and 70% are reading Scripture on a cell phone or online instead of physically opening a Bible according to https://www.barna.com/ research/how-technology-is-changing-millennial-faith/#.UmFdf2R4b5l. This is significant when you consider that millennials are relying on Google to do their fact-checking of sermon scriptures instead of the Bible and 70% are reading scripture on the internet without knowing if it is true or not. How easy it is to be misled. Worst still, the life of millennial's children will be significantly different, and they will be coming under fire for their religious beliefs and affiliation.

Do you still think this is hogwash? Does your church ask for all electronics to be turned off? Do you hear phones ringing in church? A sign of disobedience. Okay, your argument is that they forgot to turn it off. Great point! But then the question becomes why did they answer the phone and walk out of the church and forgot about worship? Emergency you said? Ahhh, so. Times surely have changed from the days of Moses down to our grandparents. They had an emergency on Sabbaths, but it waited until after sunset to be handled. And then what about those who answer their phones and sit in the church whispering and carrying on a conversation in their seat while the minister is preaching the sermon, or while the service is going on? What? You said they are too lazy to go outside? Great assumption, but be assured, this is Satan at work through all these little creeping compromises. Oh, have you checked out the minister on Sabbath checking their mobile during service, or posting to Facebook? Oh yeah, some of them do.

So, while church administration ask for electronics to be turned off in the church theirs is on– and not always for church business; that is the devil at work in the House of God on the Sabbath day spinning his web to see who all he can trap and separate from giving God their full attention on His Holy day, and not clergy, member, or visitor is immune. Technology is separating many Christians from spending quality time with God, knowingly and unknowingly.

However, God is very real and is speaking to and stirring the hearts of men to move who wants Him. But, if a person does not open their heart to listen to the word of God, their faith will forever be wavering. Romans 10:17 (KJV), "17 So then faith cometh by hearing, and hearing by the word of God."

Sexual Harassment

For clarity, this discussion is not based only on behavioral treatments for sexual harassment, adultery, and other offenses towards women in the church.

Indeed, there is sexual harassment within the confines of the church which the church is slow to admit. However, Churches that are indeed concerned about issues affecting its members ensures that such issues are addressed at all levels of the church, including bringing it before the congregation at a business meeting when necessary. Furthermore, changes implemented within the Church should reflect behaviors, attitudes, and policies that align with the word of God and not with the societal belief of what they think is right and moral, in other words, discounting the laws of man and upholding the laws and requirements of God.

The implicit biases in the church that exist towards women are generally associated with how people interact with one another based on culture, and religious beliefs; These teachings, many which are subjugated in favor of males, "affect your understanding, actions, and decisions" about the role of women both consciously and unconsciously. For example, have you ever wondered why women are the only one beaten up in the church when there is an issue with adultery? God said both are guilty after all. Have you considered the story of Bathsheba and Vashti's perspective?

Look at the story; King David sees Bathsheba - a married woman whose husband was a soldier that was off fighting a war. Bathsheba decides to take a bath on her rooftop; nobody knows why. David sees her and likes what he sees, so he has Bathsheba brought to his palace. Sometime later, after she returns home, she sends word to King David that she is pregnant. Meaning they committed adultery. If you were to look at the story of David and Bathsheba from Bathsheba's point of view, David knew she was married, and he brings her to his palace where he committed adultery with her. While we could intercourse between two consenting adults, this was disobedience to the Word of God. With the #MeTooMovement of today, if Bathsheba said she was violated, she would have proof and David would be hauled away. David was the person in power, and he made a demand. In the church, most people would agree that both were at fault for committing adultery, but the focus would be solely on Bathsheba for being a seducer and point the finger of shame at Bathsheba for the "affair," not "adultery." Bathsheba is guilty of taunting David by taking a bath, naked, on the roof in plain view of his palace.

Very few Christians would question why David did not move away from the window once he realizes Bathsheba was taking a bath. Why didn't David turn away? Also, knowing that David gave an order to bring Bathsheba to the palace would not matter because Bathsheba tempted him and he was merely a man. Additionally, little attention would be given to David for seducing Bathsheba, even though he knew she was married and should have respected her marital covenant as much as she should. God said both people who take part in adultery are accountable.

However, Christians blame the woman for affairs in the church and excuse the behavior of men being men. That is sexual harassment to label women in the church as tempters and the purveyors of sin, instead of victims of manipulation and seduction by men, especially men in power. And they are always labeling men as victims of women's perverseness freeing them from any accountability.

Sadly, the church is often a place where gender bias against women is excused and enabled. These are the teachings most Christians carry with them into every situation that involves adultery in the church. These stereotypes are rooted in cultural bias and prejudice against women by those buying into a system of conscious and unconscious inequity based on gender.

Sexual harassment is insidious because it—and the people who use it—know the kinds of feelings it will bring about, typically feelings tied to insecurity, self-esteem, and shame. At the same time, the emotions and reactions that surface in the moment of being the object of sexual harassment are as complicated as you are unique.

Of course, there are restraints, but when these distinctions are blurred, problems usually occur and they never adequately address or entirely eradicate the effects of sexual harassment, some deliberation, and reflection on where you stand about these emotional manifestations will help.

While there will be sexist comments about you and directed to you that will come from people who "do not know any better" and who do not realize the effects that their comments might have, there will be others who know what they are doing. They see the power that sexual harassment must bring you down and cause you to question your performance in ministry, but more insidiously, to get you to examine your call to ministry. These persons are not capable of telling you the truth about their feelings toward you, so they hide behind sexual harassment. These concealed feelings will include the belief that you should not be in ministry (especially true if you are clergy). Because they are unable to utter this disbelief aloud, sexual harassment becomes how they can make you feel what they feel. Sexual harassment may also mask or deflect unwanted feelings of attraction by twisting them into ridicule and degradation.

Undoing the rampant sexual harassment in the church, however, is more difficult; reports of sexual harassment are even downplayed and disbelieved, because "everyone means well" in the church. No one means to be rude; it is just the way it is. This excuse makes it all the more difficult for you to navigate its inevitability.

The church must revise its script drastically to take on sexual harassment and how it is handled when it is reported. Undoing the unruly unwelcomed behavior in the church, however, is more difficult; reports of sexual harassment are even downplayed and disbelieved, because "everyone means well" in the church. No one means to be rude; it is just the way of being friendly. This excuse makes it all the more difficult for you to navigate its inevitability. It is not okay for that church brother to pull your body into them with such force your bodies bounce off each other. Likewise, it is not okay for that kiss on the cheek to land near your lips. Still, these issues happen more frequently than are reported.

Additionally, a church brother hugging a church sister too low around the waist so that his hands rest on her bottom is violating, especially if it stays in position for more than three seconds. In other words, if it was accidental, there should be an immediacy in removing it.

It becomes harder still when you are a Pastor, of course, because you would never respond unkindly and call out sexist comments or make someone feel bad when they did not have harmful intentions. In other words, sexual harassment is so tricky because you not only must figure out how to reply to its origin at the time but also how to respond to your reactions now.

Alertness to and negotiation of sexual harassment in ministry demands knowledge about it is many and various levels, and reflection on how and when you will go about speaking up for and against the unspeakable. To be able to traverse the complicated landscape of sexual harassment will demand wisdom concerning the nature and function of sexual harassment, but also honesty about its effect on you. You will need to be aware of the emotions that will surface when you are the object of sexist comments.

One problem with sexual harassment is that it is not always obvious and can sometimes even appear nice and characterizes women as "pure creatures who ought to be protected, supported, and adored and whose love is necessary to make a man complete."

While cherishing women and placing them on a pedestal might seem harmless, there are severe costs to sexual harassment.

Moreover, sexual harassment makes women disgruntled and less likely to want to be leaders hindering their leadership aspirations. Sexual harassment serves to reinforce the false notion that women are not "cut out" for leadership by treating women in ways that make it harder for them to succeed as leaders and then taking their failure as a sign of their inability instead of recognizing the significant influences of the church's culture.

The church then must get to a place where women can break the silence against gender-based violence. There are many women in your churches today with compelling testimony of having been sexually harassed, manipulated, and assaulted by powerful men in church leadership. They cannot help but turn their minds to the story of the rape of King David's daughter Tamar by her half-brother Amnon" in 2 Samuel 13: 1-22. It is a passage in which a conspiracy of men plots the exploitation and rape of a young woman. She is stripped of the power to speak or act, her father ignores the crime, and the fate of the rapist, not the victim, is mourned. It is a Bible story devoid of justice and calls for us "to explore and speak about the trauma of sexual assault in the church as well as the exploitation of women who violated and manipulated and then seen as the tempter, devalued while men are protected.

First and foremost, your churches must examine its history and come to a fuller understanding of how it has handled cases of sexual harassment, exploitation, and abuse of women, children, and men; and acknowledge that in your church and your culture, the sexual exploitation of women is part of the same unjust sexist system that contributes to gender gaps within the church and outside the church.

Second, the Church must commit to treating every person as a child of God, deserving of dignity and respect. You must also commit to ending the systemic sexual harassment, misogyny, and misuse of power that plague the church.

Sexual harassment is a problem that is both subtle and entrenched in the culture; it can be hard to know where to begin; You do not have all the wisdom and authority necessary to change the culture in your church.

However, you may look to find opportunities to share your opinions and listen to one another. Because to say that Jesus spent most of his time investing in twelve men perpetuates the misconception that he traveled in the company of only male disciples and that excluded women from his inner circle.

It is therefore imperative that Christians be honest about their failings and brokenness, and to discern prayerfully the ways that God is calling us to stand with Tamar in all of the places you find her – both inside the church and beyond your doors, which you must o often used to shut her out." Sending subtle messages to men that they are more valued than women while sending not-so-subtle messages to women that they are not as worthy to God as men are not true and has no place in the church and is not a reflection of Jesus appreciation for the discipleship of women in the Bible or to the all-inclusive message of the gospel.

Note to women in ministry: This is another truth: no matter how much you give reasons for, explain, or acknowledge sexual harassment, it will still have an effect, and it will always catch you off guard. A comment in a moment when you are feeling vulnerable. A remark from someone you thought you could trust. Moreover, in the end, there is no explaining it or justifying it. Sexual harassment is and will continue to be.

Sexual harassment, in this regard, is a manifestation of your human brokenness, your human propensity to find ways to exert power over the other and to bring down those who have the power you look for. Sexual harassment is a manifestation of sin, with sin defined as separation from God and the rejection of the emancipatory potential of God's love.

It is necessary to confront sexual harassment and the patriarchy in your church. Patriarchal systems and unhealthy use of spiritual and religious power are oppressive and saying sorry are not enough when it involves violence against women. You must be willing to acknowledge and confront the way theology, power, is being used to harass women sexually.

Also, God instructs women to "submit to your husbands," as male leadership in the home but God never intended it to be used to justify and excuse violence against women or abuse of any kind. Any patriarchal behaviors that silenced and oppressed women and girls into submission and took away their God-given identity are against everything that God's loving nature is.

The further away you are from the ways in which you know how God's power works, the less capable you are of embodying power that seeks to lift up and not bring down, that acknowledges worth in the other even in the moments when you feel the most unworthy, and that is committed to the means by which the other is valued fully in all of her individuality and femininity and not as an object for the taking.

Essential to unlocking your power is thinking about what it will take to be proactive rather than reactive in moments when you stop others being targets of sexual harassment. Stop blaming women and acting like sexual harassment is a "women's issue." Place the blame where it belongs on the guilty party and hold him accountable for his behavior.

Sexual harassment and violence against women affect everyone, at all levels of society – women, men, and children. Men and women must stand together to end any sort of abuse against women.

You can cut all excuses, and repent and change and follow the way of Christ. Choosing to live a life that is pleasing to God and that glorify and witness for Christ, and that stands, in contrast, the destructive, demeaning, derogatory, and divisive spirits that the devil is sowing, is what you can and must do. Work to eradicate harassment against women and girls in Christian families, in your churches, and your society. Philippians 4:3 (KJV), "³ And I entreat thee also, true yokefellow, help those women which labored with me in the gospel, with Clement also, and [with] other my fellow laborers, whose names [are] in the book of life." Joel 2:29 (KJV), "²⁹ And also upon the servants and upon the handmaids in those days will I pour out my spirit."

Additionally, you can speak up whenever derogatory statements about women and girls, or when they look to silence them; The church is not an environment for sexist views and remarks and should not be ignored, minimized, or disregard. Instead, question and condemn all sexist attitudes and remarks and demand an apology from those who express such opinions and a commitment to relinquish these views, and to abstain from making such remarks again.

Furthermore, do not celebrate dysfunctional and damaging views of "manhood" and "femininity" for example, comments like "boys will be boys," "she is not very feminine," and so forth. When you do, you can encourage men to speak up and condemn sexual harassment and patriarchal systems in all their forms.

In the end, you will create a church culture that is inclusive and that respects, value, and listen to women and girls. The women will feel maintain their dignity and respect they deserve.

Is Homosexuality A Sin?

There seems to be some confusion or misunderstanding amongst the Lesbian, Gay, Bisexual, Transgender, Queer, or Questioning Intersex, and Asexual or Allied, (LGBTQIA) community that God has not spoken on, or address homosexuality in His words. Not so! God has supplied information on everything and anything that would trouble human beings, and God supplies instructions in His word to guide us away from sin. 1 Corinthians 6:9-11 (KJV) says, "⁹ Know ye not that the unrighteous shall not inherit the kingdom of God? Be not deceived: neither fornicators, nor idolaters, nor adulterers, nor "effeminate," nor abusers of themselves with mankind, ¹⁰ Nor thieves, nor covetous, nor drunkards, nor revilers, nor extortioners, shall inherit the kingdom of God. ¹¹ And such were some of you: but ye are washed, but ye are sanctified, but ye are justified in the name of the Lord Jesus, and by the Spirit of our God."

God did not stutter when He named homosexuality "Effeminate" in 1 Corinthians 6:9 as a sin. So, "Homosexuality is a sin." Equally significant, God did not call homosexuality a sin only once, and God did not bury it in His words where it could not be found. Instead, God repeatedly calls homosexuality a sin throughout His Words. Leviticus 18:22 (KJV), "²² Thou shalt not lie with mankind, as with womankind: it [is] abomination." God even went a step further and made it clear, again in His Word, that the punishment for homosexuality is death; Leviticus 20:13 (KJV), " If a man also lies with mankind, as he lieth with a woman, both of them have committed an abomination: they shall surely be put to death; their blood [shall be] upon them." Not only will they be put to death, along with the other sinners, they also shall not inherit the kingdom of God.

Then the LGBTQIA community implausibly claim that Christians of using the Bible against them. Their remarks have been met with derision, from Christians who accuse LGBTQIA of "being disrespectful" to their right to have a viewpoint on the subject.

First, this divisiveness is of the Devil because God is a God of love. And, "[12] For we wrestle not against flesh and blood, but against principalities, against powers, against the rulers of the darkness of this world, against spiritual wickedness in high places." Ephesians 6:12 (KJV)

Second, despite the rhetoric, Christians are to only use "Thus Saith The Lord" from God's Bible when they are referencing things of God. As such, God gave us His commandments to live by. 1 Timothy 1:8-10 (KJV), "[8] But we know that the law is good, if a man use it lawfully; [9] Knowing this, that the law is not made for a righteous man, but for the lawless and disobedient, for the ungodly and for sinners, for unholy and profane, for murderers of fathers and murderers of mothers, for manslayers, [10] For whoremongers, for them that defile themselves with mankind, for menstealers, for liars, for perjured persons, and if there be any other things that are contrary to sound doctrine." And despite what anyone eludes that God did away with the commandment, that is false. Ecclesiastes 3:14 (KJV), "[14] I know that whatsoever God doeth, it shall be forever: nothing can be put to it, nor anything was taken from it: and God doeth it, that men should fear before him."

God went even further and provided an example of His punishment saying in Jude 1:7 (KJV) and Jude 7:7 (KJV), "[7] Even as Sodom and Gomorrah, and the cities about them in like manner, giving themselves over to fornication, and going after strange flesh, are set forth for an example, suffering the vengeance of eternal fire."

Additionally, God also instructs Christians in Ephesians 5:11 (KJV), "[11] And have no fellowship with the unfruitful works of darkness, but rather reprove them." Christians work under the law of God, not man, and are, therefore, a Christian, while a dutiful servant of all, answers only to God on all matters of their Christian journey. The word reprove meaning to reprimand or censure (someone). So when Christians are staying true to the word of God and the ungodly feel under attack, that is God at work chastising them.

Furthermore, LGBTQIA people claim they are born the way they are, and therefore they are not going against the laws of God. Well, then the argument can be made that babies are born with innocence and have no notion of sex or sexuality like they do not know about human color to know racism and to hate.

Most recently, Pope Benedict wrote, "In various seminaries, homosexual cliques were established, which acted more or less openly and significantly changed the climate in the seminaries." This is a further indication of why God instituted marriages between a man and a woman.

However, more importantly, Numbers 15:30-31 (KJV), "³⁰ But the soul that doeth ought presumptuously, whether he be born in the land, or a stranger, the same reproacheth the Lord; and that soul shall be cut off from among his people. ³¹ Because he hath despised the word of the Lord and hath broken his commandment, that soul shall utterly be cut off; his iniquity shall be upon him."

Additionally, Christians have faced criticism for their comments and accused of homophobia, and discrimination against the LGBTQIA community. This accusation is slanderous and opens Christians up for backlash if they argue they are not homophobic, and discriminatory, they are merely quoting, "Thus saith the Lord." Truthfully, disapproving of homosexual behavior does not make one fearful or homophobic. However, many Christians have retreated because they are currently having to endure criticism from the public who put them under fire for being too holy and spreading hate. This is one of those matters that Christians must be ready to stand boldly for God. Choose this day whom you will serve. God's Law reflects His character.

Additionally, if everybody is afraid to tell the LGBTQIA community the truth, who will educate them on God's plans and desires and share the good news that Jesus wants them to come as they are, and He will bring them into the light and break the chains of their sinful lust, so they can be a new creation?

Christianity is about holiness and sacrifice and therefore turning away from homosexual acts may be your sacrifice. You can be redeemed if you choose to turn away from your sin, God will show you His truth! No different from the adulterer stopping their adulterous ways, a child molester stops molesting children, a drunkard giving up drinking, or the thief stops his stealing, and so forth.

Further, James 1:14 (KJV), "¹⁴ But every man is tempted, when he is drawn away of his own lust, and enticed. In other words, you cannot move away from this sin in your own strength because the devil will continue to entice you. But God says in Galatians 5:16 (KJV), "¹⁶ [This] I say then, "Walk in the Spirit, and ye shall not fulfill the lust of the flesh. In other words, those unnatural desires will not control you." So, because you love God, you can die to self and put away those practices and actions that contradict His word.

Far too many ministers and members of the clergy are like spineless cowards – too afraid to be emboldened to take a stand and trust in God to challenge the Devil and speak boldly for Christ when it comes to matters surrounding homosexuality and same-sex marriage. Ministers are compromising God's words by approving and performing same-sex marriage. Some out of fear of losing their jobs, some to ensure they can continue to build their numbers, and so forth. However, they will lose in the end because God will hold them accountable for their part in the abomination.

Becoming more worldly-minded than the people you are trying to reach becoming spiritually minded defeats the purpose of winning souls? God does not require that you disobey the law of Christ, risk losing your holiness and salvation, to gain theirs. It is impossible to be all things to everyone. You are under the law of Christ, and everything you do should point to Christ not away from Him, which is what you are doing when you please a man.

God forewarned that He gave up those, who changed His truth into a lie because of lust in their hearts, and they dishonored their bodies and engaged in unnatural relations with the same sex. Quoting from Romans

1:26-28 (KJV), "²⁴Wherefore God also gave them up to uncleanness through the lusts of their own hearts, to dishonor their own bodies between themselves: ²⁵Who changed the truth of God into a lie, and worshipped and served the creature more than the Creator, who is blessed forever. Amen. ²⁶For this cause God gave them up unto vile affections: for even their women did change the natural use into that which is against nature: ²⁷And likewise also the men, leaving the natural use of the woman, burned in their lust one toward another; men with men working that which is unseemly, and receiving in themselves that recompense of their error which was meet. ²⁸And even as they did not like to retain God in their knowledge, God gave them over to a reprobate mind, to do those things which are not convenient."

God warns all clergy, ministers, pastors, Bishops, ministers, evangelist, Bible Teacher, everyone who knows His word and those He has brought into the light, the truth of His words, that none of you will be able to plead ignorance. God said in James 4:17 (KJV), "¹⁷Therefore to him that knoweth to do good, and doeth [it] not, to him it is a sin."

Therefore, this clergy that is performing a same-sex marriage is doing so to appease man despite displeasing God and at the risk of losing out on Heaven. 1 Corinthians 9:25 (KJV), "And every man that striveth for the mastery is temperate in all things. Now they [do it] to obtain a corruptible crown, but we an incorruptible."

If you are knowingly disobeying the word of God that says homosexuality is a sin and choosing to continue to engage in homosexual acts, you are sinning against God.   Furthermore,
Ministers of the gospel know the word of God, or they should know the word of God, and if they do not know what God's Word on homosexuality and same-sex marriage is, they have a duty to find out by reading their Bible or consulting with other ministers and Biblical scholars. And, while a man and those involved may accept same-sex marriage and feel good for the moment, it is an abomination unto the Lord.

Notable, Clergy who are against being disobedient to the word of God is fearful to speak out, and at times careful to avoid pointing to the word of God, or entirely avoiding the subject of homosexuality altogether. But God does not leave us to figure anything out, and God does not leave us wallowing in ignorance. When the Pharisees came to Jesus and asked Him about the divorce between a man and his wife, Jesus response is clear about the marital covenant being between a man and a woman. Mark 10:5-9 (KJV), "⁵ And Jesus answered and said unto them, For the hardness of your heart he wrote you this precept. ⁶ But from the beginning of the creation, God made them male and female. ⁷ For this cause shall a man leave his father and mother and cleave to his wife; ⁸ And they twain shall be one flesh: so, then they are no more twain, but one flesh. ⁹ What therefore God hath joined together, let not man put asunder." 1 Corinthians 11:9 (KJV), "⁹ Neither was the man created for the woman; but the woman for the man." Jesus' response is relevant in context when we accept that God's word does not change or bend to fit our needs and desires.

And while members of clergy are carefully tiptoeing around the topic of homosexuality, God did not tiptoe when He said in Leviticus 20:13 (KJV), "¹³ If a man also lies with mankind, as he lieth with a woman, both of them have committed an abomination: they shall surely be put to death; their blood shall be upon them."

Therefore, Clergy who knows the gospel and remain silent on the subject and those who continue to marry people of the same sex to appease man in their sinful behavior will be held accountable; Romans 1:32 (KJV), "³² Who knowing the judgment of God, that they which commit such things are worthy of death, not only do the same but have pleasure in them that do them."

Clergy cannot be so naïve to believe that the LGBTQIA community are ignorant individuals. They are very much aware of what God says about homosexuality, about Sodom and Gomorrah. The struggles of members of the LGBTQIA community have nothing to do with what Christians are doing or saying, it has to do with "Thus saith the Lord;"

Their conscience cannot approve the thought that God is holding them accountable for the lustful ways that are causing them to sin. So, in turn, they have Christians under attack.

Clergy and Christians know that God is not an author of confusion and that the devil will use anyone, including their loved ones, to cause conflict and put God's children against each other. Indeed, adults who are electing to be in same-sex relationships are not confused about Who God is, and they do not lack knowledge of God's commandments or God's position on homosexuality or "effeminate." The information is in the Bible, and in the age of technology it can be googled and cross-reference with the Bible, it is at everyone's disposal, even children.

Christians must live by God's law, not man's desires or because of man's condemnation. Acts 5:29 (KJV), "²⁹ Then Peter and the [other] apostles answered and said, We ought to obey God rather than men. Romans 7:12 (KJV), "¹² Wherefore the law [is] holy, and the commandment holy, and just, and good. 1 Thessalonians 4:3 (KJV), "³ For this is the will of God, [even] your sanctification, that ye should abstain from fornication."

Furthermore, this debate is not about what Christians are saying; it is what God said. The discussion should be settled, but Christians continue to be under attack for speaking God's truth.

Understandably, Christians know this is spiritual warfare between God and Satan. The continued bickering between the LGBTQIA community and Christians is because people, whether they are aware or unaware, are under the influence of the devil to bully Christians into ceding God's truth and allow disobedience, lawlessness, and sin to consume society despite "Thus saith the Lord."

Additionally, as precise as the words of God is on homosexuality, and with this knowledge readily available to everyone, there are people, Christians, and non-Christians alike, demanding that believers in God's word refrain from saying homosexuality is a sin, citing, "God is a God of love."

Others try to impose their guilt upon Christian in this manner, "Well, if God is a God of love then Christians ought to stop practice hate." Then they expect everyone to be politically correct in their speech on the subject, like everyone cleaning up adultery and instead of making it more user-friendly by saying, "affair," "my boo," "my side-chick," or "my friend." No matter how much we try to clean up sin and package it to make it acceptable and unoffensive, sin is a sin, and God will pass His judgment on every single one of us. God admonished Christians and provided the foundation upon which Christians ought to build their communication with the LGBTQIA community and what He expects from Christian behavior in relation to that communication and education on disobedience of His laws in Colossians 3:1-17 (KJV). Without discounting any of the verses, and paying particular attention, to: verse 1, because Christ is the head of your life, verse 5, calls for us to call sin by its name, verse 6, warns those who are breakers of God's law of His rebuke, verse 7, encourages Christian to treat others without being self-righteous and forgetting you were once a sinner, verse 8, requires Christians to talk with their brother and sister without anger and bitterness, verse 9, and without lying to them to appease them; and, verse 11, because you are a new creature in Christ, verse 12 requires that you tell the disobedient children of God's truth in love, verse 16, teaching and admonishing them to turn away from their sinful ways. Let's read Colossians 3:1-17 (KJV), "[1] If ye then be risen with Christ, seek those things which are above, where Christ sitteth on the right hand of God. [2] Set your affection on things above, not on things on the earth. [3] For ye are dead, and your life is hid with Christ in God. [4] When Christ, who is our life, shall appear, then shall ye also appear with him in glory. [5] Mortify therefore your members which are upon the earth; fornication, uncleanness, inordinate affection, evil concupiscence, and covetousness, which is idolatry: [6] For which things' sake the wrath of God cometh on the children of disobedience: [7] In the which ye also walked some time when ye lived in them. [8] But now ye also put off all these; anger, wrath, malice, blasphemy, filthy communication out of your mouth. [9] Lie not one to another, seeing that ye have put off the old man with his deeds; [10] And have put on the new man, which is renewed in knowledge after the image of him that created him: [11] Where there is neither Greek nor Jew, circumcision nor uncircumcision, Barbarian, Scythian, bond nor free: but Christ is all and in all. [12] Put on, therefore, as the elect of God, holy and beloved, bowels of mercies, kindness, humbleness of mind, meekness, longsuffering; [13] Forbearing one another, and forgiving one another if any man has a quarrel against any: even as Christ forgave you, so also do ye. [14] And above all these things put on charity, which is the bond of perfectness. [15] And let the peace of God rule in your hearts, to the which also ye are called in one body; and be ye thankful. [16] Let the word of Christ dwell in you richly in all wisdom; teaching and admonishing one another in psalms and hymns and spiritual songs, singing with grace in your hearts to the Lord. [17] And whatsoever ye do in word or deed, do all in the name of the Lord Jesus, giving thanks to God and the Father by him."

Therefore, it is not anyone's place to condemn or force anyone to go against the word of God which is the real foundation upon which Christianity stands. Calling homosexuality sin is not a formal decision of Christians; it is "Thus saith The Lord."

Still Christians, God does not want His people condemning homosexuals with a self-righteous attitude and forgetting to hold all sinners to the same standards. Sin is sin in God's eyes, so even though you may be a Christian and stand firmly against homosexuality, you cannot be dogmatic about homosexuality and turn a blind eye to other sins; that include adulterers, fornicators, thieves, drunkards, covetous, revilers, extortioners, it is just not right, and God is a just God to everyone.

People can live how to choose; God gave them free will. However, they must be told the truth in love. Also, gently remind them that 1 John 1:9(KJV), "If we confess our sins, he is faithful and just to forgive us [our] sins, and to cleanse us from all unrighteousness. However, even though God forgives, cleanses, and restores, free will comes with responsibility, accountability, and consequences. God will hold each of us accountable for our actions, and God chastises His children whom He loves.

However, if you are about pleasing man, and bending to the lawless sinful ways of man, you might as well sign them over personally to the devil. 1 John 3:4 (KJV), "⁴Whosoever committeth sin transgresseth also the law: for sin is the transgression of the law." James 2:10 (KJV), "¹⁰For whosoever shall keep the whole law, and yet offend in one [point], he is guilty of all. So, Romans 7:7(KJV), "⁷ What shall we say then? [Is] the law sin? God forbids. Nay, I had not known sin, but by the law: for I had not known lust, except the law had said, thou shalt not covet."

Also, remember, to whom much is given much is required. Part of being a soldier in God's army is that you will come under attack from the enemy firing at you and you will have to duck for cover in the short run, but you will win that soul for Christ in the long run and be blessed. Psalms 19:7-9 (KJV), "⁷The law of the LORD [is] perfect, converting the soul: the testimony of the LORD [is] sure, making wise the simple. ⁸The statutes of the LORD [are] right, rejoicing the heart: the commandment of the LORD [is] pure, enlightening the eyes. ⁹The fear of the LORD [is] clean, enduring for ever: the judgments of the LORD [are] true [and] righteous altogether." And as God promised in Psalms 112:4(KJV), "⁴Unto the upright there ariseth light in the darkness: [he is] gracious, and full of compassion, and righteous."

Additionally, as a Christian, you are in a relationship with God, and there is a covenant between you and God. Jesus is your example, and (1) Jesus did not come to pacify, Jesus came to satisfy, and (2) Jesus did not cave into a man, Jesus saves man. Therefore, Christians, you must remain committed to "Thus saith the Lord" or you will be guilty of condemning your brothers and sisters to hell by pacifying them with the lie that homosexuality is not a sin. In other words, you cannot in good conscience call yourself a Christian and pacify no man or woman with a lie, nor should you want to be appeased with one when God's word clearly says otherwise.

So, while people want you to turn a blind eye and to stay silent on the matters of homosexuality, Christianity is not about being selective to make self or others feel good or to be happy; Christianity is about living a life of commitment to God, about serving a living and loving God and being holy and obedient to God and to God's words. You serve God and only God, not man or man's ideals. You cannot be selective and only read or believe the parts of the Bible that make you, and everyone feels comfortable or fit everyone's narratives while discounting the Biblical verses that are a rebuke to lawlessness and inappropriate behavior. Likewise, overlook the Biblical verses or nullify the ones that question your motives, your actions, and that hold you accountable. To do so is to live an artificial life and one of compromise.

God needs His soldiers to be bold and take a stance and refute this claim that homosexuality is not a sin. However, many ministers are staying silent and causing too many Christians in their charge, who are looking to them for guidance and direction, to sit quietly or retreat when the Bible is clear. Therefore, Christians who are concern about this subject and whether they should speak up or not should seek counsel from other Biblical clergy members. Proverbs 11:14 (KJV), "14 Where no counsel is, the people fall: but in the multitude of counselors there is safety."

Additionally, even when Christians are afraid to hold up the gospel banner, Christians should never err in the seat of conflict and compromise on sin - and staying silent when you know the truth of God's words that are unequivocal and forever is a slippery slope. You are not giving account to God's laws of morality, value, and truth and standing on what matters to God.

Finally, God's timeless Word reveals His plan for salvation and His intentions for marriage and sexuality. Scripture is clear that homosexuality is a sin. Clergy and Christians who stay silent or cede truth on this matter is allowing the devil to sow his discord and accusation on God's people even though God's word never changes. Sin should not sit and fester and continue to grow and infect our homes, churches, and communities; instead, sin should be addressed and pulled out at its roots before it consumed our hearts and minds.

Here is the sum of the matter: Hebrews 13:8 (KJV), "8 Jesus Christ the same yesterday, and today, and forever." And, God is Holy, Just, Unchanging and All-loving. Isaiah 33:22(KJV), "22For the LORD [is] our judge, the LORD [is] our lawgiver, the LORD [is] our king; he will save us." God loves everyone; God wants all of us with Him in Heaven. God thought enough on the subject of homosexuality to include it in His words over two thousand years ago because God already knew man was going to change the truth of His words to appease their lust, and each other, and to soothe their own carnal desires. Christians, hate the sin, love the sinner. Remember people know you are Christian by your love, therefore, continue to discuss in love.

Prayerfully, in this section, God has directed and cleared up this troubling matter that is separating Christians from their LGBTQIA brothers and sisters. For those who are having issues with the truth, know this: God's Nature, His Words, His commands, His promises, and more significantly, God's Authority, is always right and will never change.

Within these words, God has spoken. God said it, so that settles it and your response equates to no debate because Jesus Christ is the same yesterday, and today, and forever. God's blessings as you search for His truth. Pray and ask God to help you recognize when something in your life is contrary to His Word and lead you in the path you should go. Amen.

James 5: 16, 19 – 20 (KJV), "16 Confess your faults one to another, and pray one for another, that ye may be healed. The effectual fervent prayer of a righteous man availeth much. 19 Brethren, if any of you do err from the truth, and one convert him; 20 Let him know, that he which converteth the sinner from the error of his way shall save a soul from death, and shall hide a multitude of sins." It is my hope that this piece educates and not offend, and that God brings any person struggling into His truth. God bless!

Confronting Your Own Biases

How do you live your belief, in every aspect of your life? Sometimes the truth can get twisted, blurred, manipulated, and lines crossed. Things once seen as black and white may start to appear grayer. It may seem harder to recognize what is up or what is down. What is right and what is wrong?

Should Christians' interpretations of their religious belief influence their decisions when they are in positions of authority over others? You face a lot of your own biases and an equal amount of criticisms from a cruel world outside the walls of the church, and from within the church. However, as Christians, at the heart of your worship, your existence, and your every being, should be your love for God. Confronting your own biases is a very effective way to stop behaving in discriminatory ways.

Therefore, despite your cynicism and criticism, despite how much you are ridicule you must still have a tenderness to forgive, and a heart, despite how damage, to love, as Jesus loves. It will help you to feel less disappointed, less angry, and less regretful.

Understand, these sins infested contentious individuals are still trying to find their way to Jesus or are allowing the devil to use them.

However, you and free will and only you can decide how you are going to live your Christian journey. Plus, do not forget, people have negativity about God to where a perfect Jesus went to the cross. So why does imperfect you expect to be treated differently?

As an adult, you still have a penchant for detecting and dwelling on the negative, falling prey to that one small request for improvement. Sound familiar? However, if you do, it is no cause for alarm; there are ways to counter the potential negative impact of your biases.

Your biases are merely a product of intelligent human design that, "Whatever can go wrong, usually does," and, "Your tendency to mentally jump to conclusions." That is right — humans were designed to be keenly aware of unfavorable circumstances and consequences as it helped us to survive. Being sharply attuned to attacks of negativity bias and knowing when to retreat, is essential to protecting yourselves.

Negativity bias is your tendency to have higher sensitivity to the adverse events and to overlook the positive things that may be happening in your life. Psychologically speaking, adverse events weigh us down three times more than positive events does. While these biases may serve us in situations related to survival, it can cause anxiety and depression in your everyday relationships.

As a result, sometimes your judgment becomes impaired, and you do not always make the best decision.

Therefore, it is essential to figure out how you can effectively deal with your negativity biases.

Self-righteousness

In fairness to those struggling with homosexuality and other immoral behaviors, sin, God wants His followers to behave in loving ways to everyone, even our enemies God wants us to hate the sin not the sinner. The Bible should not be used as a weapon against believers to justify behaviors that God says is not moral and calls a sin, neither should the Bible used to beat those struggling with sin into the ground. One cannot be mature in Christ unless one learns to love, accept, and embrace the reality of all people.

It does not mean you cannot discuss sensitive topics such as homosexuality and bringing people into God's truth, not your truth, God's truth because God's Words is forever and does not change and woe unto anyone, who changes it.

Therefore, surrendering truth to accept and normalize homosexuality will lead to a profound distortion of God's Words and a crumbling of God's authority between man. Ignoring the systemic roots of homosexuality and any sin and staying quiet so as not to upset the masses results in a stunted spiritual maturity. Slowly, sin creeps into the church and its structures and fester until it erupts and tries to disrupt God's divine plans for His people.

When people share their experiences, are you moved with pity, love, and compassion, or are you angry, distressed, and troubled? Do you take the opportunity to listen to others with identity markers different than your own? To the skeptic, most Christians – certainly most who appear willing to "defend" their faith – may seem dogmatic and able to forgive their sin because they know Christ better than anyone. Christians sometimes use a narrow interpretation of Christian morals to deny limit their relationship with the LGBTQIA community, some Christians going as far as refusing to service them. Behaviors like this are not Christlike, and therefore it is sometimes justifiably when people see

Christians, and they consider the plethora of Religions and religious beliefs, but they do not see the Christ in us.

Additionally, your strikingly consistent pattern of hypocrisy is seen because you were taught to consider what is deemed sexual immorality in the church, you continue feeding systems of discrimination and oppression by not formally recognizing other people's differences. Justifiably so because it is almost impossible to ignore something that has been ingrained in many people since childhood, the perfect illustration of this bias comes from the monument of contention itself— For example, most Christian would describe themselves as "a kind and decent human being," so oftentimes, it is difficult to explain to others that "you feel" a certain way about Lesbian, Gay, Bisexual, Transgender, Queer, or Questioning Intersex, and Asexual or Allied, (LGBTQIA) community. That your behavior is not in alignment with theirs, that their belief system does not reflect yours that you have of God. However, God is a God of love, and He loved and died for everyone. God wants us to love LGBTQIA people as they are and make them feel invited. Did God not command us to love even the sinner, hate the sin but love the sinner.

You must know Christ for yourself before you can fully understand why the study of Biblical scriptures around the subject of homosexuality is carefully directed to ensure you do not offend the masses.

Instead of seeing you as proclaiming the gospel, are members of the LGBTQIA community sees you as using the Bible as rebuke and manipulation. Especially when they hear us reciting the commandments, but they do not see us living the commandments. The truth is, you should ensure your fervor is right with God before questioning the motives of others or condemning their relationships of others to Christ.

Be sure you are able to answer the question Jesus asked His disciples, in Matthew 16:15 (KJV), "[15] He saith unto them, "But who say ye that I am?" And, in Mark 8:29 (KJV), "[29] And he saith unto them, But who say ye that I am? And Peter answereth and saith unto him, Thou art the Christ." And again, He asked in Luke 9:20 (KJV), "[20] He said unto them, but who say ye that I am? Peter answering said, The Christ of God." Do you know Jesus as "The Christ of God?"

Also, they hear about the cross and the plan of salvation, but they do not see us living with an urgency that the cross and the plan of salvation needs.

Therefore, many nonbelievers conclude, then, that the believer is naturally biased in favor of his own religious beliefs, needs and wants without having considered where best to place his trust - do not expect people whose views differ from yours to agree with you or rally for the causes you believe in if you don't rally for theirs.

Still, some Christians seem so convinced of their views, regardless of how bizarre some of these views look to the unbeliever and to other Christians who do not share the same views.

Sure, there are times you must formulate opinions about others, and sometimes you are right, but then there are those times when there is no validity to the things you believe. Your judgment is so unfounded and so off base that God warns us about, that is a liability to the Christian journey. Moreover, in Matthew 7:1-3 (KJV), "1 Judge not, that ye be not judged. 2 For with what judgment ye judge, ye shall be judged: and with what measure ye mete, it shall be measured to you again. 3 And why beholdest thou the mote that is in thy brother's eye, but considerest not the beam that is in thine own eye?"

What is unusual about God is that when God designed us, He equipped us in such a way that if you evaluate yourselves, you can see an accounting for even the smallest details. For example, God designed us to face toward the direction your feet take us; to prevent us from looking back or tripping over obstacles and running into others. And God designed marriages Mark 10: 6-9 (KJV), "6 But from the beginning of the creation, God made them male and female.

7 For this cause shall a man leave his father and mother and cleave to his wife; 8 And they twain shall be one flesh: so, then they are no more twain, but one flesh. 9 What therefore God hath joined together, let not man put asunder."

However, for so many Christians, putting away the selfishness that dwells within and just caring about others is one of their greatest downfalls to true selflessness or a blockage to dying to self. Transformation is a process, and your faith grows as you transform. How can you indeed die to self and transform if you cannot love those affected by several discriminations and disadvantages?

Finding your path to God needs you to die to self, that God might live in us. So how do you start transformation? You have God's help, now what? Dying to self-starts by recognizing you live in a world of indifference. Once you realize that other people are different from us, you can begin to die to self. Moreover, as you let go of the ego, you will learn to trust God more and then grow in Him.

Also, by considering that people have overlapping identities and experiences, you can begin to understand the complexity of prejudices people face in both societies and within the walls of the church.

Thankfully, God's mercy is sure, and God has provided us with enough evidence, the cross which provides a way of salvation via Christ to prove His love and faithfulness to us.

Therefore, rather than reading God's friendly warning with a self-righteousness, you ought to offer grace to those who have strayed from His will.

Recognize, you live in a fallen world with a fallen nature, but in Christ, you all can be new creatures.

Still, you cannot sit by and quiver with fear of being called out for discrimination because you hold God's word to be true. Ellen G. White says, "The greatest want of the world is the want of men - men who will not be bought or sold; men who in their inmost souls are true and honest; men who do not fear to call sin by its right name; men whose conscience is as true to duty as the needle to the pole; men who will stand for the right though the heavens fall."

You must call sin by its name when you see a blatant misquote of God's word to justify sin. For Pete's sake, it is one of the reasons why God destroyed Sodom and Gomorrah so let us not pacify each other; it is forbidden for two men, or two women to be engaged in an intimate situation with each other; Biblical Truth is Biblical truth. God said it, and that settles it. See 1 Corinthians 6:9-11 (KJV).

Moreover, for those who believe that God did away with the laws, then answer this question, "Why would God instruct us to obey the ten commandments in the Old Testament, and Jesus tells us in the New Testament, that you should not only obey the law but teach it as well?" To reiterate, live as you choose, but do not mistreat Christians for repeating "thus saith the Lord."

It is difficult to reconcile Christians belief of religious traditions that are revered and the LGBTQIA community and the love that emulates from them. The problem some Christians have is that they are so disgusted by homosexuality and fear rubbing shoulders with the LGBTQIA community. Many have this attitude that associating with LGBTQIA will wrongly reflect their desires. These individuals do not know how to mesh their own identities and challenges with the identities and challenges of others. They do not know how to communicate a sense of absolute love, trust, and familiarity toward one another. Worst, they do not pray and ask God to help persons from the LGBTQIA community to uncover their identities, understand their stories, and find wholeness.

It is interesting to note that many believe if they let people from the LGBTQIA community in the church somehow the when you question the motives of others and gather facts to find that you should be fearful of someone? Of course, there will be. So, does that mean you should go searching and judge?

Not, you should only remain faithful to God's word, starting with Matthew 7:1 (KJV) "Judge not that ye be judged."

Moreover, as uncomfortable as you are in naming another person's perceived identity, beyond your assumptions, you must recognize how people's unique experiences of character, and particularly ones that involve multiple overlapping oppressions, are valid despite your experiences and beliefs.

Assuming their sexual preferences defines all "LGBTQIA" people would be an oversimplification that erases their identity and relationship with God and limits their experiences beyond the gender binary. Recognize that one of the reasons that people in the "LGBTQIA" community experience their Christian journey differently based on their overlapping identity markers and ostracization within the church, your biases are placing a wedge between them and their relationship with God.

Also, many Christians are openly opposed to the "LGBTQIA" community in private settings; but in public and for political correctness, forsaking the word of God, they are reticence on the subject; opting to practice restraint instead of being bold and comfortable enough to say God condemns that lifestyle out loud, when the Word of God is being misstated and opposed. Reference thus saith the Lord in, "1 Corinthians 6:9(KJV), "Know ye not that the unrighteous shall not inherit the kingdom of God? Be not deceived: neither fornicators, nor idolaters, nor adulterers, nor effeminate, nor abusers of themselves with mankind."

Therefore, avoid attitudes that assume your own experiences with God are baseline, you can open yourselves up to be welcoming to everyone, listening to others' points of view, and starting the process to dying to self.

Become comfortable recognizing you are all different but with similar ideas as Christian striving for an eternal home. By accepting your differences and similarities, you will find that diversity matter all areas of your life, including your community, Christian journey, and more. Where many churches are falling short is that polish and performance take precedence over presence. For example, churches will use the same members repeatedly but will not encourage someone who loves to sing songs of praise to take part because they have Sister Songbird to do all the singing. That takes away from worship because God wants to hear His frog that is full of love with Him croaking than Sister Songbird who may know to sing but do not know God.

Likewise, a church can be racially and ethnically diverse, but not accessible to people with disabilities. But be clear, while you are not to discriminate or be self-righteous towards the LGBTQIA community, you must stand firm on your convictions that the word of God is everlasting, and God firmly stated in Leviticus 18:22 (KJV)"[22] Thou shalt not lie with mankind, as with womankind: it is abomination."

Additionally, before you point fingers, get educated so you can begin to understand the issues those in the LGBTQIA community, domestic violence, sexual assault, rape, or trafficked community face, and about the work that is currently being done around these topics and take part.

Listen, sympathize, and pray for those who live with these intersectional identities each day to broaden your horizon beyond your, "what is in it for me mentality."

As you do, you will be more open and accepting of your own identity in Christ and the subjects you care about most but more importantly, how to put away self and minister to others in a loving Christlike way without imposing your personal views while representing and sharing the love of Christ.

Once you recognize your differences, you can begin to move away from attitudes and language that looks to define people by a singular identity while castrating them away from the love of Christ that is unconditional for all humankind.

Also, even if they experience pain and tragedy, allow others, in love, to face the consequences of their actions. As the children of God, He gives free will and only requires you to explore your own biases continuously. Get educated on the narratives of those with different interlocking identities, including others with differing interwoven characters, or who are ignorant about the oppression others may be facing, while setting aside your own biases.

Next, do not be afraid to seek out existing intersectional narratives from other Christian's points of view but refrain from interjecting your biases because your biases do not correlate with "truth or falsity."

Also, biases are unacceptable and have no place in the church. Your prejudices always prove to be hurtful, offensive, and burden. Addressing your preferences belongs to you, and not on the individuals who are subject to them.

Like Christians, many people believe the Bible teaches about modern sensitivities rightly recognize as morally repugnant, and others have used them to justify abuse, terror, torture, and execution.

Also, as a Christian, if you listen with the love of Christ in your heart, you will be better prepared to engage in conversations with nonbelievers and other Christians with opposing views.

Still, you must stay through to Biblical principles and not sway from "Thus saith the Lord." Instead, respectfully agree to disagree without arguing the Bible and Biblical principles.

As Christians, you are the salt that is preventing the world from a state of absolute lawlessness. Paul's second letter to the Thessalonians declares, that while iniquity is now working in the world, there is coming a complete manifestation of the "wicked one," but at present that full demonstration hindered the power that is blocking is the Holy Spirit in the godly people living upon this earth. How you share God with others is what matters. God wants us to win souls, not drive them away. Get people into the churches, plant the seed, and allow God to do the watering and The Holy Spirit will supply the elements for their growth.

To conclude, as Christians, you are often known more for your prejudices than principles. You have the guidance of the Holy Spirit, and if you listen rather than telling the Holy Spirit how to behave and what you will accept and what you will not, you would be further along in your relationship with Christ. This criticism, while harsh, is a reason to throw out your moral compasses and sway with whatever the prevailing winds of the day may be. God warned us in 2 Timothy 3:12 (KJV), "12 Yea, and all that will live godly in Christ Jesus shall suffer persecution."

144

Remember, you serve a never changing God who will hold us accountable one day; The word of God is firm and never changing. Think on 2 Thessalonians 1:3-4 (KJV) "³ You are bound to thank God always for you, brethren, as it is meet, because that your faith groweth exceedingly, and the charity of every one of you all toward each other aboundeth; ⁴ So that you yourselves glory in you in the churches of God for your patience and faith in all your persecutions and tribulations that ye endure:" Let's just love each other in Christ and be not transform by this world. "⁸ For by grace are ye saved through faith; and that not of yourselves: it is the gift of God:" Ephesians 2:8 (KJV).

Together, your behavior shed light on the conditions under which worship and cope with biased comments at church. More effectively — a helpful tool until the problem can be addressed.

The Transformed Life

2 Peter 3:9 (KJV), "⁹ The Lord is not slack concerning his promise, as some men count slackness; but is longsuffering to us-ward, not willing that any should perish, but that all should come to repentance." This message is a reminder to all of us who have been listening to the gospel of grace for some time now. The Lord is revealing to us the secret to living a transformed life. It is time for us to remove all the buttons in our lives that the devil constantly presses. Let us get to the deepest root that causes all our problems.

Condemnation kills—it is time to take it seriously. We preach to the church about the dangers of stress, but there's a deeper root than stress." Your problems are not the root. When you go through an evil day, you are like a sickly plant with sick leaves. You may have left of sickness, poverty, a broken marriage, or depression in your life. But these are just the leaves. These are just the manifestations of the root. It would be foolish to attack the leaves because they are not the cause of your problems. We all know that there will be no leaf if there is no root.

Now, the deeper root of stress is fear. All stress is caused by fear—fear of failing, fear of not having enough, fear of death and so on. But that's as far as medical science can go. They cannot touch the deepest root because it is spiritual.

Even the world knows that, and many people in medical science are beginning to realize that there is a root of sickness. In fact, a study by a well-known medical facility showed that about 70 percent of all sicknesses are due to stress.

When there's condemnation, there will be fear. When there's fear, there is going to be stress. And when there's stress, there will be manifestations of the curse.

Now, if you disagree with me that the root cause is condemnation, let me refer you to Genesis, the book of beginnings.

147

The devil has not changed his tactics even with a church like yours where you preach so actively against condemnation. Do you know why? Because he has no other tactic! He has no other weapon! The devil cannot enforce the curse in your life apart from condemnation. The devil cannot make you sick apart from condemnation. You have to cooperate with him and receive the condemnation first.

Colossians 2:14–15 (KJV), "¹⁴ Blotting out the handwriting of ordinances that was against us, which was contrary to us, and took it out of the way, nailing it to his cross; ¹⁵ And having spoiled principalities and powers, he made a shew of them openly, triumphing over them in it. The good news is that God disarmed the devil at the cross. God took his only weapon—the law—and He nailed it to the cross! Yes, God has triumphed over the devil and all his demonic principalities and powers! That is why it is essential to understand that you are not fighting for victory; you are because of victory in Jesus. The victory is already ours through the finished work of Christ on the cross.

The fact that you can feel condemned is proof that you have a heart of flesh, not a heart of stone. Ezekiel 11:19 (KJV), "¹⁹ And I will give them one heart, and I will put a new spirit within you; and I will take the stony heart out of their flesh, and will give them an heart of flesh:" Ezekiel 36:26 (KJV), "²⁶ A new heart also will I give you, and a new spirit will I put within you: and I will take away the stony heart out of your flesh, and I will give you a heart of flesh." It is proof that you are genuinely born again.

The word "therefore" connects Romans 8:1 to the earlier verses in Romans 7:1 (KJV), "¹ Know ye not, brethren, (for I speak to them that know the law,) how that the law hath dominion over a man as long as he liveth?"

Paul talked about how he was condemned by the law that he knew so well. God loved us so much that He gave us His Son Jesus Christ to die for our sins. Jesus came, and He was condemned for our sins at the cross. When He hung on the cross, God took all our sins of our entire lives, and He heaped them on Jesus. Then God unleashed the vengeance of His fury against lawlessness and sin on the body of Jesus Christ until Jesus cried, "It is finished!" The reason you have a second chance to be saved from all your sins—in Jesus; name!

To overcome the devil by the blood of the Lamb you must believe there is power in the blood of Christ. Jesus' blood is so powerful because in Matthew 26:28 (KJV), "28 For this is my blood of the new testament, which is shed for many for the remission of sins."

The blood is for the forgiveness of sins! The blood is there to ensure that you live in no condemnation! That is what makes it so powerful!

Notice also what is said in verse 10, "...for the accuser of our brethren, who accused them before our God day and night, has been cast down." The devil is called the accuser of the brethren. And he relentlessly accuses God's people day and night. But the good news is that he has been cast down! He has been defeated! The moment he has no power to accuse, salvation, strength, the kingdom of God and the power of Christ will manifest in your life!

Some of you might say, "I have no problem with this root. I don't feel condemned." However, you will be surprised. Condemnation is very subtle, especially if you are a person who believes in doing what is right. Continue to do what is right, but do not respond to the accuser. When you choose not to respond to him, he cannot condemn you. The root cause of all your problems is destroyed, and you will come to the place of no condemnation in your life.

Are You an Asset or a Liability?

Are you an asset or a liability to your church? What do your dispositions—inward attitudes, state of mind, feelings, your personal "postures toward God" reveal about your relationship with God? How do you stand for God in the Church and out and about in the world? When people see you, they should be seeing Christ.

People seem to always fit into one of two categories, asset or liability, giver or taker, burden or blessing, problem, or problem solver. Whatever you are you fall into one of these two categories; You are either you an asset or a liability to your church, but it is an exhortation to be a blessing instead of a burden.

Paul warns us not to assume self-importance and the dangers of self-estimation in Romans 12:16 (KJV), "Agree one toward another. Mind not high things but condescend to men of low estate. Be not wise in your conceits".

Still, today, churches have a steady barrage of accusation about the hypocrisy which is amongst the most dangerous biases of human beings. Not to mention incredibly hypocritical.

Therefore, it is vital for you to work towards being an asset. Imagine a church where all its members are assets. How incredible that church would be. Everyone is working in unison for the common goal of winning souls for Christ and getting everyone to Heaven.

God needs you to represent Him and draw others to Him. You cannot fulfill your mission if you are behaving like a liability or like the people who need to be saved; this is clear.

Additionally, joining cliques and considering your in-group members (However insular that group may be), as righteous while seeing others as blasphemous or worthy only of ridicule, and its adherents, infidels or heretics, your bias against those you consider as outsiders only serve to promote further hypocrisy. Remember, the church is the people, not the building.

This behavior is plaguing your churches, and it is why Christians are accused of being hypocritical. "Are you an asset or a liability to God's Church?" That is the question you need to answer to fully understand where you are in your walk with Christ and your impact or influence in His church.

Jesus encountered some religious leaders who considered themselves to be relevant to God but saw a weeping woman and a man in a tree considered insignificant as unworthy; Jesus reversed their faulty assumptions.

Another Christian attitude that is proving to be a liability to the church is that many professed Christians, have no ambivalence about their journey to Heaven. Many have become acclimated to doing things one way, which is their idea of the right direction, and they start to bully their leaders, and some go as far as discount or challenge "Thus saith the Lord" if it is not in line with them getting their way.

Some Christians have been in the church a life span and do not know God let alone have a relationship with God, while many new believers entering the church comes in with a fire for God developed from some experience that led them to the church in the first place.

With this comes your bias, to take the path of least resistance, depriving yourself of a certain amount of freedom to remain "moral" but defining morality any way you chose. With no law-giver, there is no reason to follow rules that you did not set for yourself.

Sure, you can be just as religious sitting at home in front of the television watching football games as someone who dresses up, goes to church on Sabbath, sings in the choir, lead out in praise, prays, and reads the Bible.

However Christian behavior has spiritual ramifications. Whether it is going to Church, singing songs of praise, praying, or talking to others, are all religious acts. Moreover, how you relate to other people helps to define each one of us as a distinct identity in relationship with others. As such, it reveals who you are, what you care about, what you love, what you dislike, as well as that stuff that comprises character. Also, while you can be religious at home, how do people see you? What is your role about Christ?

As this section concludes, consider, are you a blessing or a burden to the those around you? Do you see yourself as a problem solver, or are you the problem? Are you an asset or a liability? Whatever you are, God loves you, and you are necessary to Him and to His church. Even if you feel you are a liability, which will be a sad situation, know that you are of crucial importance to God because He does not see any of His children or anyone seeking after Him as a liability.

Plus, God's church is a special place for all misfits, so God welcomes you into His family. So of course, God does not expect you to change every one of the 8+ billion people on the planet, but He does expect you to change the one person you can change; Yourself!

Strive to be an asset for God.

Let Me Pray About It

If you read nothing else, read and understand this, "Do not pressure people or try to get them to participate in ministry."

Christianity is a calling, just like Pastoring is a calling. The Bible tells us, Matthew 22:14 (KJV), "For many are called, but few are chosen." The Great Commission is for everyone to proclaim the gospel to the nations. Every Christ-follower who are called and accept their calling does so to glorify God by making disciples of Jesus among their neighbors. So, yes, it is baffling when Christians say, "Let me pray about it?" when asked to take part in a church activity or ask for your help in ministry.

Isn't it amazing that prayers to serve are the only prayers God never seems to answer? God must not solve this particular prayer because the person is asking for help never hears back from the person who said, "Let me pray about it." The truth is, in ministry, the Christian does not need to pray for God's permission to aid in His work, permission is understood to have been granted for anything holy that gives glory to God and shows love to a brother or sister in Christ. You need to be obedient to His will, and your prayers, after saying "Yes" need only be to ask God's guidance so that you can glorify Him in the process.

Also, you should be faithful in your prayer. Jesus taught us to pray, Matthew 6:9 (KJV), "[9] After this manner, therefore, pray ye: Your Father which art in heaven, Hallowed be thy name….." And, 1 Thessalonians 5:17 (KJV) reads, "[17] Pray without ceasing." Likewise, Romans 12:12 (KJV), "[12] Rejoicing in hope; patient in tribulation; continuing instant in prayer."

But do not disrespect God by hiding behind prayers as a means of not supporting the work of God through the ministries of His church. Matthew 5:37 (KJV), "[37] But let your communication be, Yea, yea; Nay, nay: for whatsoever is more than these cometh of evil". In other words, stop lying to the brethren that you are going to pray about it, including

God in your deceptive behavior, and using prayer as a source of escape. Also, Proverbs 3:5 (KJV), "⁵ Trust in the LORD with all thine heart, and lean not unto thine own understanding."

Without prayer and proper planning, you will overextend yourself and become broken and crushed by the weight and pressures of ministry and because of all the needs and demands that it brings. Serving out of compulsion will bring about bitterness, and that is not an exercise of free will. Luke 11:9 (KJV), "⁹ And I say unto you, Ask, and it shall be given you; seek, and ye shall find; knock, and it shall be opened unto you." God has already equipped you before someone come to ask for help. Use your spirit of discernment to identify the things that are of God. A brother or sister seeking your help so that you will enhance their program and get them more praise is not of God, pray on these types of things that the Holy Spirit will guide you into the light. "Pray about it" when people in the church ask us to take part in a church activity or ask for your help in ministry? Jesus already provided us with the answer to this question. In Philippians 4:8 (KJV), "⁸ Finally, brethren, whatsoever things are true, whatsoever things are honest, whatsoever things are just, whatsoever things are pure, whatsoever things are lovely, whatsoever things are of good report; if there be any virtue, and if there be any praise, think on these things." [And do it].

However, there is no scripture in The Bible calls you to pray and ask God whether you should participate in His work? Christians use prayer in these situations as an excuse not to participate and to say no indirectly. Perhaps this is why they never come back to you with their answer from God. 2 Chronicles 7:14 (KJV), "¹⁴ If my people, which are called by my name, shall humble themselves, and pray, and seek my face, and turn from their wicked ways; then will I hear from heaven, and will forgive their sin, and will heal their land". It is wickedness when you use prayer to say "no" to service. This is why sometimes people do not hear back from God or never return to provide an answer to your request for help.

Let's be clear; this does not mean you treat every request made to you as an assignment from God. You always must pause, questioned the validity of the request if it is something that will glorify God, and yes, you may even need to pray about it in context of helping where you are needed and as necessary.

Also, if you are asked to pray or even if you are inclined to pray, apply the words of Matthew 6:5 (KJV), "⁵ And when thou prayest, thou shalt not be as the hypocrites are: for they love to pray standing in the synagogues and in the corners of the streets, that they may be seen of men. Verily I say unto you; They have their reward".

Additionally, never use prayer to bring pain to another person. Preying on others through prayer is a sin. God commands in Matthew 5:44 (KJV), "⁴⁴ But I say unto you, Love your enemies, bless them that curse you, do good to them that hate you, and pray for them which despitefully use you, and persecute you." So, certainly, God does not want to listen to prayers with ill intent.

Remember, prayer is an imaginary vertical line that connects you to Jesus, Who serves as a mediator between you and God. This is not a matter to be played with or be unreasonable with.

Prayer is an individual relationship to God and God's relationship to an individual - it is a two-way street. Through this relationship to God, you have the privilege to go to God in prayer, and Jesus invites you to pray, and He serves as an intercessor in your relationship with God.

Additionally, prayer grants us the opportunity to present your requests to God. Prayer is not just about asking for God's blessings – though you are welcome to do so – it is about communication with the living God. Without discussion, relationships fall apart. God instructs you in Philippians 4:6 (KJV), " Be careful for nothing; but in everything by prayer and supplication with thanksgiving let your requests be made known unto God."

However, prayers, while it is the Christians greatest blessing admittedly — has become your greatest Christian failure because you lie and say you will pray about it, using prayer to say no when you should be saying yes. Ephesians 6:18 (KJV), "18 Praying always with all prayer and supplication in the Spirit and watching thereunto with all perseverance and supplication for all saints."

God cares for you, and He gave you prayers as a means of communicating with Him. Prayer, then, is your vertical connection to God that allows you to worship, genuinely repent and request forgiveness for your sins. And, to openly thank God for His mercies, and praise God intimately and within open groups. Prayer keeps us connected to God when you communicate with Him. Pray to acknowledge He is God, and that you accept His gracious gift, Jesus Christ, as your Lord and Savior (Genesis 17:1, Romans 6:16-18).

Additionally, use your prayers to confess your sins to God and to accept God's forgiveness. Romans 3:23-26 (KJV), "23 For all have sinned, and come short of the glory of God; 24 Being justified freely by his grace through the redemption that is in Christ Jesus: 25 Whom God hath set forth to be a propitiation through faith in his blood, to declare his righteousness for the remission of sins that are past, through the forbearance of God; 26 To declare, I say, at this time his righteousness: that he might be just, and the justifier of him which believeth in Jesus."

Likewise, pray that God's will be done in your life, that His Holy Spirit guides us, and that you be filled with the fullness of all God has for us. You go to God in faith, knowing that He hears and answers all your prayers, 1 John 5:14 (KJV), "14 And this is the confidence that you have in him, that, if you ask anything according to his will, he heareth us". Be confident that God knows and wants what is best for us; so ask that all be done in all you seek from Him. Then, thank Him for it, even though it has not happened yet.

Do not forget to also pray for (spiritual) understanding and wisdom. Proverbs 2:6-8 (KJV), "6 For the LORD giveth wisdom: out of his mouth cometh knowledge and understanding. 7 He layeth up sound wisdom for the righteous: he is a buckler to them that walk uprightly. 8 He keepeth the paths of judgment, and preserveth the way of his saints".

Pray to find intimacy with God by communicating with Him in prayer. Pray with thanksgiving Colossians 4:2 (KJV), "² Continue in prayer, and watch in the same with thanksgiving", for all the ways He blesses you. And, use your prayers especially when you or someone is ill, lonely, going through trials or interceding for others James 5:14-16 (KJV), "¹⁴ Is any sick among you? let him call for the elders of the church; and let them pray over him, anointing him with oil in the name of the Lord: ¹⁵ And the prayer of faith shall save the sick, and the Lord shall raise him up; and if he has committed sins, they shall be forgiven him. ¹⁶ Confess your faults one to another, and pray one for another, that ye may be healed. The effectual fervent prayer of a righteous man availeth much". Also, 2 Corinthians 12:9-10 (KJV), "⁹ And he said unto me, My grace is sufficient for thee: for my strength is made perfect in weakness. Most gladly, therefore, will I rather glory in my infirmities, that the power of Christ may rest upon me. ¹⁰ Therefore I take pleasure in infirmities, in reproaches, in necessities, in persecutions, in distresses for Christ's sake: for when I am weak, then am I strong".

Above everything, pray to worship God in truth and adoration for He is God. Psalm 95:6-7 (KJV), "⁶ O come, let us worship and bow down: let us kneel before the LORD, our maker. ⁷ For he is our God, and we are the people of his pasture, and the sheep of his hand. Today if ye will hear his voice."

As you can see, there is nothing you cannot pray about. There are abundant references to prayer in the Bible. The Bible encourages you to "pray without ceasing" and "in everything give thanks to the Lord." When you choose to have a positive attitude, you will see the many blessings you have received just for giving God praise.

However, prayer is not meant for you to ask God if you should do His work because you should know based on your relationship with God, what you should willing do because of your love God.

Let us be frank, yes, you should go to God in prayer about the work you are requested to do, but only after you have accepted the responsibilities. Do you seriously believe that God will tell one of His healthy soldiers, "No, don't help in My ministry?" Instead, pray for the Holy Spirit's guidance in the performance of the duties. Romans 8:26 (KJV), "²⁶ Likewise the Spirit also helpeth our infirmities: for we know not what we should pray for as we ought: but the Spirit itself maketh intercession for us with groanings which cannot be uttered."

You should also be using your prayer as a means to reaching God because prayer connects you to God for things to happen as He deems. Prayer, in this instance, clears personal and other obstacles out of the way for God's work to be done without chaos and confusion. It is not that God cannot work without your prayers, but He has established prayer as part of His plan for carrying out His will in this world.

Isaiah wrote, Isaiah 40:29-31(KJV), "²⁹ He giveth power to the faint; and to them that have no might he increaseth strength. ³⁰ Even the youths shall faint and be weary, and the young men shall utterly fall: ³¹ But they that wait upon the LORD shall renew their strength; they shall mount up with wings as eagles; they shall run, and not be weary; and they shall walk, and not faint."

There is only one supreme Creator and sovereign God and prayers has a place with Him. There is only one way to Him, and that is through His only Son, Jesus Christ. God, your Heavenly Father, is the only one you can be assured of who hears and answers your prayers. He is the God of incredible love, mercy, and forgiveness. God's Word calls you to pray, and when you pray you are inviting God into your life, to communicate with you so you can fellowship with Him and build a relationship with Him. 2 Corinthians 6:1 (KJV), "We then, as workers together with him, beseech you also that ye receive not the grace of God in vain."

When you pray, God gives us the joy and privilege of working together with Him. He could do it without us, but you cannot do it without Him. However, what glory that God allows us the privilege of doing it with Him!

Also, when you pray, God grows you. For many Christians, their prayers becomes a long list of self-needs and wants that goes something like this: "Our Father, who art in Heaven... my name is Jimmy, Give me, give me, give me! I need, need, need, want, want, want, don't forget to bless me and oh my aunt!" Their prayers resemble a "shop 'til you drop poetic moment."

Prayers have become like the Dead Sea, where all the rivers flow in, but none of them flow out. You want blessings, but you never pray just to tell God, "Thank you." There are so many things to thank God for even when everything around you seems hopeless, yes seems, because you always have hope in Christ, you just fail to thank God for hope.

But like the Dead Sea, where the only way the water gets out is through evaporation. It has no salt; nothing can live in its water, through your prayers, you want God to let everything flow inward towards us – you want others to be a blessing to you, you want, you want, you want, and the only way you give a little is when God showers you with undeserving abundance.

What if before God blesses you God asks you, "What have you done for Me lately?" Fortunate for you, you will never have to answer that question because God will never ask it of you. God gives His blessings to you freely, whether you deserve it or not, and His grace and mercy are not dependent on what you do for Him but on His selfless love for you.

Another concern you must asked yourself, "Have you ever prayed and did not receive what you asked for at once but ultimately?" "What did you do?"

Some of you may have kept on praying until God delivers you a blessing, some of you may have gotten angry with God and throw in the towel, some of you may be pouting about your displeasures with God, but if you search your heart and life you will see something that is hindering God's quick response. You lack gratitude for the small things is preventing God from trusting you with the big things and sometimes trusting you with anything. Also, God does not respond quickly because at times your prayer may be selfish. Some of you can know someone who is sick and close to death, but you do not stop to pray for that person. Instead, you pray for God to stop your headache.

Until you stop living your life trying to be always blessed, and you begin to turn the direction of the flow from inwards, to outwards and upwards, so that you are being a blessing to others and offering God His glory and praise, there is not much you should be expecting from God.

God will let you wait, not to be mean, but He will let you wait so He can change you, mold you, and grow you because you are not doing it through the application of His word in your life. If God did everything for you every time you ask, or even without you having to ask for it, what need would you communicate with Him? Why would you need to pray?

Also, God expects you to be considerate of others, and have praise and faith in Him. God wants your glory like He wants you to be entirely dependent on Him and Him alone. But you may be thinking you don't need God and can do it on your own. Well, 2 Corinthians 3:5 (KJV), "⁵ Not that we are sufficient of ourselves to think anything as of ourselves; but our sufficiency [is] of God,"

Do not forget, God knows your every need before you ask, so your prayers to impress God and ask for things are not necessary, although welcoming. You must understand the difference. God loves you and invites you into fellowship with Him through prayers, and it will be great if you spend your time in praise and thanksgiving for the things God has done and the things God will do in your life, and the life of your loved ones and friends. So, instead of taking God for granted, and trying to impress Him you're your prayers, apply Psalm 37:4 (KJV), "⁴ Delight thyself also in the LORD: and he shall give thee the desires of thine heart."

For those who ask for help in ministry and always get this response, "Let me pray about it," don't you find it amazing that this seems to be the only prayers God never answers? Well, it is an assumption that God never answers this prayer because the person never comes back to tell you what God said. Facetiousness, but the truth is, in ministry, the Christian does not need to pray for God's permission to help in His work, consent is understood and granted for anything holy that gives glory to God and shows love to a brother or sister in Christ. Hebrews 4:12 (KJV), tells us "12 For the word of God is quick, and powerful, and sharper than any two-edged sword, piercing even to the dividing asunder of soul and spirit, and the joints and marrow, and is a discerner of the thoughts and intents of the heart." You need to be obedient to His will, and your prayers, after saying "YES" need only be to ask God's guidance so that you can glorify God through your deeds.

Somehow, prayers, while it is the greatest blessing any Christian is privileged to have available to them — has become the most significant Christian failure because you use it to say no and to hide behind God and forget just to say "Thank you, Lord." As followers of Christ, you have the pleasure of the words of Philippians 2: (KJV), "17 Yea, and if I am offered upon the sacrifice and service of your faith, I joy and rejoice with you all. No doubt there are times when you are called to say "yes" in ministry—even when it's difficult or inconvenient—to "toil, struggling with all his energy that he powerfully works within [us]", 2 Timothy 4:6 (KJV), "6 For I am now ready to be offered, and the time of my departure is at hand".

When Saying "No" Is Appropriate

Can you say "No" in ministry? Of course, you can. You are encouraged to decline ministry opportunities, and yes, there really is a time and a place for saying "no." John 6:28-29 (KJV), "28 Then said they unto him, What shall you do, that you might work the works of God? 29 Jesus answered and said unto them, this is the work of God, that ye believe on Him whom he hath sent".

The question of yes or no whether the Lord wants you to do the work of which your participation is asked is relevant to your Christian journey. Of course, God wants and needs our participation in ministry.

"No!" Why is it that one of the most common words but trying to say?

Perhaps you were asked to serve in some capacity and got caught off guard, or you want to please people, you do not want to be mean or unhelpful. You do not want to burn a bridge or miss an opportunity or miss something fun. You do not want people to be mad or upset with you or to speak poorly about you. Moreover, so, time and time again, you say yes when you should not. Often at the expense of something else like your health. Then there are those some who are fed up with serving other people because of the pain and suffering they had to endure because of their service to others. Also, there are times you will are exhausted volunteering and serving ministry overcommitments. When you are asked to do something, you are not able to do, or unavailable for; it is much easier to say no by referring someone else who might do the job even better.

However, your response is in relation to your response to God's calling and trusting God's posture toward you in that call: God knows your name, and He calls you by your name.

Also, God knows your capabilities before you were born, and He loves you far more than you can imagine. Therefore, God fully

165

understands you, and He knows what He can trust you with. He will not ask you to do anything and not equip you for the work. Remembering Colossians 1:29 (KJV), "²⁹ Whereunto I also labor, striving according to His working, which worketh in me mightily". Jesus was poured out for us. John 6:28-29 (KJV), "²⁸ Then said they unto him, what shall you do, that you might work the works of God? ²⁹ Jesus answered and said unto them, this is the work of God, that ye believe on him whom he hath sent".

Still, most of us know at least one or two people who say yes to everything, need to be involved or who are looking to plug in somewhere else. Saying yes too many times can make you feel overwhelmed and stressed-out. By overcommitting yourself, you may neglect the people and things in your life that are important.

Worse, it can cause you to become resentful of those your feel are becoming or have become a burden to you. Also, even after saying yes, you may still experience a sense of being used, or underappreciated. In other words, be kind and considerate but say no when necessary.

There are times you will be poured out and exhausted in ministry because of your cultural norm of ministry overcommitment. Instead of saying yes, all the time and compelling yourself, pause before answering and allow yourself to gain a moment of clarity about the situation, or to find someone else who may be interested and walk away at least feeling helpful that you did your part. Everybody wins!You can go from being the person who says no to the person who helped. If you feel like you must say that hardened word no, a simple, direct no is usually the most effective; the Bible advocates a direct approach.

Also, if you must say no but are unable to do so, before you respond to a request, set down your idol of the image—your extreme concern about others' opinions of you, and let the person know you will get back to them. It is perfectly okay to say, "I will check my schedule," or, "I will think about it," or, "I need to get back to you" before giving a final answer. Waiting to answer is the easiest way to conclusively say no without feeling bad and without upsetting the person doing the asking.

Also, power off the noise in your head and then reboot. Some members are very assertive, aggressive, or good at making you feel guilty; it can be tough to say no to these people and in person. Your slowness to commit will be met with one of three responses: the look of gracious understanding, the look of judgment, the look of someone died. In these cases, changing the channel and stepping back is necessary but never say, "let me pray about it" knowing that you are on your way to a no. That is not a good thing to use God and prayer in that manner.

Instead, tell the person you need more time to give a response and then respond to the person with a firm no through a nonconfrontational channel of communication, such as an email or a text message. Having a non-verbal conversation helps you avoid the trap of back-and-forth convincing, especially when the person who is doing the asking is much more forceful or persuasive than you are.

Also, in ministry, it is okay to be slow to jump in and weigh your motivations for participation. Are you taking part in glorifying God, or pleasing people? You can serve alongside others, and sometimes that means stepping down to let someone else step up. To do that, though, you must believe that your identity lies in whom God says you are, not in whom others might think you are and should not be concern about others' opinions. Your personality is not in your service. Your character is in being a beloved child of God. Period.

However, a deliberate slowness to commit can bring about a look of judgment, or a look of gracious understanding. Either way, it is proper to say "No" and decline ministry opportunities if you are unavailable or unable to perform the duties. Recognizing that your identity lies in whom God says you are, not in whom others might think you are.

There is a whole body of Christians who love God and to whom God has given beautifully nuanced gifts. You are not meant to go it alone or be the "I will Christian." God gave us cultural trends related to values, beliefs, attitudes and behaviors and a body of believers to serve alongside, and sometimes that means stepping back or stepping down and letting someone else step up. To do that, though, you must believe that your identity lies in whom God says you are, not in whom others might think you are.

God calls us to live your life in a way that glorifies Him. Your identity does not rest in the work of your hands, but in Jesus and His work on the cross.

Choose Your Words

Do you know the words you say can alter the outcome of your situations and in fact, set the direction of your life?

The Bible tells us very plainly how our tongues and the words we speak can open the door to good or evil in our lives. Look at what Proverbs 18:21 (KJV), "²¹ Death and life are in the power of the tongue: and they that love it shall eat the fruit thereof."

As a believer, every word you utter has tremendous power; With your tongue, you can choose to build or destroy dreams, heal, or break the spirit, bring delight or despair, bless or curse; We see this principle in action in so many instances in the Bible.

Before they received their miracle child, God changed the names of a childless couple, Abram and Sarai, to Abraham (meaning "father of many nations") and Sarah (meaning "princess") just before He told Abraham that from them would come to a multitude of nations (see Genesis 17:5, 16–17). But how could this happen when Sarah was barren?

It happened with his change of name. From then on, Father of many was how Abraham introduced himself, and Sarah would say the same every time she called out to Abraham and spoke about him. Likewise, Abraham would call out "Princess!" every time he called her name.

And somewhere along the way, Sarah experienced a renewal of youth, her barren womb was resurrected with divine life, and this couple—one a hundred years old and the other, 90 and barren from her youth—conceived the miracle child God had promised them.

What a powerful demonstration of the power of words in just the speaking of a name!

That is not all. In the Gospels, Jesus Himself showed us how it is through our words that we can bring the power of God into our situations of sickness, adversity, and even death:

He cursed the fig tree; it withered.

He spoke to the wind and waves; they were stilled.

He spoke to sicknesses, and men and women were healed.

He spoke life, and people were raised from the dead.

What I want you to see is this: The power to change your circumstances lies in your mouth! You can speak life and see life even when you seem to see death, especially when you understand the truths about your words.

Your words spoken in line with God's promises have life-changing power. Words spoken in line with God's promises have enormous power. When you speak God's Word in faith over your adverse circumstances, you will find His mountain-moving power come into those situations. Speak His promises, and you will release His divine healing, life, and victory where there is been sickness, brokenness, or lack. See Mark 11:23 (KJV), "²³ For verily I say unto you, That whosoever shall say unto this mountain, Be thou removed, and be thou cast into the sea; and shall not doubt in his heart, but shall believe that those things which he saith shall come to pass; he shall have whatsoever he saith."

That is why, if you want to see a positive difference in the way you live, it is essential to line up your words with the promises of God's Word rather than speak based on what you see or feel about your adverse circumstances.

As you speak His Word, you will also find it dispelling your fears and imparting faith and peace to your heart. Faith comes by hearing and hearing the Word-faith (instead of despair and fear) is imparted as your ears hear and hear God's Word coming out of your mouth!

Your words will open wide the treasury of heaven. Because Jesus has done everything you need at the cross, God is continually supplying grace, health, protection, deliverance, and whatever you need in life to you.

So, what do you believe for today? A healthy body? A financial breakthrough? A restored marriage or relationship? A baby? A finished project? A new job? Relocation? Whatever it is, God wants you to know that the provision is already there. All you need to do now is to believe all that He has done for you and learn to speak in alignment with God's promises. Your words will open wide the treasury of heaven and set in motion the process for your provision to reach you.

You have a double part of speaking power. As a new covenant believer in Christ, you are the child of a King, which means you have a double portion of speaking power. The Bible tells you in Christ, you are part of His royal priesthood, 1 Peter 2:9 (KJV), "⁹ But ye are a chosen generation, a royal priesthood, an holy nation, a peculiar people; that ye should shew forth the praises of him who hath called you out of darkness into his marvellous light." It also shows us that the words of these two groups of people—kings *and* priests—hold special authority and power. A king's word is backed by great power. Ecclesiastes 8:4 (KJV), "⁴ Where the word of a king is, there is power: and who may say unto him, What doest thou?" And priests, by the authority of their word, settle "every controversy and every assault" Deuteronomy 21:5 (KJV), "⁵ And the priests the sons of Levi shall come near; for them the LORD thy God hath chosen to minister unto him, and to bless in the name of the LORD; and by their word shall every controversy and every stroke be tried:"

According to God's Word, you will see the battle settled in line with God's promises as you put the immense power of your words as a king and a priest to work. You do not have to be a victim of your situation or circumstances, or a slave to your sins. You can choose to experience victory even if you do not see it by the words you choose. You can speak victory in existence once you have God because God promises you a life of victory in Him. So be bold and start using your double portion of speaking power. Choose to align your words with the promises of God over your marriage, your family, your health, your finances, your relationships, your job —for whatever you need—and see amazing transformation that will happen in your life as God blesses you because of your incredible faith and powerful words of belief and testimony!

Watch Your Mouth

The information provided is not intended to be legal advice and must not be relied upon as such. Also, nothing contained herein is meant to be an attorney-client relationship, and such a connection can only be established by individual consultation and execution of a written agreement for legal services with an attorney.

Defamation of character happens when there are false statements of fact made about you to a third party, and you suffer economic losses because of such false statements. Verbal attacks about you will not support a defamation claim, nor will admonitions or lectures about you to third parties without false statements of fact (not opinion).

However, under the law of defamation, there is another class of communications known as confidential communication.

Defamatory words do not become privileged because you hold the person to the strictest confidence, maybe even pinky swear to keep the person to some level of secrecy.

Also, defamation is libelous when written communication between the two or more people is used, including written communication between husband and wife or between best friends.

New York supreme court (in the case of Klinck vs. Colby, 46 New York, 42'7) held that "the occasion in which it [privilege communication] made, rebuts the inference arising, prima facie, from a statement prejudicial with the character of the plaintiff; and puts It upon him to prove that there was malice in fact, and that the defendant was actuated by motives of personal spite or ill will, independent of the circumstances in which the communication was made."

Therefore, you have a moral obligation to refrain from gossiping and becoming a volunteer to defame another person in a matter in which you have no legal or personal interest.

No pressing emergency warrants are defaming another person's character, therefore, refrain from scandalling a person altogether.

Sure, when you find that you have things in common with someone else, that you share similar struggles, and that you are not alone in your Christian struggle, it makes it easier as you travel down the road.

However, it is important to note that not everyone is your friend and does not must be your friends or amicable associates, not even in the church. You may tuck certain people away carefully to protect yourself from your closest family member or friend to where, often, it is hard to take an in-depth look into your inner self at that person no one knows, not even you, and share what is most troubling to us.

However, while each of us wants to self-protect, you must come to learn to leave some people alone and practice self-care and balance that with spending more time speaking to your spouses and your children, especially your older children.

However, to address your issues, and explain your pain to someone else, who may, or may not care about us or have your best interest at heart, you must open yourselves up to someone.

Let us use the analogy of you driving your car down a country road. You meet two cows sitting in the middle of the street blocking your path. What do you do? You go around them and peacefully carry on your journey until you reach your destination; this is how you should handle people who feel in necessary to stand in your way, go around them.

However, you do not. Instead, when people block your path, you stand toe to toe with them instead of going around them peacefully. The need to go blow for blow is more significant than being peaceful. You waste valuable time engaging in frivolous conversation, or you give up and sulk with a 'woe it is me" attitude and sinks into depression because your feelings were hurt.

Sure, when a person acted bona fide in the performance of duty or regarding a matter where his interest is involved, and he believes he was justified in having a reasonable and probable cause to believe what was voiced, written or published was right, in such a case the person is protected by the privilege which attaches to what he releases from the consequences of an honest mistake. But it is best to remember, Proverbs 21:23 (KJV), "23 Whoso keepeth his mouth and his tongue keepeth his soul from troubles."

There is no higher calling than the ministry of God. He who occupies this exalted position should present only the message of God, eliminating from his mind, and from the minds of others, those thoughts which tend to contaminate and lead to criticism and defamation.

What did Jesus emphasize? When asked about the greatest commandment, Jesus mentioned two commandments as primary: love God and love your neighbor. The basics of Christianity are encompassed in these two ideas. Various lists have been developed to explain the meaning and application of these two commandments-the basics of loving God and loving others.

Anyone publishing defamatory words under a qualified or limited privilege is liable, but only so upon proof expressed malice and was held by the supreme court of Connecticut and of other States.

Also, churches face an increasingly litigious and regulated environment. This troubling trend means church leaders must inform themselves about legal risk and implement proper risk-management strategies for the church and its ministries.

Churches are a burden when their most significant legal risks facing the churches and church leaders is the potential legal liability issues surrounding sexual abuse. Victims are grieved, angry, discouraged, and in the absence of accountability, some victims end of leaving the church bitter. They lose trust when they are unsure how their church leadership will respond and when the very people wreaking havoc are the ones entrusted with shepherding God's flock.

As painful as it is to hear these heartbreaking stories about the ongoing crisis of abuse in the Church, there is hope in Christ for each of us.

So, how should churches respond? Paul reprimands the Corinthians in 1 Corinthians 6 (KJV), "1Dare any of you, having a matter against another, go to law before the unjust, and not before the saints? [2]Do ye not know that the saints shall judge the world? and if the world shall be judged by you, are ye unworthy to judge the smallest matters? [3]Know ye not that we shall judge angels? how much more things that pertain to this life? [4]If then ye have judgments of things pertaining to this life, set them to judge who are least esteemed in the church. [5]I speak to your shame. Is it so, that there is not a wise man among you? no, not one that shall be able to judge between his brethren? [6]But brother goeth to law with brother, and that before the unbelievers."

You need to do what you can to prevent sexual abuse, but you also need to have a plan in place for how to respond if it does occur. Paul goes so far as to instruct perpetrators to be handed over "to Satan for the destruction of the flesh" It seems that certain transgressions are beyond the church's power to address adequately. Paul says, acts as an 'avenger who carries out God's wrath on the wrongdoer' Romans 13:4 (KJV), "[4]For he is the minister of God to thee for good. But if thou do that which is evil, be afraid; for he beareth not the sword in vain: for he is the minister of God, a revenger to execute wrath upon him that doeth evil."

Once your real interests are at stake and your church's reputation is on the line, it can become far too easy to rationalize bad behavior. Immediately when an accusation is levied, as a caution, always believe the victim until you can prove otherwise. The accuser will need your support as they find their life further affected with the lies, the cover-up that follows, and the abuse goes unchallenged. Many churches are quick to dismiss or ignore the complaint. And not until there is a mounting of abuse accusations does the church address the issue with seriousness.

Also, members will quickly support their Pastor, and the individual affected by the violence is alienated, shunned, and very little care is given to them as they go through the aftereffects of the abuse trauma. Additionally, when sexual abuse is investigated internally by church leaders, they risk missing the truth. On behalf of both parties, you have similar aims and values: You want to find the truth, to be fair, and to carry out justice for all parties.

The effects of bias can continue beyond your first evaluation. Friendship is one of the reasons you should doubt your ability to uncover the whole truth, to be fair, and to carry out justice for all parties. Also, if you have doubts about your ability to be objective; you are also supposed to recuse yourself when the members might have doubts about your ability to be impartial.

Also, when another person's morally questionable behavior helps you, you trust them more than if it does not, and you are less likely to remember they are bad behavior.

On the contrary, this is a dangerous road, because your bias does not just affect your final decisions; it can permeate your whole judgment.

Similarly, it is in the broader interest of the Christian community that people can trust that church leaders will seek the truth. When people see churches trying to handle investigations of their own leaders internally, it leads many to doubt whether the church desires to bring the truth to light.

Even if you think you can be objective, if the public view your actions as trying to sweep things under the rug, this does real damage, not only to your church but to the entire Christian community.

Therefore, whether you are aware or not, when you have an economic interest overestimating your objectivity will let you evaluate those you care about favorably and that might affect the outcome despite your conscious efforts you may have a hard time being objective and to make an impartial judgments, it erodes the congregations trust in the fairness about a range of judgments and in a variety of contexts.

Your biases might be preventing you from seeing the truth. You need to be aware of how your relationships with the accused and your desire to keep them in power might affect how you interpret the situation. There might be an even greater danger in your decision making as you try to rationalize, justify, cover-up, or deny sins. and judge Church leaders.

People often try to rationalize keeping leaders accused of sexual abuse in power, and many terrible injustices have been rationalized to protect the church. Do not take your ability to overlook warning signs or minimize accusations as evidence that there is no problem.

However, protecting perpetrators and not holding them accountable is dangerous. Given all this, and given how difficult it is to evaluate your leaders objectively, it is essential to have sexual abuse allegations investigated by an independent party that does not have a vested interest in the church. If you want the church to be a safe place of healing, you cannot afford to cover up the truth. The first step, though, is finding it.

The Trouble With Gossip

You all gossip, you have, and everyone has at one time or the other and has enjoyed a long history. Also, many of us tend to allow other people's opinions to not only damage your self-image and self-esteem but often, to define who you are. Marcus Aurelius said, "Everything you hear is an opinion, not a fact. Everything you see is a perspective, not the truth."

Gossipers use gossip to cause harm. They spend their time in idle talk parading themselves as the all-knowing of real knowledge and judgment and sharing information which is flawed, unworthy of any respect. They maliciously reveal the embarrassing, and shameful details of their family, associates, and friends. However, God warns us about gossip; that there are no benefits to you.

The severity of the problem with gossip is that it causes a man to anger God, who despises when you use rumors, tale-bearing, and backbiting to hurt your fellow sisters and brothers.

The trouble with gossip is that it is an appalling, atrocious and distressing act that has no beginning and destruction is its only end. Gossip promotes division, cause strife, alienate family, and separate the best of friends. It is like fuel to fire with dire consequences. Proverbs 16:28 (KJV) tells us, "28 A froward man soweth strife: and a whisperer separateth chief friends."

Also, gossip breathes contention and stifle the gospel and have been known to break the hearts of the strongest and caused the deaths of many. To date, there is no explanation for this perplexing naivety by Christians who rank gossip as a tiny, inconsequential sin, when this critical act can be spiritually fatal when the offending Christian does not repent!

Webster gives gossip a negative definition as one who habitually reveals personal or sensational facts about others. That is the problem with gossip and gossipers. They have a bad reputation and an unsavory character.

Still, many of us turn to gossip out of vengeance, anger, hatred, and because of a grudge, and you circulate unwarranted gossip by saying, "I do not know if this is true, but I heard..." or, "Have you heard..." No compassion for the severe damage they are about to inflict with their gossip. So, what if scandal ruins someone's reputation or relationship? Soon, However, everyone begins to identify the shattered reflection of an ungodly Christian for the evil he is.

Worst still, men have lost marriages, families destroyed, and some Christians, especially your Pastors and lay leaders, have had their reputation assassinated because of gossip. Proverbs 16:27 (KJV), "27 An ungodly man diggeth up evil: and in his lips there is as a burning fire." They are driven to seek out and speak of other shortcomings, and failures; that is the problem with gossip. People get so addicted to its poison that spreading rumors and scandal consumes their every desire "like a burning fire" until their lips quiver—they must spread the word! Guilty of changing people's identity to where they are called by gossip's name, no longer a child of God, just "gossiper, or ungodly person." When you see them or hear their voice, immediately, you know gossip is on its way!

It is painful to be the subject of gossip, particularly one that has no basis of truth. Proverbs 18:8 (KJV), "8 The words of a talebearer are as wounds, and they go down into the innermost parts of the belly." For many church members and churchgoers, building friendships and setting up positive relationships with other members is a feat; this is a reality. They are surprised when they see how difficult it is to fit in, or many do not feel welcome. No matter what you do or say, or how you carry yourself, you will always be scrutinized by others. Soon, you hear or experience severe scandal or something so negative that it may take a stronghold in your life and become detrimental to your health. Gossip like this can have devastating consequences and cause people to suffer some adverse effects such as isolation and be affected mentally, developing anxiety and depression.

Scandal divides people. Someone will always make you the subject of their gossip which can be a particularly devaluing experience, dampening your sense of self-worth, affecting your sense of belonging, and negatively affecting your enjoyment at church, to where you want to leave the church. It destroys relationships, sows discord, and creates a spirit of bitterness, and evil. It causes people to act and speak in toxic ways.

Going forth, do not trust everything you hear — gossip is not always correct, and often people spread false gossip just to hurt someone they despise.

While you cannot always control what people say about you, you can control how you respond or react—and you can be resilient. Growing awareness of its prevalence and potential dangers reminds us of the importance of gauging the credibility of a story's source, fact-checking its content, and analyzing its message for bias. It has also renewed our appreciation for time-tested, reliable sources that have consistently proven Christian integrity.

When someone spreads false rumors about another person, it is difficult for that person to shake off the smear placed on their reputation. Also, misinformation commits the same kinds of deception with much more at stake, and the person may experience severe damage to their character, personal and professional life. Likewise, it is incredibly stressful and can lead to anxiety and depression.

Therefore, it is vital that you be keenly aware of the circumstances that are motivating a person to behave in such a detrimental manner that is harmful to another and do not encourage the behavior by breathing life into it or taking part in the act by adding your opinion.

By doing this, you may contribute to the bad behavior dissipating, or you may change the adverse action of the person when they see you are not a willing participant in their toxic behavior. Thank God you can stand firm. 2 Thessalonians 2:16-17 (KJV), "[16] Now our Lord Jesus Christ himself, and God, even our Father, which hath loved us, and hath given us everlasting consolation and good hope through grace, [17] Comfort your hearts, and establish you in every good word and work."

Not only are there people who enjoy spreading dirt about others, but there are also those who enjoy listening to the trash too. You love hearing things about others, and you rush quickly to pass the gossip along. No one bothers to check the facts; chatter will not allow time for that.

Nobody is saying it is not difficult to deal with negative people; it is. However, you have an opportunity to make a difference in your churches, community, even in school or work environments. Whoever is speaking ill about you, let them, and learn to ignore their insensitivity towards you. It is an inefficacious exercise to "defend" yourself against negative people.

Therefore, cultivate the habit never to defend yourself or to dignify their behavior by giving them your time and attention.

Also, if you breathe life into the bad behaviors of others, and continually feed them with your response, you will empower them to inflict further hurt through ongoing attacks and ostracization.

It is imperative that you learn that even though some people call themselves Christian, they may not know God or have any relationship with God and may have miserable misanthropic natures. Once you get to a place of Christian growth, you will triumph, and others will gain an inside glance at how you were able to withstand. They will increase the strength and faith to turn the impossible to possible. You can be a victim or a victor, a Child of God, or a damaged soul; it is all about character branding and redefining yourself and your purpose here on earth.

To add, while you are working on yourself, allow God to be God. He will hold them accountable and will decide their just rewards. God calls each of us to account for your actions because it matters to him that you treat Him, and other people, with love.

In other words, he will not let your abuse go on forever. God cares about you enough to take anything that is a hindrance to your Christian journey seriously. God said in Romans 14:12-14 (KJV), "[12] So then every one of us shall give account of himself to God. [13] Let us not, therefore, judge one another anymore: but judge this rather, that no man put a stumbling block or an occasion to fall in his brother's way. [14] I know, and am persuaded by the Lord Jesus that there is nothing unclean of itself: but to him that esteemeth anything to be unclean, to him it is unclean."

You must focus on your purpose to effectively carry out any task at hand; unmask and address anything that is weighing you down, else, the existence of any negative person(s) will continue to hold you hostage and be a burden on your life.

Therefore, focus on your work and keep moving forward you do not have time to look or listen to the negativity around you. Pray for those who are still struggling and allow God, who promises in Exodus 23:22 "[22] But if thou shalt indeed obey his voice and do all that I speak; then I will be an enemy unto thine enemies, and an adversary unto thine adversaries," to handle the rest. You do not need to engage yourself in every battle or address issues that have nothing to do with you, which is usually adverse and temporary.

People will change their thinking towards you once God blesses you in their face, and they see you doing meaningful things. James 3:1-8 (KJV) James, the half-brother of Christ, explained why gossip stays around... He said, "[1] My brethren, be few masters, knowing that you shall receive the greater condemnation. [2] For in many things you offend all. If any man offends not in word, the same is a perfect man, and able also to bridle the whole body. [3] Behold, you put bits in the horses' mouths, that they may obey us; and you turn about their whole body. [4] Behold also the ships, which though they are so great, and are driven of fierce winds, yet are they turned about with a very small helm, whithersoever the governor listeth. [5] Even so, the tongue is a little member, and boasteth great things. Behold, how great a matter a little fire kindleth! [6] And the tongue is a fire, a world of iniquity: so is the tongue among your members, that it defileth the whole body, and setteth on fire the course of nature; and it is set on fire of hell. [7] For every kind of beasts, and of birds, and serpents, and things in the sea is tamed, and hath been tamed of mankind: ⁸ But the tongue can no man tame; it is an unruly evil, full of deadly poison."

Another problem with gossip is that even the Master Physician has not been able to administer a cure that His people are willing to swallow to stop the scandal from running around destroying the churches. Proverbs 11:13(KJV), "¹³ A talebearer revealeth secrets: but he that is of a faithful spirit concealeth the matter." The severe problem about gossiping-is that you must answer to God for being its friend. God has warned us that for every idle word you speak, you will give an account in the end. He said in Matthew 12:36-37 (KJV) "³⁶, But I say unto you, That every idle word that men shall speak, they shall give account thereof in the day of judgment. ³⁷ For by thy words thou shalt be justified, and by thy words, thou shalt be condemned."

So, chatter continues to infest your churches like a plague devouring willing members, including those who listen and those who speak, somehow gossip has a way of recognizing the weak. "Still, you can at once reject negative chatter. You must not invite it to come in and offer it a chair to sit down. Moreover, if you do, it will continue to fester until everyone tempted to administer a dose on others finds himself or herself its victim.

Now that you have named the problem, God admonishes us in Leviticus 19:16 (KJV), "¹⁶ Thou shalt not go up and down as a talebearer among thy people: neither shalt thou stand against the blood of thy neighbor; I am the Lord." And since you consider yourselves Christians, you must keep a tight rein on your tongue. James 1:26 (KJV), "²⁶ If any man among you seem to be religious, and bridleth not his tongue, but deceiveth his own heart, this man's religion is vain."

Therefore, it is time for every Christian to tell gossip, "sorry, you are breaking up with your scandalous ways; you can no longer be your friend." When you feel compelled to share a juicy piece of gossip, do not. These are strong words, but you must do it! Exodus 23:1(KJV), "¹ Thou shalt not raise a false report: put not thine hand with the wicked to be an unrighteous witness."

Therefore, you cannot associate yourselves with the evil of gossip. If you are not trying to help a person when you talk about them, that is gossip.

However, if you are trying to help the person, not with the purpose of gossip, but to help honestly, that is empathy. It is crucial that you know the difference.

For example, Mylan lost her job and had been struggling to pay her bills. She tells you of her situation. You go to Nancy to ask for help for Mylan. It is gossip if the nature of your heart is to belittle Mylan in the process, or if you do not honestly care whether Nancy helps or not, you want Nancy to be aware of Mylan's situation, that is gossip. If going to Nancy means you are hoping that she will help you come up with solutions for Mylan, that is empathy, not hearsay or gossip.

Likewise, some of us slicksters use your prayers as an opportunity to gossip. Let us use Mylan again, and now you are praying aloud for Mylan at the Wednesday night prayer meeting. "Dear Lord, it is sad that Mylan loss her job and now must face homelessness. Please bless her and all the other people in her situation Lord;" Praying for someone is great, and you should always pray for each other, but that is a gossip prayer in its most terrible form.

There is a proper way for praying for Mylan that does not require that you put her business into the public. For example, the prayer for Mylan could go something like this. "Dear Lord, I want to lift my sister Mylan in prayer today. Please place a special blessing on her Lord. You know each of your needs, and you thank you for hearing and answering your prayer, Amen!" Alternatively, "Dear Lord, you all have struggles, please bless my brothers and sisters who are struggling with job loss...." You have just prayed for Mylan without calling her name out aloud and spreading her business amongst the group.

Here is another example. Mylan called to say she needs prayer for her husband who is in hospice. She does not think he will make it. It

185

becomes gossip if you post on social media that, "Sister Mylan is asking for prayer for her husband who was transferred to hospice. He may not make it through the week, and she is just broken up. Please pray for Mylan and her husband." Let us try to get prayer for Mylan and her husband that will not violate their privacy or belittle their situation. How about a simple form of that request? "Hello everyone, Mylan has asked that the church prays for her and her family." Alternatively, is she is not specifically asking the church to pray, just asking for prayer, then the request should be something like this, "Hello everyone, please pray for all your sick members and their family."

Be mindful of your mouths, your heart, and your intentions. God's know your hearts. He sees your intents. The proud and self-righteous should always be mindful during prayer time: Matthew 6:6 (KJV), "⁶ But thou, when thou prayest, enter into thy closet, and when thou hast shut thy door, pray to thy Father which is in secret; and thy Father which seeth in secret shall reward thee openly".

So, when you stop to pray for someone, ask yourself, "What was the intent of my prayer?" If it is anything less than pure, it is best you pray for yourself, "Create in me a clean heart, Oh Lord."

Additionally, do not spend your time circulating another false report or put your hands with the wicked to be an unrighteous witness. Romans 1:30, 32 (KJV) "³⁰ Backbiters, haters of God, despiteful, proud, boasters, inventors of evil things, disobedient to parents, "³² Who knowing the judgment of God, that they which commit such things are worthy of death, not only do the same but have pleasure in them that do them." God manifestation is in His word, and God does not stutter when He speaks.

So, when you hear gossip, no matter who originates the accusation, never repeat it or be party to spreading it even if you have substantial evidence to its truth.

Always question the motive of the person spreading the rumor, whether it is meant to inflict harm or to bless.

Also, if you are not willing to take part in negativity, you should not be a partaker in the behavior through listening or repeating. However, should you overhear the gossip, question its validity, and remain closed lip.

Matthew 12:33-37 (KJV) "[33] Either make the tree good, and his fruit good; or else make the tree corrupt, and his fruit corrupt: for the tree is known by his fruit. [34] O generation of vipers, how can ye, being evil, speak good things? For out of the abundance of the heart the mouth speaketh. [35] A good man out of the good treasure of the heart bringeth forth good things: and an evil man out of the evil treasure bringeth forth evil things. [36] But I say unto you; That every idle word that men shall speak, they shall give account thereof in the day of judgment. [37] For by thy words thou shalt be justified, and by thy words, thou shalt be condemned."

What is essential to understand about gossip is that it reveals what is in the heart. What the mouth speaks depends on the condition of the heart. So, to correct your speech, you will work on fixing your hearts. Also, rather than maliciously spreading slander about people you hear about who have sinned, you will pray for their repentance and forgiveness. You mean it gossip, you can no longer speak, or listen to your evil words. Ephesians 4:29 (KJV) says, "[29] Let no corrupt communication proceed out of your mouth, but that which is good to the use of edifying, that it may minister grace unto the hearers."

If someone hurts you so profoundly, chances are you have been hurt by gossip at some point in your life, and it is natural that you worry, and react in different ways. You may find yourself withdrawing into yourself, confiding in friends, or confronting the person.

Your goal if you are the subject of harmful gossip is to prayerfully and peacefully address situations that hurt you and move on. Although the idea of conflict, confrontation, defiance, and opposition may come to mind when you think about confronting someone who has wronged you, going to the person in love, saying a prayer with them and then stating your case in a noncombative way can settle the matter peacefully.

Once you have made this move on, do not spend any more time worrying about the frivolity of it.

Gossip spreads division to the degree that some people leave the church, and some members are overwhelmed with feelings of doom and gloom. The reality of gossip is that it is an unspeakable evil, an act that is very harmful. When you call out the gossiper, his smile widens into a rictus of repulsiveness.

However, it does not matter what other people say or think of you. What matters is what you think and feel about yourself. People can only define you if you give teeth to their opinion. If you can remember that people who gossip have no purpose other than to hurt or harm you, you can begin to overlook them and look past them. There is reason except to make themselves feel superior, so just do not entertain their foolishness.

Sure, it is hard not to get disheartened when others intentionally-hurl hurtful opinions at you. It is easy to think in your mind that those opinions do not matter and do not define you as a human being, but it is harder to put into practice.

Considering that you have all been the target of an ill-intentioned opinion at one point or another, most of us know just how this feel. It is hard to suppress your emotions when people are doing their best to get you going.

Still, as Christians, it is essential to take the high road. Matthew 5:39 KJV, "[39] But I say unto you, That ye resist not evil: but whosoever shall smite thee on thy right cheek, turn to him the other also." Do not allow negative people to stir you into a fury. Instead, continue to do what you know is good and right.

If you have an issue with gossiping and feel you can't help but to partake in juicy gossip, your goal from this day forth is to use your words to share God and comfort others by bestowing grace - that is to build others up and help them be right according to God's word. Say goodbye to gossip and use your time being fishers of men. God will be pleased!

Matthew 5:38-48 (KJV), "[38] Ye have heard that it hath been said, An eye for an eye, and a tooth for a tooth: [39] But I say unto you, That ye resist not evil: but whosoever shall smite thee on thy right cheek, turn to him the other also. [40] And if any man will sue thee at the law, and take away thy coat, let him have thy cloak also. [41] And whosoever shall compel thee to go a mile, go with him twain. [42] Give to him that asketh thee, and from him that would borrow of thee turn not thou away.

[43] Ye have heard that it hath been said, Thou shalt love thy neighbor, and hate thine enemy. [44] But I say unto you, Love your enemies, bless them that curse you, do good to them that hate you, and pray for them which despitefully use you, and persecute you; [45] That ye may be the children of your Father which is in heaven: for He maketh his sun to rise on the evil and on the good, and sendeth rain on the just and on the unjust. [46] For if ye love them which love you, what reward have ye? do not even the publicans the same? [47] And if ye salute your brethren only, what do ye more than others? do not even the publicans so? [48] Be ye therefore perfect, even as your Father which is in heaven is perfect."

Lukewarm Christians

In this distracted, shallow culture, many Christians are still engaged based on selfish desires. And then there are others, because of lifestyle choices that they feel traditional churches do not embrace, like millennials. With time, the dissonant screech of fear will become a reality as many churches are forced to close their doors and go bankrupt due to lack of attendance and financial support through tithes and offerings. Missions will suffer as the churches expect to do more with less.

Many churches are on a slippery slope now and risking separation from God because worshippers want a feel-good time and churches are trying to accommodate them. This may seem justifiable when God must compete with Satan instead of Satan competing with God.

Compare a Sabbath morning to a concert. All over the world concerts are selling out and packed to ability by people who waited in lines for hours, some for days to get a ticket. But people have a problem getting out of bed to spend a couple of hours with God in church, and if they manage to get there, God forbid if that minister does not shorten the sermon so they can get out on time.

Think of it this way, how many professed Christians would be in church on Sabbath morning if they hear their favorite celebrity is coming to a park near them? The ministers have trouble getting them in now, so what do you think will happen? Guarantee that day the churches will be empty. Truthfully, worshippers must be guaranteed a feel-good time to show up on Sabbath morning and churches are doing everything in their power to indulge them because some are worried about losing souls to the world, and others about numbers, dollars, and cents.

God owns everything, He does not call His ministers to worry about what He can supply, but everyone is having to feel-good church and worrying about self and forgetting all the times when God said, "I got this."

Yes, the Internet has made finding answers to questions—any questions—more accessible than ever. Whether it is curiosity about a new restaurant or matters of faith, Millennials are taking their inquiries to the search bar. Six out of 10 practicing Christians (59%) say they search for spiritual content online, but it is not only Christians doing this kind of surfing. Three out of 10 of all Millennials are too, which may open a new field of opportunity for churches hoping to understand and connect with these souls in cyberspace." https://www.barna.com 1 John 2:15-17 (KJV) warns, "¹⁵ Love not the world, neither the things that are in the world. If any man loves the world, the love of the Father is not in him. ¹⁶ For all that is in the world, the lust of the flesh, and the lust of the eyes, and the pride of life is not of the Father but is of the world. ¹⁷ And the world passeth away, and the lust thereof: but he that doeth the will of God abideth forever." It is also worth noting that staying perpetually "on the fence" – unwilling to reach a firm conclusion in your relationship with God – brings with it risks and consequences as well. It seems like it is famous for everyone to call themselves a Christian these days but ask them who God is and they do not have a clue. Like they do not have any relationship with God, and both of their feet are still patty pattering in the world. Most are one day Christian, the day they go to church, and the other six days they want to be Christians. Then you have the word of mouth Christians, the ones that say they are Christians but do not show any of the characteristics of a Christian.

However, let us get back because you want to look at the Lukewarm Christian, one foot in the church, one foot in the world, their mouth says they are a Christian, but their behavior tells you otherwise. Romans 12:1-2 (KJV), "¹ I beseech you, therefore brethren, by the mercies of God, that ye present your bodies a living sacrifice, holy, acceptable unto God, which is your reasonable service. ² And be not conformed to this world: but be ye transformed by the renewing of your mind, that ye may prove what that good is, and acceptable, and perfect, will of God."

Lukewarmness is a stage of cooling down. No soul stops short at this stage. The heart leaps at once into fire and life. However, it chills gradually but a lukewarm man you cannot describe. He is a mere collection of negations. His soul is like a reservoir or bath, into which streams of hot water and cold are being run at the same time, and you cannot tell which current is stronger, for they are often about equally strong. A lukewarm man has force, but it never moves him to any definite action. He has sympathies, but they tend to evaporate. He thinks, on the whole, he is a good, a religious man, on the side of Christ and of right.

People are, on the whole, not quite sure what side he is on. The lukewarm man does not make it a principle to confine his religion to the four walls of the church and the two boards of the Bible. He holds that it should not be so restricted. Also, so he carries a few scraps of it into his daily life. He knows that prayer should not be an empty form, so he occasionally tries to pray inwardly and sincerely -- that is when he is neither very tired nor swamped. He had never given way on a question of principle, except when he was pushed, or it appeared that very few people were looking on: and he has often regretted giving way at all. He does not intend to do it again. A lukewarm man does a little Christian work, not, of course, enough to involve any sacrifice or exhaustion, nor would he take any pains to provide a substitute for occasional or even frequent absence. It is only genuine workers who do that. The lukewarm person has made a great many vows in the matter of religion in the course of his or her life -- too many. It would have been better to have made fewer and kept some.

Christ regards it best to be hot, next best to be cold, worst of all to be lukewarm.

1. They are lukewarm who are at no pains to guard against error, and to acquire just sentiments of religion.

2. They are lukewarm who, from worldly hopes or fears, detain in unrighteousness the truth they know, and who will not profess it openly.

3. They are lukewarm who give God the body but withhold from Him the soul.

4. The inactivity of professed Christians is substantial proof that they are lukewarm.

5. Many discover their Lukewarmness by the limitations within which they confine their obedience, or by the weakness of their religious affections when compared with their attachments to worldly objects.

6. They are lukewarm who are little affected with the advancement or the decay of religion, or with that which concerns the common welfare of humanity.

Lukewarmness prevails in men but not only from the world does the faithful disciple receive a cross. The lukewarm generation of professing Christians, which has a name to live but is dead, avoids with lofty scorn and persecutes with the most refined cruelty the humble believer who by his consistency reminds them of their inconsistency. And the child of God who prefers the infallible but straightforward word of scripture to the diversified but bewildering creeds of his fallible fellows, bolstered up, as they are, by custom, tradition, or convenience, must expect the isolation that invariably goes with faithfulness in a degenerate age. For indeed the church has not improved since all deserted at least one than the apostle Paul, leaving him to stand alone in his first defense at Rome.

Nevertheless, the Lord stood with him as He will with every true-hearted follower, to give sufficient grace for the most onerous burden that may be borne for His sake; 2 Timothy 4:16-17 (KJV), "[16] At my first answer no man stood with me, but all men forsook me: I pray God that it may not be laid to their charge. [17] Notwithstanding the Lord stood with me and strengthened me; that by me the preaching might be fully known, and that all the Gentiles might hear: and I was delivered out of the mouth of the lion."

You talk of treasures in heaven but view the riches of this earth as more desirable. God does not desire only a part of you; God wants all of you. Jesus wants to be your Saviour.

The Undisciplined Mind

As a Christian, ask yourself: "What does God expect of me?" Your answer is found in 1 Timothy 4:1-16 (KJV), "¹ Now the Spirit speaketh expressly, that in the latter times some shall depart from the faith, giving heed to seducing spirits, and doctrines of devils; ²Speaking lies in hypocrisy; having their conscience seared with a hot iron; ³ Forbidding to marry, and commanding to abstain from meats, which God hath created to be received with thanksgiving of them which believe and know the truth. ⁴ For every creature of God is good, and nothing to be refused, if it is received with thanksgiving: ⁵ For it is sanctified by the word of God and prayer. ⁶ If thou put the brethren in remembrance of these things, thou shalt be a good minister of Jesus Christ, nourished up in the words of faith and of good doctrine, whereunto thou hast attained. ⁷ But refuse profane and old wives' fables and exercise thyself rather unto godliness. ⁸ For bodily exercise profiteth little: but godliness is profitable unto all things, having the promise of the life that now is, and of that which is to come. ⁹ This is a faithful saying and worthy of all acceptation. ¹⁰ For therefore we both labor and suffer reproach, because we trust in the living God, who is the Saviour of all men, especially of those that believe. ¹¹ These things command and teach. ¹² Let no man despise thy youth; but be thou an example of the believers, in a word, in conversation, in charity, in spirit, in faith, in purity. ¹³ Till I come, give attendance to reading, to exhortation, to doctrine. ¹⁴ Neglect, not the gift that is in thee, which was given thee by prophecy, with the laying on of the hands of the presbytery. ¹⁵ Meditate upon these things; give thyself wholly to them; that thy profiting may appear to all. ¹⁶ Take heed unto thyself, and unto the doctrine; continue in them: for in doing this thou shalt both save thyself, and them that hear thee."

Walking a journey of faith is not an easy endeavor. For many Christians, it is easy to slip into anxiety and depression from constant cynicism and criticism not only from members who choose to exhibit bad behavior, but also from good meaning members who stand by in silent and just watch but do nothing to come to the aid of their Pastor or fellow congregant that is under attack. God provides comfort when the storm rages and heightens your anxiety; He says in Philippians 4:6 (KJV), "⁶ Be careful for nothing; but in everything by prayer and supplication with thanksgiving let your requests be made known unto God."

Especially when grieving a loss of anything or being criticized when you are doing the best you can, sometimes while under pressure. However, God never said it would be easy. He only promises help in your time of affliction.

Everywhere you go, you will meet finger pointers which will do everything in their power to damage your reputation. Sometimes it is your spirituality that is under attack or even your relationship with God. Also, the very people who are doing it are sometimes the ones you trust to have your back. You just forgot to tell them while they are watching your back, do not help plunge the knife further down.

You all heard the saying the church is a hospital; the problem with the hospital is that some people reject the Therapist and refuse the therapy that will get them well. They prefer to stay laid upon their death bed, damaging their Christian walk, whining, and complaining about everything wrong in the church and do very little to nothing to fix it. Instead, the sore that infest their bodies are passed around, and soon the other members of the church are infected, and so it spreads, making the church at times, a very toxic environment.

Still, it is best to stay under the umbrella of the church and work out your salvation with fear and trembling. Because during some of these moments, it can be effortless for you to focus on the negative, forgetting that your status is not your character and it is only a shattered reflection of who you are.

Also, Satan is always lurking in the shadows waiting patiently to see whom he can devour. That even during times when someone praises you, somehow you still manage to feel hurt or embarrassed, and the words of praise fade away because you can only focus on your weaknesses and not the good the person sees in you. The good news is that you are in control of your emotions.

Lastly, you must recognize that despite what people say or do, the damages that are happening to us is because you are sometimes your worst enemy. The shattered reflection you see looking back at you when you glance in the mirror is because you have beaten up on yourself to the point you do not even recognize who is looking back at you. All you can see is a broken reflection of a man, unworthy, un-respected, unloved, and undeserving.

Oh, but not so fast, now look at yourself through the shine in God's eyes as God lovingly steers at you, His beautiful creation. Now, what do you see? You see a man worthy of being loved unconditionally, wrapped in an abiding love, a sustaining love, an everlasting love.

Am I My Brother's Keeper?

1 John 4:18-20 (KJV), "[18] There is no fear in love; but perfect love casteth out fear: because fear hath torment. He that feareth is not made perfect in love. [19] We love him because he first loved us. [20] If a man says, I love God, and hateth his brother, he is a liar: for he that loveth not his brother whom he hath seen, how can; he love God whom he hath not seen? [21] And this commandment have we from him, That he who loveth God love his brother also."

From time to time you have burdens that are too big for you to bear alone. You need help to carry the load, and God calls for us to help those who cannot help themselves. Hebrews 13 (KJV), "[1] Let brotherly love continue. [2] Be not forgetful to entertain strangers: for thereby some have entertained angels unawares." Paul wrote his friends in Philippi: Philippians 2:3-4 (KJV), "[3] Let nothing be done through strife or vainglory, but in lowliness of mind let each esteem other better than themselves. [4] Look not every man on his things, but every man also on the things of others."

Also, Jesus served as an example through His sacrificial love on the cross. He knew you could not bear your sins alone, so he bore them for us. Galatians 6 (KJV), "[1] Brethren, if a man is overtaken in a fault, ye which is spiritual, restore such a one in the spirit of meekness; considering thyself, lest thou also be tempted. [2] Bear ye one another burdens, and so fulfill the law of Christ. [3] For if a man thinks himself to be something, when he is nothing, he deceiveth himself. [4] But let every man prove his own work, and then shall he have rejoicing in himself alone, and not in another. [5] For every man shall bear his own burden. [6] Let him that is taught in the word communicate unto him that teacheth in all good things. [7] Be not deceived; God is not mocked: for whatsoever a man soweth, that shall he also reap. [8] For he that soweth to his flesh shall of the flesh reap corruption, but he that soweth to the Spirit shall of the Spirit reap life everlasting. ⁹ And let us not be weary in well doing: for in due season you shall reap if you faint not.¹⁰ As you have therefore opportunity, let us do good unto all men, especially unto them who are of the household of faith. ¹¹ Ye see how large a letter I have written unto you with mine own hand. ¹² As many as desire to make a fair shew in the flesh, they constrain you to be circumcised; only lest they should suffer persecution for the cross of Christ. ¹³ For neither they themselves who are circumcised keep the law; but desire to have you circumcised, that they may glory in your flesh. ¹⁴ But God forbid that I should glory, save in the cross of your Lord Jesus Christ, by whom the world is crucified unto me, and I unto the world. ¹⁵ For in Christ Jesus neither circumcision availeth anything, nor uncircumcision, but a new creature.¹⁶ And as many as walk according to this rule, peace be on them, and mercy, and upon the Israel of God.¹⁷ From henceforth let no man trouble me: for I bear in my body the marks of the Lord Jesus.¹⁸ Brethren, the grace of your Lord Jesus Christ be with your spirit. Amen."

God knew your burdens would weigh us down at times, especially in times of crisis, tragedy, and when guilt overcome your life. He told us in James 5:16 (KJV), "¹⁶ Confess your faults one to another, and pray one for another, that ye may be healed. The effectual fervent prayer of a righteous man availeth much." And, Galatians 6:2 (KJV), "² Bear ye one another burdens, and so fulfill the law of Christ," provides us with guidance on your responsibility to one another.

However, God did not want us to weigh each other down and wear each other out. So, God admonishes us to "²² Cast thy burden upon the LORD, and he shall sustain thee: he shall never suffer the righteous to be moved." Psalm 55:22 (KJV).

Still, God does expect us to face your feelings and your fears. He requires us to have some level of accountability for your behaviors and to deal with your emotions, attitudes, and responsibilities head on, and He provides people to help us, not for us to use and abuse.

Problems arise when you behave with disrespect like the world owes you something and leads to your suffering alone when you realize people will not give in to your demands and overreaching drama. Like you have boundaries set for your life, other people have limits. 1 Peter 4:8 (KJV), "⁸ And above all things have fervent charity among yourselves: for charity shall cover the multitude of sins."

Also, while God put people in your life for times of hardship, God also gives each of us free will, including the people He places in your life.

Sometimes in your life, you lose sight of who your real enemy is, and you start fighting with one another. Unless you learn to recognize that the Devil as your only enemy and study how he operates, chances are, life will be more difficult for us than it needs to be.

God tells us to be watchful because God knows the devil cleverly disguises himself and divide us from your spouses, children, families, friends, and he even divides the churches – causing us to fight against each other. But God reminded us in Ephesians 6:12 (KJV), "¹² For you wrestle not against flesh and blood, but against principalities, against powers, against the rulers of the darkness of this world, against spiritual wickedness in high places." So yes, you are your brother's keeper, and your brothers are not your enemies. Even when they wrong us, they are not your enemies. God said, 2 Corinthians 2:10-11 (KJV), "¹⁰ To whom ye forgive anything, I forgive also: for if I forgave anything, to whom I forgave it, for your sakes forgave I it in the person of Christ; ¹¹ Lest Satan should get an advantage of us: for you are not ignorant of his devices."

Because of sin, there is division in the church; Sin always divides and separates us from God and each other. As a result of sin, marriages split up, friends part ways, relationships are strained, etc. Sin impacts relationships (usually your horizontal relationships with others, but still your vertical relationship with God). You repeatedly see this example in the Bible. When Adam and Eve sinned in the Garden, they became separated from God. Their close, personal relationship with Him wasn't the same anymore. You see this with the Nation of Israel. When King Solomon sins by worshiping idols, the result is that his kingdom is divided, split into two kingdoms (Israel and Judah), torn in two because of this sin.

God did not want for Jesus' Bride, the Church, to be divided. Jesus' prayer for the Church was that you would be unified, united just like Jesus is united with the Father (John 17:20-23 also 1 Corinthians 12:15). However, when Jesus left, Satan remained. His desire is to spread dissension and division (Romans 6:16-20). The Church has a real enemy that is continually warring against it to try to create as much division as possible.

Additionally, Christians still have sinful natures. You are far from perfect! You repeatedly sin. Sin also has the effect of clouding your minds so that you cannot perceive things correctly. It tends to skew your interpretation of God's expectation and your lust of the world. Thus, you experience many disagreements of how to interpret various things in Scripture.

Also, the result of sin is divisions. Christians struggle at times to agree on everything. Board meetings become war zones that even Pastors find themselves under attack. Sometimes they also fought over different interpretations of Scripture.

However, it is the proclivity of humanity to focus on your differences instead of the more critical points to which you agreed. God is wrapping up and on His way. These are the times of harvest. People are hungry for God. The incentive is to reach people for whom Jesus died. While disagreements are not always preventable, if Christ is in the center of your relationships, believers in Christ will not divide. But, all too often, your sinfulness comes out, and you set Christ aside until you bring others into agreement with us or you make them suffer your wrath.

Very rarely do you find Christians, in humility, who cede to their brothers and sisters in Christ. However, your differences should not be a cause for your division. Instead, God wants us to bear each other's burden and practice humility, with Christ as your example.

The result of the division in the Church causes the church to lose, and everyone experiences the pain. In most of these cases, there are correct points on both sides (as well as some errors and overreactions). You cannot put God in a box, and the reality is that you need the perspective of the whole Church to understand Him better. By surrounding yourselves with only the people who think like us, everyone loses.

The Bible tells us precisely what your parameters are and how to protect them, but often your family, or other past relationships, confuse us about your metrics. Matthew 5:22 (KJV), "But I say unto you, That whosoever is angry with his brother without a cause shall be in danger of the judgment: and whosoever shall say to his brother, Raca, shall be in danger of the council: but whosoever shall say, Thou fool, shall be in danger of hell fire."

Are you your brother's keeper, yes you are. Read Luke 6: 13-38 (KJV), "[12] And it came to pass in those days, that he went out into a mountain to pray, and continued all night in prayer to God. [13] And when it was day, he called unto him his disciples: and of them he chose twelve, whom also he named apostles; [14] Simon, (whom he also named Peter,) and Andrew his brother, James and John, Philip and Bartholomew, [15] Matthew and Thomas, James the son of Alphaeus, and Simon called Zelotes, [16] And Judas, the brother of James, and Judas Iscariot, which also was the traitor. [17] And he came down with them, and stood in the plain, and the company of his disciples, and a great multitude of people out of all Judaea and Jerusalem, and from the sea coast of Tyre and Sidon, which came to hear him, and to be healed of their diseases; [18] And they that were vexed with unclean spirits: and they were healed. [19] And the whole multitude sought to touch him: for there went virtue out of him, and healed them all. [20] And he lifted up his eyes on his disciples, and said, Blessed, be ye poor: for yours is the kingdom of God. [21] Blessed are ye that hunger now: for ye shall be filled. Blessed are ye that weep now: for ye shall laugh. [22] Blessed are ye, when men shall hate you, and when they shall separate you from their company, and shall reproach you, and cast out your name as evil, for the Son of man's sake. [23] Rejoice ye in that day, and leap for joy: for, behold, your reward is great in heaven: for in the like manner did their fathers unto the prophets. [24] But woe unto you that are rich! for ye have received your consolation. [25] Woe unto you that are full! for ye shall hunger. Woe unto you that laugh now! for ye shall mourn and weep. [26] Woe unto you, when all men shall speak well of you! for so did their fathers to the false prophets. [27] But I say unto you which hear, Love your enemies, do good to them which hate you, [28] Bless them that curse you, and pray for them which despitefully use you. [29] And unto him, that smiteth thee on the one cheek offer also the other; and him that taketh away thy cloak forbid not to take thy coat also. [30] Give to every man that asketh of thee, and of him, that taketh away thy goods ask them not again. [31] And as ye would that men should do to you, do ye also to them likewise. [32] For if ye love them which love you, what thank have ye? for sinners also love those that love them. [33] And if ye do good to them which do good to you, what thank have ye? for sinners also do even the same. [34] And if ye lend to them of whom ye hope to receive, what thank have ye? for sinners also lend to sinners, to receive as much again. [35] But love ye your enemies, and do good, and lend, hoping for nothing again; and your reward shall be great, and ye shall be the children of the Highest: for he is kind unto the unthankful and to the evil. [36] Be ye therefore merciful, as your Father also is merciful. [37] Judge not, and ye shall not be judged: condemn not, and ye shall not be condemned: forgive, and ye shall be forgiven: [38] Give, and it shall be given unto you; good measure, pressed down, and shaken together, and running over, shall men give into your bosom. For with the same measure that ye mete withal it shall be measured to you again."

Dealing With Difficult People

Romans 12:19 (KJV), "Dearly beloved, avenge not yourselves, but [rather] give place unto wrath: for it is written, Vengeance [is] mine; I will repay, saith the Lord." Recognize that sometimes believers may merely disagree. It does not necessarily mean that one is a "false teacher," but only that both might be doing their best to follow God's Word and what He is leading, they just may not agree on everything. We see this in Scripture, and we see it all around us today. Matthew 5:38-39 (KJV), " Ye have heard that it hath been said, An eye for an eye, and a tooth for a tooth:"

Throughout history, people have always found someone to talk about. They have ganged up on those they perceived as different, or in some way a threat to their existence. This is steeped in society and culture and goes back towards the dawn of modern man. But our wise and loving God admonishes you to Philippians 2:14 (KJV), "Do all things without murmurings and disputings: and Matthew 7:1 (KJV), "Judge not, that ye be not judged. Why do you torment others for no real purpose? Why do you cast out those who are different? What is it about human society that makes this something so ingrained into your life?

You do not live in a perfect world where everyone is the same, with the same set of skills or upbringings or talents. No. You live in a broad and diverse world, where genetic mutations from the dawn of time have led to an overall diversity in the species on this planet. Within every species, there are countless more diversities. The difference is that humans are conscious and aware of their existence and tend to find solace in tormenting and weakening the spirit of others. However, God commands in 1 Thessalonians 5:15 (KJV), "See that none render evil for evil unto any [man]; but ever follow that which is good, both among yourselves, and to all [men]."

The fact of the matter is that people will always find something or someone to talk about. Romans 12:20 (KJV), "Therefore if thine enemy hunger, feed him; if he thirsts, gives him drink for in so doing thou shalt heap coals of fire on his head." They will always convey their opinions and cast out those whom they feel are weak, misfits or just do not "fit in" with others because of they are too fat, too skinny, too dark, too white, too religious, too fanatical, too smart, too dumb, or whatever have you. It does not matter. People will always find someone to talk about.

Whenever you are heavy laden with worries or cares, weighed down by the yoke of the law, or amid an enemy that is weighing you down, go to Jesus, and you will find rest in Him. Rejoice, sit down, and prop your feet up, because God has promised that He will deal with your enemies and make them your footstool! Mark 11:25 (KJV), "And when ye stand praying, forgive, if ye have fought against any: that your Father also which is in heaven may forgive you your trespasses." Matthew 5:44 (KJV), "But I say unto you, Love your enemies, bless them that curse you, do good to them that hate you, and pray for them which despitefully use you, and persecute you;"

Matthew 5:45 (KJV), "That ye may be the children of your Father which is in heaven: for he maketh his sun to rise on the evil and on the good, and sendeth rain on the just and on the unjust. Luke 6:35 (KJV), "But love ye your enemies, and do good, and lend, hoping for nothing again; and your reward shall be great, and ye shall be the children of the Highest: for he is kind unto the unthankful and [to] the evil."

Your self-worth is not defined by an approval rating. No matter what the naysayers and the purveyors of negativity around you might say, your self-worth is not defined by an approval rating. There is no objective rating scale that allows another person to judge you. They do not know what you have been through. They do not know your story, your trials, your tribulations, or the path you have walked through the shadow of the valley of death. No, it just does not work that way.

However, too often, you do define your self-worth by an approval rating. You do allow what others say or think about us to influence how you feel about yourselves. The he-said-she-said pipeline often influences happiness barometer. That grapevine makes it to us in some way or another, whether electronically or verbally, and you feel the effects of that, like a ground-altering earthquake. It jolts You! It sickens You! It makes you depressed. It should not. However, it does. You allow it to do that.

Moreover, because you allow it, you stoke the fire of feelings and angst. You help to spread the conflagration of negativity when people know that it is affecting us. They know that pressing that button is going to hurt.

So, they keep pressing it and pressing it. Do not allow it to upset you. Do not allow it to phase you. Forget what they think. Seriously, forget it.

They do not know your journey, where you have been or where you're heading. I recall a compelling story that I once heard about a man who took his children to church. He sat there watching as a father was completely neglecting his three children jumping back and forth over the pews. The children were playing joyously but acting somewhat out of control inside the church, and their father was oblivious to the fact. A deacon came to the end of his proverbial rope. He had to say something. Flabbergasted by the children's behavior and the father's callous attitude, he approached the father, looked at the man, and with disdain, he said, "How could you ignore your children's behavior in the House of the Lord? The man, looking up at him with an apologetic glance profusely apologized. 'I know. I'm sorry. I guess I should do something, shouldn't I?' Then he said, their mother died a few days ago, and this is the first time I saw the joy coming back in them, I was enjoying hearing them laugh again. People don't know your story, and you do not know theirs. Just let things go and let God handle it. If it is not hurting you physically, just pray for the person.

After praying, trust your intuition and who you are deep down inside. Oftentimes, your gut instincts are really the Holy Spirit at work stirring inside and guiding you to do what is right. If you're doing the right things under the guidance of the Holy Spirit, the devil will flee.

Keep light of the fact that many before you were judged, and many after you will continue to be judged. It will always be this way. That is the nature of a diverse society. You are not all the same. Moreover, considering that fact, you should not allow those opinions to affect you. At the end of the day, when you come to the end of this life, none of that will matter. What will matter will be your experiences and what value you brought to this world, not other people's opinions of us.

Remember that you can never please everyone with your decisions so do not try. No matter what decision you make, someone is going to be upset. Notice even as perfect as Christ was He was crucified, why not you? Someone is going to have an opinion of which path you follow or which direction you choose. They will judge you on what you do for your children, what you do for your career, what you do for your education, who your friends are, the places you spend your time, what you do for a living, and everything else in between.

How can you expect to please them all? How can you expect to appease and cater to the opinions of all those people out there who differ so widely from your views? It is quite impossible. However, for one reason or another, you allow other people's opinions of us to dictate how you feel. When you decide, and people judge us negatively for it, you question whether you did the right thing.

Why? Why should it matter that you cater to others? They do not know you. They do not know all the things that you have been through. They do not know why you made that decision over another. So, why is their opinion the right opinion? It is not. It is subjective. Your decision is steeped in the present situation and circumstances that surround your life, not theirs. You are doing the best for you and your family. That is all that matters.

What is good for someone else might not be good for you
We are all so different. Everything about your life is different. You are the product of different experiences, different upbringings, different values, and beliefs, and so on. So, doesn't that mean that what is right for someone else might not be good for you? Does it mean that there is some

neat little box that all decisions go in? Does it mean that the opinion of the masses is correct and that they are justified in judging you? Of course not.

You base your sanity on those same opinions of others. You allow that to dictate how you feel at any given moment. Are you happy because someone approves of one of your decisions? Alternatively, are you sad, because others disapprove? Why should their opinion be the right opinion? Why should what is good for them, also be good for you? What is it about these negative people, and why do you allow it to affect us so profoundly?

If you continue to give people the power and allow it to affect us negatively, they will continue to judge. They will continue to say things to hurt us or make us feel unworthy of being in your skins. That is not fair whatsoever. You should never do that to someone else and do not allow them to do it to you. Chase your dreams and make your decisions based on what is right for you, not them. Because taking the high road is always a better choice

God put us all here on the earth to thrive. Not just to survive. You were made to uplift each other and make others feel good about themselves. Especially when they are trying to do the right thing in life and help their families and add value to the world.

There is this universal oneness that binds us all. No matter what anyone else says or thinks about you, taking the high road is always a better choice. Turn the other cheek, even if they spite you on both sides of the face. Matthew 5:39 (KJV), "39 But I say unto you, That ye resist not evil: but whosoever shall smite thee on thy right cheek, turn to him the other also."

God does not want you living in sadness and animosity with each other. Do not allow that to happen. Do not get sucked into negative thinking and people's poor opinions of you. It does not matter. Take the high road. Ignore the naysayers. Turn the other cheek no matter how much it burns you or hurts you inside to do so. You'll be glad you did.

You will be glad you stayed in the realm of positivity rather than flinging yourself into the ring of negativity.

The Burden of Ambiguity

"Your weak and fragile Christian faith is often shaken that it surprises us when your faith survives. Your faith, when put to the test, sometimes teeters, and at times come tumbling down as you experience life's most gruesome hardships that shake your foundation. So much so that any in connectivity to God can leave us more vulnerable in this complex and ambiguous world that is more than mere faith can handle." Bev Gilliard

Can an authentic Christian recognize and acknowledge ambiguity in the doctrinal realm while experiencing no ambivalence about God's reality, love, presence, and Jesus Christ as Lord and Savior? Or are ambiguity and ambivalence inextricably linked such that any recognition of an acknowledgment of uncertainty in the doctrinal realm automatically brings with it spiritual doubt?

In other words, can you have inner certainty (certitude, confident assurance) about God, about Jesus Christ, about the Holy Spirit—their reality and presence—without claiming certainty about Christian dogmas and doctrines?

However, there is no ambivalence that spirituality and religion are like conjoined twins. You cannot be one without being the other. Your faith is in many ways merely the action of your spirit from moment to moment. Anyone who claims to be spiritual but not religious is still religious — they still have a set of beliefs, have habits and rituals, and relate to others in distinct ways that inform their identity. Often, However, the problem is solipsism, not lack of religion.

Rarely will you meet a person who refused to admit any ambiguity about doctrines, who was indeed an absolutist about doctrinal certainty, who lacked inward, spiritual assurance?

What is the role of doubt and faith? Doubt and faith cannot live together in you because faith will not allow you to doubt.

There is certitude that God is real and He loves you. Indeed, most Christians go through a period of struggle with what they learned from childhood and what they face in adulthood. These struggles sometimes stem from their beliefs that the church is infallible, and their increasing desire to place restrictions on Christianity by setting aside whatever feelings of guilt that would arise from time to time from their skepticism that questioning their beliefs was not pleasing to God. Far be it for an authentic Christian, to place a question mark over all formal, doctrinal beliefs. But God permits everyone, that includes Christians, in Isaiah 1:18 (KJV), to "18 Come now, and let us reason together, saith the LORD: though your sins be as scarlet, they shall be as white as snow; though they are red like crimson, they shall be as wool."

The Bible tells us that men heart will fail them. Moreover, many of us, as you watch the news fear your pending doom from nuclear weapons. The rich have been building bomb shelters and preparing to go live on the moon out of fear of a world that will one day be destroyed.

Then there of some of us who are facing a personal health crisis or a loved one got news of an incurable decease, and you begin to fear the unknown of what will happen when the person is gone or if you are gone.

You are on the job, and the talk of downsizing or closing the business is looming, and now you fear to be jobless. Anxiety is setting in, how are you going to pay the bills? Are you such a fearful Christian?

Indeed, the first enemy of faith is ambiguity, and you are all fearful one time or the other. So, the question is, how much, how long, and to what degree do you allow your fears to control us.

For many Christians, anxiety and depression pave the golden road to fear. Prayer and study of scripture offer some insights into fear but does not help them in the battle. Soon, they plummet into sorrow, despair, and self-pity. Moreover, until you breakdown entirely and cry out to God will they find relief from their fear.

Yes, you read that right. Fear is a self-inflicted torment that only the person can solve, and for the Christian, it needs crying out to God and believing that God will deliver you.

Of course, you must fully surrender and truly lean on God, handing all your burdens over to Him and trusting Him to handle it.

However, the problem is that you get on your knees and confess out of fear, but you still do not place everything in God's hands. You believe you can give God the portions you cannot handle and deal with the part that you feel you know about best.

However, not until you are broken and beg God sincerely for His help, can you be helped. Then you go to God when you are completely broken and expect an immediate response. Also, when God does not respond at once, you get stirred and bothered, or you retreat and give up.

Matthew 8:23-27 (KJV) says, [23] And when He was entered into a ship, His disciples followed Him. [24] And, behold, there arose a great tempest in the sea, insomuch that the ship was covered with the waves: but He was asleep. [25] And His disciples came to Him, and awoke Him, saying, Lord, save us: you perish. [26] And He saith unto them, Why are ye fearful, O ye of little faith? Then He arose and rebuked the winds and the sea, and there was a great calm. [27] But the men marveled, saying, What manner of man is this, that even the winds and the sea obey Him!

There is no storm in your life that God cannot handle, no raging seas that He cannot calm, no winds so strong that He cannot hold back and keep from blowing. God has supplied evidence upon evidence in His Word. His scripture gives you comfort for when you are fearful and in doubt, but you do not spend enough time delving into the word of God, or you do not believe.

The cross is enough evidence that you have nothing to fear. A promise of Jesus's return is enough to comfort your soul. The miracles Jesus performed, and more personally, all the times He showed up right on time for you, are all evidence of His love and mercy towards you.

213

How could you be fearful of any raging storm? Are you not believing that God is bigger than your situation? Are you not thinking there is nothing He cannot handle? Alternatively, are you just not letting loose of your burdens and turning it over to Him because you can deal with it on your own? And if you have turned it over to Him, why are you still holding on to it? Make up your mind – will God handle it, or will you?

Life is happening all around us, and you are bound to face storms in life, it is how God keeps us secure in Him. Remembering Who the Captain of your Ship is, who is navigating your boat when the waters are rough and that God never leaves you alone to struggle in your storms, is the key to coming through your trials possible shaken though never broken.

God waits patiently on the sideline watching you maneuver and always ready with the solution when you ask Him for help. The question is, are you asking? Also, are you asking in faith believing and trusting God that He has the solution?

Therefore, despite the crashing waves that are tossing your ship, always remember Who is in the boat with you? Hebrews 13:5 (KJV), "5 Let your conversation be without covetousness; and be content with such things as ye have: for he hath said, I will never leave thee, nor forsake thee," and you'll never be fearful about anything in life; You will never be lost at sea with Captain Jesus at the helm.

Also, never forget that God loves you and wants you to know just how precious you are to Him. He willingly rewards, redeems, and restores His broken vessels.

However, no matter how strong your faith is to open doors, without a connectedness and trust in God, no amount of teaching will keep those doors open. Gain wisdom and be emboldening to encourage others to live a faith-filled life.

Another issue with Christian ambiguity is that Christians are so conflicted. For example, when a church gets a new Pastor, and he tries to institute changes, he is likely to get his wrist-slapped for making changes to things you have become complacent about; And, when the Pastor doesn't, he will get criticized and condemn for his lack of vision.

However, in these ambiguous circumstances, where complacency is the norm, and problems, opportunities, expectations, and the future are stubbornly fog-bound, and it is essential to nip misunderstandings in the bud. You must decide what you are willing to perceive as ambiguity in matters of faith, whether you will allow that ambiguity to remain and accept it as part of the journey of faith, or quickly move toward a resolution that uncertainty and religious conflicts will not be tolerated and will be handled with urgency once they do.

Do not let fear stop you, adopt an ambivalence so that even harsh self-criticism meets with compassion, a caring response, and supportive approach, for others and for self.

Handling Your Fears

Hebrews 4:15-16 (KJV) reads, "¹⁵ For we have not a high priest which cannot be touched with the feeling of our infirmities; but was in all points tempted like as we are, yet without sin.¹⁶ Let us, therefore, come boldly unto the throne of grace, that we may obtain mercy, and find grace to help in time of need." Fear, anxiety, and depression. Three of Satan's most famous weapons against you. Fear has anxiety and worries screaming in your head, that internal battle overwhelming you with a thick shadow of darkness, controlling your every move and decision. Self-doubt. Inadequacy. Never feeling you are enough; so much so that your hearts and muscles tense.

Also, fear have you trembling with low self-esteem. You live so cautiously; you do not feel like you are living at all. Sound familiar? Well, God provided you a medicine against fear, it is call Faith and hope in God. Taken in proper doses, they faith and hope will knock out fear everytime. Psalms 34:4 (KJV), "⁴ I sought the LORD, and he heard me and delivered me from all my fears."

Fear is trying to get you to react; but if you react to fear; instead of responding to the love of God that will be a mistake.

Instead of reacting, respond. God tells you in Philippians 4:13 (KJV), "¹³ I can do all things through Christ which strengtheneth me." That includes your beating fear. Faith in God, true faith, will end Satan's power that is enslaving you. Stay determine and persevere even when it seems impossible.

Fear is no lightweight; it is known to paralyze and weaken the most seasoned Christian. Sometimes the things you did in your past may haunts you. You worry about getting caught, or about someone finding out. You worry about the shame and pain, and all the other consequences, on and on, none stop. This is what fear does and fear only need a tiny opening to quickly attack and jab away at your faith until it weakens you under pressure.

Fear will remind you always of all the stress and worries that plague you. Like "kryptonite," fear will not stop until it beats you down and gives you that illegal punch to the back of the head that knocks you flat. Fear is no simple matter. As a matter-of-fact, fear is a stronghold that can paralyze you and your entire household.

While fear is a killer tool use by Satan, it is also false evidence appearing real, and a fringe contender to faith and hope in God. Faith is the only hope you have of knocking out fear and restoring that eternal peace amidst your hardships. All life's challenges, wavering, troubles, and difficulties could not disrupt your peace of mind when you put your full trust in God and allow God to be the driver of your life. You would not have to live under the weight of "what ifs."

Realized this, everyone has dealt with fear at some point, in their life and avoiding feeling afraid can cause extreme distress. Fear paralyzes you, its victim until you are stagnant under its weight, you cannot move forward, and you are too terrified of moving backward. A great spirit-drainer, fear robs you of your energy, saps your creativity, threatens your sanity, and jeopardizes your sobriety.

Also, know this, if you are experiencing fear, you must get it in check before it kills you. Examine your relationship with God because faith and fear cannot exist in you at the same time. Fear, therefore, is a lack of faith in God, His promises, and His will for you. So, the opposite is true, if you fully trust God and surrender your life to Him, you will fear no evil. Psalm 23 (KJV) , "¹ The LORD is my shepherd; I shall not want. ² He maketh me to lie down in green pastures: he leadeth me beside the still waters. ³ He restoreth my soul: he leadeth me in the paths of righteousness for his name's sake. ⁴ Yea, though I walk through the valley of the shadow of death, I will fear no evil: for thou art with me; thy rod and thy staff they comfort me. ⁵ Thou preparest a table before me in the presence of mine enemies: thou anointest my head with oil; my cup runneth over. ⁶Surely goodness and mercy shall follow me all the days of my life: and I will dwell in the house of the LORD for ever."

So, what does God say about fear? God's Word always tells us "Fear not, fear not." But the very things the Bible tells us to not to fear, we fear, and the things we should fear, we somehow seem not to fear.

When people hear the word fear, many take it lightly, but fear is quite a serious matter. Fear is at the crux of so many of your stuck moments. You are afraid of individuals, never loving or loved, failure, embarrassment, hopeless diagnosis, and death of self or loved ones. Some people even worry about change, poor self-image, loneliness, not being good enough, viewed as the bad guy, facing inner truths, and losing your salvation. These catastrophic thinking causes you to push away old friends and avoid new experiences. And instead of taking a chance, your perceived risk will cause you to passively give in to fear, limiting your life and allowing fear to become a disability. Through faith, you can muster up an incredible source of power to build self-confidence and neutralize self-sabotage. Remembering God's command, "do not fear, for I am with you; do not be dismayed, for I am your God. I will strengthen you and help you; I will uphold you" Isaiah 41:10 (KJV), "¹⁰ Fear thou not; for I am with thee: be not dismayed; for I am thy God: I will strengthen thee; yea, I will help thee; yea, I will uphold thee with the right hand of my righteousness."

Your desire to pursue your dreams will somehow diminish; you find yourself complaining instead of solving, and either you will give up on your dreams or do not dream. Scariest of all: you may turn to ungodly behaviors.

A woman decided to marry this man after dating him for several years. Her girlfriend says, "Girl he will never marry you, look how long you all have been dating and he never asked you to marry him." She asked her friends, "Well, why not, what's wrong with me?" The friends said, "Well, we don't want to hurt your feelings, but while you are sweet and everything, you are girlfriend material, men nowadays want women that are in shape. If you want him to say yes, you must lose all that weight first. Otherwise, he will never ask you to marry him." The woman tried to pretend her friend's advice did not hurt her.

However, the words stung deeply, and no matter how she tried, every time she looked in the mirror, the beauty she once saw was now a blob of fat. Despite the facts, that she was moderately overweight, despite the facts that her boyfriend loved her and told her how beautiful she was, even though they were together for some time, that truly made no difference. Slowly she became depressed. She told her boyfriend what the friends had said, and he explained to her that he loved her for who she is, and he loves her just the way she is. Realizing how much pain her friends have caused her, her boyfriend pulled her friends aside and told them how much pain their advice caused. Quickly the friends went to her and lovingly offered a myriad of sincere apologies. It was too late, the damage now is done, and they could no longer undo the emotional harm that was done to their friend. Now she is forever consumed with fear that she is not good enough for her boyfriend and one day, instead of marrying her, he will walk out, find someone better or more appealing, and never return.

Fear looks for every opening to grow, and negativity is its soil. When you spew negativity before thinking you inflict pain that sometimes is so deep that it scars the individual for a long time if not for the rest of their life. And, even with the best of intention and sincerest of apologies they will never free from the pain. These issues when left to fester, create anxieties within the individual and lead to even more fear and then depression.

The idea that others are viewing you negatively and criticizing you, if not outright, internally, hurts. Sharp and unkind words can consume your soul and can cause detrimental unrepairable harm to your psyche, self-esteem, and can even trigger depression and anxiety or compound your fears.

While most of you may understand the terrible harm negative people cause, still, you can only see the "good in people." You sometimes do not see the effects of their bad behavior until it is sometimes too late.

For others, you cannot help but focus on the negatives, maybe because you grew up with pervasive criticism, or in an environment that promoted negative responses and the consistent negative reinforcement over time eventually will lead to you only "focusing on the negatives."

Same when a friend hurt you. Think about a time growing up when someone ridiculed you with negative remarks that cut deep into your flesh. Guaranteed you have one of these memories which you recall effortlessly years later. An excellent and unfortunately common example: Think about a friend complimenting you all the time about how proud they are of you, after several enthusiastic comments, your friend makes one negative, stinging rebuke. Which comment are you most likely to evaluate? Like many people, it is more likely than not that you focused on that one negative remark and discarded all the many positive comments. That is what is happening when you focus on the negatives and downplay or dismiss the positive feedbacks and compliments you've earned. Now you are convinced that even though many great things continue to happen to you, the pain of that one negative thing clouds your memory with the fear that is how your friend and everyone else perceives you, especially if the negativity came from someone whose opinion you value or trust.

Sometimes, people do not set out to intentionally hurt you. But the likelihood of you trusting that person again is slim at best because you fear they will hurt you again. You are just sure that even though the person is working hard to change their behavior, there is no hope for them to be better than the picture you have painted in your mind of who that person is. Fortunately, that is not how God deals with us. 2 Peter 2:9 (KJV), "⁹ The Lord knoweth how to deliver the godly out of temptations and to reserve the unjust unto the day of judgment to be punished:" (1Corinthians 10:13 KJV)

Still, there are some intentional negative people who find joy in knowing they are inflicting pain upon you. And they will use every opportunity to hurt you over and over again intentionally. You have to be honest with yourself and the person to see where the problem lies. If you know it is just your fears overwhelming your friendship or relationship; it is essential to get it in check because those fears will chip away at all current and future relationships if left unchecked. If it is solely the person being obnoxiously mean, it is vital for you to weed them out of your life. However, don't end good relationships and don't fix yourself.

Truthfully, fear have been known to cripple communities, states, countries, and send the world into frenzy. With so much craziness going on around us today: the overwhelming pressure from unemployment, economic uncertainty, conflicts, homicides, crimes, persecution, violence, and societal unrest, fear is usually at the crooks of the unrest you are feeling. There actually is a lot you worry about in your day to day, not to mention we have family members and friends piling on their issues atop what you are already dealing handling. The reality of these concerns bring about worries, and unchecked contributes to your anxiety and depression.

At times, you may find yourself suffering from both physical and emotional problems: loss of appetite, sleeplessness, and fatigue. Your head left unchecked will become overloaded with intense anxiety.

Check your reality and it will tell you that you spend too much time worrying about things never even happen or may never happen. Living under the weight of the "what if's" is a hard place to dwell in and hope in Christ blots out all fears. Isaiah 41:10 (KJV), "[10] Fear thou not; for I am with thee: be not dismayed; for I am thy God: I will strengthen thee; yea, I will help thee; yea, I will uphold thee with the right hand of my righteousness."

Also, like many, you may be suffering from anxiety and depression. Examine, and you will find your fears about life: your everyday concerns about health, marriage, money, children, and so forth, is the source of all your unhappiness and discomforts. When you feel like things around you will or has spiraled out of uncontrol you see the affects on your day-to-day life.

Additionally, you may experience issues with focusing. Also, worries about family's well-being, your futures, finances, safety, and even your mortality begins to be overwhelming. Fear even can cause paranoia, and you begin to distort events and choose a victim role to justify "irresponsible," "selfish," or "immoral" behaviors. You stop standing up for what you believe in and allow others to decide your fate -it is not unusual, and fear can prevent you from getting anything done.

Untreated fear can cause you to become susceptible to divorce, broken relationships, victimization, rejection, disapproval, missed opportunities, illness, and depression. This is the spiraling effect as if you are sinking in quicksand.

Shortly after, panic attacks become your daily companion, compounded with the experiences of pounding heart, shortness of breath, dizziness, sweaty palms, and other unpleasant physical symptoms. 2 Timothy 1:7 (KJV) "7 For God hath not given us the spirit of fear, but of power, and of love, and of a sound mind." Soon, nothing in your life will seem calm – frustration, remorse, regret, apprehension, guilt, shame, incompetence, and terror will begin to clutter your spirit and mind; with time, your destinies derailed; this level of fear can even cause you to die prematurely.

However, when you have faith, faith will remind you of a man named Jesus, who died on a cross so you may live, saying, Philippians 4:6-7(KJV), "6 Be careful about nothing; but in everything by prayer and supplication with thanksgiving let your requests be made known unto God. 7 And the peace of God, which passeth all understanding, shall keep your hearts and minds through Christ Jesus." Also, the perfect love of Jesus casts out all fears.

Additionally, fear can overwhelm you with a thick shadow of darkness, controlling your every move and decision. However, you must never lose hope in Jesus. God cannot do anything with you if we lose hope and begin to doubt Him. God's Word challenges and empowers you to be faithful that God's way is perfect, so you don't fall under the power of Satan and into sin, but instead, live life and shine as a light in this evil world of darkness, and bring you into a life of victory.

Your brain is conditioned to remember the things that hurt us the most, especially the ones that cut us deeply. Focusing will help to reprogram your brain to notice the things that are healthy for your mind, and with time you will become blind to the negative.

Understand that people's negative bias serves no purpose and should not be treated as if it does, so do not to ruminate on the negative. Moreover, that is what negativity does; It is a poisonous dart that penetrates deep into us and can cut us up into little pieces that it may take a lifetime to stitch us back together.

Also, no determinant can foretell how long you will experience the effects and live or relive the pain that you suffered, sometimes unintentionally, sometimes maliciously. So even though, for some people, they did not intend the consequence of their action to have an adverse effect, the unintended consequences of their work(s) may have caused irreparable damage(s).

Therefore, do not spend time feeding your brain unhealthy food, instead think positive, happy thoughts. Make a conscious choice to focus on the Godly things, the right words and express your gratitude and rejoice in your affliction. To be able to "see only the positive" you must cultivate a spirit of appreciation and gratitude and respond only to the things that grow you. Focus on the everyday small positive experiences and continually reminding yourself that life is good.

Look at all the possibilities you face each day, make a list if you must, of what is readily available to you. Life is about doing the best you can with what you have; And, do not put unreasonable demands on yourself that may cause failure and encourage negative feedback. You have worked hard and is more than capable.

Also, when people give you positive feedback, appreciate it and savor it, and believe it! It helps to acknowledge the sincere praises others give you and rehearse it ever so often, as you push negative thoughts right out of your mind.

Sure, it is harder than it seems. Even later in life, some people, whom you may think is mature and can handle anything, are beaten down and become so broken that they only focus on the negatives.

Remember, consistent negative reinforcement will eventually lead to you only "focusing on the negatives." One of the most classic examples of this is the person who feels beaten down by a parent or teacher who tells them repeatedly, "You will not amount to nothing." Years later, you can hear the person complaining about that moment that resignates in them over and over. This is painful and heartbreaking yet so many children past and present still hear these negative words. The words are engraved in their soul, their spirit, and their being. Despite how much they try to move on, how many positive accomplishments they have made, and despite all the positive reinforcements and acholades, that one negative moment keeps resurfacing again and again. Statements as such have damaged many people from childhood into adulthood, spanning their entire lifetime.

Still, it is up to you not to worry, to put these negative emotions out of your head because there is no cure for emotions, and focus only on the good things happening around you. Allow God to take over and do what you can, just do your best at all times, in God's eyes you are already enough. Psalm 23:5 (KJV), "Thou preparest a table before me in the presence of mine enemies: thou anointest my head with oil; my cup runneth over."

So yes, you will have enemies everywhere, even in the church, that are working to keep your lights from shining. These sorts of behaviors are not new. Not all Christians are always welcoming. Some of us are combative, arrogant, miserable, and want to spread discord in the church. For those of you who exudes positivity, it is crucial that you intervene when you see someone being mean in their criticism of others. If you see someone being dogmatic, and unchanging in their ridicule of others, interrupt with a cliché statement like "well, let us look at the bright side!" People remember clichés, and you have now redirected the conversation to a positive discussion! Equally important, ensure that you do not take part in further damaging the person by appeasing the negative person in their destructive behavior or indulging in gossip.

However, you have the assurance of knowing that God will bless you and exalt you despite any situation your enemies create for you. God will bring them into your presence, and God will bless you beyond measure in their face, those who tried to destroy you, your naysayers, and those who are unjustly inflicted pain and are working or worked to damage your psyche. God anoints your head with oil, which means God blesses you with favor, and He gives you plenty that it runs over your cup, off the table, and unto the floor and your Great Provider God continues to provide you with more and more blessings that you will not have room to contain it.

Therefore, find comfort in Deuteronomy 31:6, "Be strong and of good courage, fear not, nor be afraid of them: for the Lord thy God, He is that doth go with thee; He will not fail thee, nor forsake thee."

Also, take responsibility for your health. You alone have a choice what you spend your time doing. You can choose to focus less on negative emotions that cloud the reflection of who you are, and that have nothing to do with you, or you can concentrate on being happy by focusing on the pleasantries of life that let you feel good about yourself, good about your accomplishments, and ultimately lengthen your time on this earth.

Continue to read your Bible, it is rich with God's promises; and it is a source of comfort for the afflicted, reassurance for the sick, and encouragement for the soul. In your times of struggles read Philippians 4:19 (KJV), "[19] But my God shall supply all your need according to his riches in glory by Christ Jesus." When you are feeling overly anxious read Psalm 32:8 (KJV), "[8] I will instruct thee and teach thee in the way which thou shalt go: I will guide thee with mine eye." Read Romans 5:3 (KJV), "[3] And not only so, but we glory in tribulations also: knowing that tribulation worketh patience." And be comforted in death that Jesus is the resurrection and the life. John 11:25-26 (KJV), "[25] Jesus said unto her, I am the resurrection, and the life: he that believeth in me, though he were dead, yet shall he live: [26] And whosoever liveth and believeth in me shall never die. Believest thou this?" If you left behind by a loved one's untimely passing, meditated on Psalm 68:5 (KJV), "[5] A father of the fatherless, and a judge of the widows, is God in his holy habitation."

Guard your heart believing that fear is not in God's plans for your life. 2 Timothy 1:7 (KJV), "[7] For God hath not given us the spirit of fear; but of power, and of love, and of a sound mind." While you do not know the future, you know Who holds your future. When you feel afraid and think you will lose control, trust the One Who is in control. And though fear continuously seeks a rematch, remember, faith, hope, and love never fails to sustain you and trumps all fears. Also, remember that God's grace and mercy are always available in abundant supplies.

Finally, everyone has fears; what matters is how you handle them. Do not allow fear to paralyze you and become a disability for you. Please read Luke 12:22-32; stay encouraged. God Bless. Amen!

Bitterness

As Malachy McCourt said, "Resentment is like taking poison and waiting for the other person to die." You do not deserve the amount of strain you are putting on yourself by holding onto resentment. Let us not waste time-fighting against ourselves but recognize who the real enemy is. Psalms 37:8 (KJV), "Cease from anger, and forsake wrath: fret not thyself in any wise to do evil." We can choose to give each other grace and kindness. We can hold on to what matters most and pursue unity in the body of Christ. Proverbs 14:29 (KJV), "[He that is] slow to wrath [is] of great understanding: but [he that is] hasty of spirit exalteth folly." Use caution in whom you listen to and choose to take guidance from. Sometimes when we are in a place where it is hard to see clearly, maybe because of our own pressing worries or cares, we need a trusted friend who can speak the truth in places we need to hear. This is often true in marriage. Learning to listen to one another and take into consideration what the other might be sensing or discerning can often have great power in saving us from a heap of trouble up ahead if we will only heed the warnings that someone, we love may speak our way.

A church member gossip about you and defamed your character, a boss or a manager cheated you out of a promotion, a coworker made you angry, a family member disrespected and shame you in public, or maybe it is a friend, your leading man, that let you down, leaving you "in agony". Everything that you had worked for your entire life was just being trashed, was being destroyed.

Suddenly, you feel yourself becoming disgruntled and bitter, always grumbling about something, nothing makes you happy. You are now harboring resentment which you know are about as beneficial as…well…nothing. However, you cannot help yourself. Do not be dismayed; it happens to the best of us one time or the other. Remember,

Psalms 103:8 (KJV), "The LORD [is] merciful and gracious, slow to anger, and plenteous in mercy."

First, let us define bitterness because it is a painful emotion that takes hold of each of us from time to time. Bitterness knocks on all your doors and sometimes, the solutions mean untangling webs of hurt that hides behind pain you wish would never resurface, sometimes it goes back for years, at times to your childhood in some people's case. Bitterness is usually a clear emotional condition of internal discontent which erupts as rage, envy, irritation, slander, rebellion, etc. When it explodes, it is dangerous and, after some time, this disgruntlement, this bitterness, this root that is deep within, will manifest itself toward someone or something. People have known to be bitter towards God, a parent, a spouse, their children, a boss; no one is exempt – when it erupts.

However, do not be dismayed; Scripture acknowledges your pain and provides you with a solution. Proverbs 15:1 (KJV), "A soft answer turneth away wrath: but grievous words stir up anger." Anger, Great and mighty passion!

Additionally, the church is no exception. If you attend church long enough, you are sure to meet one, two, five, ten bitter Christians. Pursed mouth, unhappy, and miserable. Everybody is trying to prove their worth, vying for positions in the church, some, for jobs for which they are not qualified or available. Now let us not confuse anger - being mad and upset, with bitterness - being resentful. Proverbs 15:18 (KJV), "A wrathful man stirreth up strife: but [he that is] slow to anger appeaseth strife.

Unlike anger, bitterness has no clear outward signs physically associated with it and can be easily masked, hiding in the depths of the soul if the individuals so choose.

Bitterness grows in people when something happens to them beyond their control and that they perceive was not their fault, but it caused them to experience some pain or feelings of disgruntlement. Examples include unwanted experiences; failures; disappointments; setbacks.

Being bullied, cheated, suffering injustice, are all examples of activities that can undoubtedly lead to bitterness in an individual.

Additionally, bitterness can be caused by being publicly humiliated, feeling betrayed, wrongfully blamed or when one feels taken advantage of or disrespected.

If left unaddressed, bitterness grows and can become difficult to handle. Struggles of coping with the trauma and trust issues further make an impact on the individual and further compounds and complicate the bitterness. Especially if the person feels disrespected that others are making light of their situation.

Also, untreated bitterness can turn into a need for revenge. Therefore, it is essential to overcome bitterness quickly. Ecclesiastes 7:9 (KJV), "Be not hasty in thy spirit to be angry: for anger resteth in the bosom of fools.

Sadly, bitterness is sometimes caused by simple miscommunication that turned into a misunderstanding because people did not talk through the issue that causes them to be offended. Bitterness may occur when one person assumed something about the other person and labeled it as fact in their mind. That other person might not even remember they offended you after some time has passed, or why you are bitter towards them. Ephesians 4:31(KJV), "Let all bitterness, and wrath, and anger, and clamor, and evil speaking, be put away from you, with all   malice:

Alternatively, at times, the other person may not be aware they hurt us, but you held on to the resentment without saying a word. Fuming, ready to fight and get even. You pass judgment and condemn the person based on your perceived notion of their intentionality to offend us and the next thing you know you find yourself wallowing in a pool of resentment and bitterness. The longer you choose to stay in the pool, the more bitter and withered you become.

Maybe you have experienced this bitterness, where you experience a great sense of loss and resentment and left unaddressed it turned into rage and anger. Bitterness can cause your body to suffer undue stress

231

that consumes you, and makes you sick, robbing you of your peace of mind and happiness.

Soon, the bitter person soon ends up in a vicious cycle, and their persistent feelings of negativity cause more rage, and more rage causes more negativity. These emotions continuously get triggered by events that remind you of the hurt or disappointment, and you become physically ill. Now you must focus intensely on negativity and rage that it disables your ability to let go of the situation.

Moreover, because you cannot 'let go,' or resolve issues….it begins to drain you emotionally because it takes a significant amount of passive-aggressive emotional energy to keep the hostility and aggression that supports bitterness. It does not make sense to remain in a state of bitterness when the only person being hurt is, well, you. Live your best life happy and always work to address any bitterness once it raises its ugly head. When you are bitter, you are so focused on the past that you cannot enjoy the present.

Also, to find your purpose, you must focus on the present and even think about the future a little. You cannot do that consumed with bitterness, and negatively that is affecting you.

Worst yet, bitterness can lead to anxiety and depression, as well as trouble sleep disorders. Your bodies are not meant to be stressed all the time, so these effects are like your body's way of letting us know it is not happy. Aside from the internal problem(s), bitterness can lead to hostility and cynicism and affect your personal or emotional development, damage your self-confidence and self-esteem, and cause you to experience trust issues. Feelings of helplessness can prevent you from taking back control of your life.

Granted, people hurt us in life, they make us angry at times, but you also must take responsibility for your happiness and your emotions. When you are bitter, it becomes a lot easier to blame everything on what happened to you or the person who did it to you, and you end up stagnant swimming in self-pity.

Small victories can make you feel empowered, and that can make you start to feel less bitter. You must work towards finding your way back to being favorable to rid yourself of the negative feelings bitterness brings about. Proverbs 19:11 (KJV), " The discretion of a man deferreth his anger; and [it is] his glory to pass over a transgression.

One thing is for sure - you cannot beat bitterness with more pain. Also, because you can only change you, to overcome resentment, you must change yourself despite whether you feel justified in your bitterness or not. Changing your attitude, especially when you feel justified, may be difficult, and may seem unfair or unreasonable, but it is a reality, and the sooner you can accept it, the better off you will be. Wait for people to change or things to turn around you, you're going to be waiting forever. Part of this metamorphosis that you are about to undertake also requires that you forget feelings of revenge, getting even, or expectations of an apology, or whatever you have bottled up inside of you that you feel you need to move forward, get over it, it will not happen. Take charge of your happiness and let things go. No one says it will be easy, but it is necessary.

Still, for many of these bitter Christians, all they can see is a life full of misery, obligation, and self-inflicted pain and jealousy.

Understandably, you cannot always keep deep misery at bay. Their self-righteous anger, Hebrews 12: 14-15 (KJV) states, "14 Follow peace with all men, and holiness, without which no man shall see the Lord: 15 Looking diligently lest any man fail of the grace of God; lest any root of bitterness springing up trouble you, and thereby many be defiled."

These long-faced Christians go around continuously angry, disillusioned, and defensive even over politics and the infringement of their worldly rights and have no consideration for their Heavenly rights.

Worst yet, their eyes are no longer fixated on Christ, they lost that spark for loving Jesus, and they cannot even be happy for their fellow brothers and sisters who are basking in the goodness of God. You do not always like to admit it, but you have all been there: you do not get what you want, and someone else does.

Quoting Dr. Steven Maraboli, "Do you think the peace of mind can be found in holding a grudge...alternatively, harboring resentment or wallowing in thoughts of what could have been? Me neither".

Along with changing your mindset and letting things go, you must practice forgiving as much as God forgives you. Sometimes this means forgiving yourself first and forgiving even the unforgivable.

Hebrews 12:15 (KJV) tells us, "15 Looking diligently lest any man fails of the grace of God; lest any root of bitterness springing up trouble you, and thereby many be defiled;" Bitterness is not God's plan and design for anyone. It causes us to fall out of harmony with God. Also, Proverbs 20:22 (KJV), 22 Say not thou, I will recompense evil, but wait on the LORD, and he shall save thee.

Instead of living bitter and seeking revenge and retribution, God wants us to trust His justice to be fair as He is loving and wants the best for everyone. God can reduce even the most miserable person to sniveling softy. Proverbs 15:1 (KJV), "A soft answer turneth away wrath: but grievous words stir up anger."

Bitter or Better? Proverbs 14:10 (KJV), "10 The heart knoweth his bitterness, and a stranger doth not intermeddle with his joy." Each of us has a choice to live better or bitter; it is a choice. Be free today, do not live bitter, live better and be the best you. Ephesians 4:26 (KJV), "Be ye angry, and sin not: let not the sun go down upon your wrath." James 1:19-20 (KJV), "19Wherefore, my beloved brethren, let every man be swift to hear, slow to speak, slow to wrath: 20For the wrath of man worketh not the righteousness of God."

Walking Your Journey

Most of us have someone you can call a friend, that one person whom you have come to appreciate and want to spend your time with, hanging out and sharing your dreams with, well at least if you are fortunate enough. Sometimes that person knows us better than anyone else, and you can count on them to be there even if you have an emergency at three a.m. However, what happens when that friendship reaches its end of the journey and you must go it alone for God to move you to the next level? Ephesians 4:2 (KJV), "2 With all lowliness and meekness, with longsuffering, forbearing one another in love."

A true friend will show up to support you under any circumstances. They will do whatever is necessary to assist you, encourage you, and make you feel love. They will tolerate your shortcomings, and inconsistencies and accepts us unconditionally, forsaking all others no matter what.

However, not everybody is meant to walk your journey with you forever, and sad to say; sometimes it is your best friend that has to go. There will be times in your Christian walk when all you need is Jesus walking alongside you. When you are so worn out, or when your next level in your relationship with God requires you go it alone. Jesus says in Matthew 11:28-30 (KJV), "28 Come unto me, all ye that labor and are heavy laden, and I will give you rest. 29 Take my yoke upon you and learn of me; for I am meek and lowly in heart: and ye shall find rest unto your souls. 30 For my yoke is easy, and my burden is light."

This is vital information to the Christian walk because sometimes you get so bogged down with life happening to you, things moving fast around you, and burdened with life, that you cannot deal with the weight of others holding you down or holding you back. All you need is some personal one and one with God.

Then there are moments when negative people are sucking the living daylight out of you. They are not in your life for any other purpose but to make you miserable and drain you and your resources. Once you recognize this is happening, you have a duty to yourself and God to remove these stumbling blocks from your life.

Although, not all stumbling blocks are evil or ill-intentioned towards you, merely that some people are not supposed to be a part of your journey. Sometimes it is that they have served their purpose in your life, and sometimes it is because they never needed to be there in the first place. Even success fades eventually. You have heard it said, "People are either a blessing or a lesson." and this is true. Therefore, you must decipher a person's purpose in your life. Sometimes, in your weakness, God sends people whom you might not otherwise tolerate to strengthen us or protect us in moments that may prove harmful or even from yourselves.

You will never fully understand what prevention or interruption God is using that person for, so it is best to pray for understanding. Appreciate the role they played in your life, and if you were blessed, thank God, and share the blessing, even if as a testimony, and if God gifted you with a lesson, thank God and grow from it, either way, cut them off and move on.

Let us be clear, moving on is about "giving someone up," relinquishing that relationship that has come to the end of your journey. You are not about totally abandoning the person or "giving up on someone." When you let go of someone to continue your calling, God expects you to give them up not give up on them.

Also, you are to do it in love, and your responsibility for them does not end, you still must pray for them, and check up on them. Understand, this is not about hating or disliking anyone; this is about obedience and your Christian journey. Do not forget that God expects you to be your brother's keeper. Like Hannah, you must realize that though you may have been entrusted with a position of care and responsibility toward someone, God is ultimately their keeper, and they are God's responsibility.

Additionally, God cannot bless us if you do not open your hands and let go of some things, God cannot move us to the next level if you have the wrong people hanging on your coattails.

Also, when God asks us to let go of something or someone close to us, the pain of doing so may feel like punishment -- but it is not! Relinquishment is not the act of God removing sinfully attachments. Relinquishing or real "giving up" is a mature decision you make in response to God's request.

When God asks us to relinquish someone or something, God is testing your love, loyalty, and reverence to Him and perfecting your ability to trust Him unconditionally with that which is most precious to us.

The fact that God requests us to relinquish someone or something is an encouraging sign that He knows you already set up a relationship of trust with Him. He does not ask us to renounce above the level of your ability.

Abraham saw his surrender of Isaac as an act of worship in Genesis 22 (KJV), "[1] And it came to pass after these things, that God did tempt Abraham, and said unto him, Abraham: and he said, Behold, here I am. [2]And, he said, Take now thy son, thine only son Isaac, whom thou lovest, and get thee into the land of Moriah; and offer him there for a burnt offering upon one of the mountains which I will tell thee of."

Indeed, it is not wrong for us to have hopes! However, part of relinquishment is coming to terms with the fact that life happens. When you surrender your expectations, you allow God to be God, and He will supply all your needs and bring fulfillment to your life, though maybe not in the manner you envision.

So, now you want to know how you will know it is time to walk away from certain people.

Well, you will discern so by continually paying attention to what God is saying to you, that is if you have a relationship with God.

Eventually, you will reach the point of acknowledging your helplessness in relating to your loved one, realizing you've reached the limits of your human love and wisdom. You are now ready to recognize your need to let God take over.

God is always steering you away from a life of suffering. With God's help and a spirit of discernment, you will know what fits the effervescent changes that are going on within you and outside of you. Over time, your life purpose will appear through your relationship with God.

You will learn to recognize confusion and anxiety, from calm and happiness. Your life will seem quieter, and when you reflect on God and all that He has given you, suddenly you will open to where God wants to take you next. By this time, the after the storms of your life would have passed and a feeling that is awe-inspiring; a sense of calm will come over you. Moreover, once you surrender to God, which you will happily do, He will let you see the cobwebs, and chaos and you will recognize the people whom God wants you to move away from.

Crisis vs. Christ

The state and condition of your world today have thrown many Christians into a problematic world, full of challenges that are causing most Christians anxious and to panic. Also, because God gives us free will, it is a Christian burden when you must decide between handling your crisis which is not always Godly or surrenders to Christ.

However, in coming to your convictions; being a defender of individual rights and conscience, wanting to take part in human justice, be mindful not to forget that nothing supersedes God's laws, His righteousness, or His mercy. However, the essence of the true Christian is an extraordinary love and believe they have for Jesus Christ, whom they have not seen, but in whom they have placed their trust.

It is therefore imperative that Christians know, or ought to know that you are living at the end of days, and God warned us in Luke 21:26(KJV), "[26] Men's hearts failing them for fear, and for looking after those things which are coming on the earth: for the powers of heaven shall be shaken." Based on this knowledge, Christians must seek to understand and to adjust to the uncertainties of these times and not to be so shaken that they lose faith in God and His promises to those who believe. No doubt, the crisis will get worst, but where you stand in Christ will determine how you withstand the dangers of this world yet to come—yes, and the unprecedented difficulties and the uncertainty that you will face. There are still tremendous challenges - of course, that is, However, to come to fulfill the gospel.

Still, it is unworthy of Christians to bewail his fate and exaggerate the challenges amid which he finds himself. As Christians, you know who Christ is, you trust and believe in Him, and you have the evidence of the cross and the testimonies of all the times Christ has brought us through. God has not changed. His words are still the same, and God does not love us less despite what is going on in the world.   Now is the time when you must stand firm on the promises of God and be looking forward to His return. 1 Corinthians 16:13 (KJV), "[13] Watch ye, stand fast in the faith, quit you like men, be strong." Remember Paul's words to the Corinthians: "God is faithful, who will not suffer you to be tempted above that ye are able; but will with the temptation also make a way to escape, that ye may be able to bear it" (I Corinthians 10:13).

Sure, the Christian journey is not easy, and it will get more difficult the closer you get to the end of time, but this is one of the many burdens you must endure in faith. What, then, is the burden of the Christian today, the Christian who, as a man, have their own set of problems, hardships and complexities they must go through and through your crisis, you will must decide if you draw to the truth which is "[8] Jesus Christ the same yesterday, and today, and forever." (Hebrews 13:8), or do you rebel, and give into the crisis and surrender to the devil, the adversary. God tells us in 1 Peter 5:8 (KJV), "[8] Be sober, be vigilant; because of your adversary the devil, as a roaring lion, walketh about, seeking whom he may devour:"

However, vigilances do not equate to Christians compromising their faith for natural solutions to the crises of their day.

Above all things, when Christians come into a relationship with Christ and realizing how much Jesus first loved them with an unconditional love that He willingly died on a cross, that surpasses any love he has for Christ, the crisis seems bearable.

The Christian, then, must rise above any crises they face and rest in the assurance of Christ eternal love and the plan of salvation. Only when a Christian is secure in Christ, unmoved by the things of this world, should Christians be bold enough to take a stand against the forces of the crisis of evil that threatens his relationship with Christ.

Then when the state of this world, crisis versus Christ, one of the most subtly of Christian's burden, presents itself, Christians know they need the guidance of the church to carry that burden without stumbling or becoming disheartened.

Therefore, it is equally essential that you have church leaders who lead and do not feel the need to be so popular that instead of leading, they follow the masses that are dependent on them for their leadership. It becomes a case of lead, or follow, but your leaders should not try to do both, less everyone will go astray.

Faith and Blessings

God said, "Have faith." Mark 11:22-24 He did not say, "Try to have faith," "Hope to have faith," "Wish to have faith," He said, "Have faith." Faith needs action. Faith without action is dead. Believe that you have received them, and you will. You must believe that you have received it before God blesses you with it. Amen.

If you do not see your blessing, it is because you have not examined the question, "What is the man that thou art mindful of him?" Man's insignificance, and God's mindfulness of man, allows you to see the blessings of the infinite goodness of God; for it is, indeed, a beautiful thing that the Creator of heaven, whose glory is so surpassingly great as to ravish us with the highest admiration, condescends so far as graciously to take upon Him the care of the human race, which have rendered man, and which expresses the frailty of man rather than any strength or power which he possesses.

Remember, God thinks upon you continually, He cares for you, and confer such high favors upon you even though you have fallen into a state of sin, and misery, and mortality, and are a sick or miserable state of His creation. God comes when you call upon Him. He visits you in your messed up broken condition, filled with biases and burdens - not in anger, as that word is sometimes used, but with His grace and mercy, abound and plentiful. Psalm 65:9 (KJV), "9 Thou visitest the earth, and waterest it: thou greatly enrichest it with the river of God, which is full of water: thou preparest them corn when thou hast so provided for it". Also, as he did for Sarah in Genesis 21:1-5 (KJV), "1 And the LORD visited Sarah as he had said, and the LORD did unto Sarah as he had spoken. 2 For Sarah conceived, and bare Abraham a son in his old age, at the set time of which God had spoken to him". And, Exodus 4:31 (KJV), "31 And the people believed: and when they heard that the LORD had visited the children of Israel and that he had looked upon their affliction, then they bowed their heads and worshipped".

When I see the heavens, the sun, the moon, and stars, O God, what is a man? Who would think that thou shouldest make all these creatures for one, and that one well near the least of all? Yet none but he can see what thou hast done; none but he can admire and adore thee in what he seeth: how had he need to do nothing but this since he alone must do it! Indeed the price and value of things consist not in quantity; one diamond is worth more than many quarries of stone; one lodestone hath more virtue than mountains of earth. It is lawful for us to praise thee in ourselves. All thy creation hath not more wonder in it than one of us: other creatures thou madest by a simple command; Man not without a divine consultation: others at once; man thou didst form, then inspire: others in several shapes, like to none but themselves; man, after thine own image: others with qualities fit for service; man, for dominion. The man had his name from thee; they had their names from man. How should we be consecrated to thee above all others, since thou hast bestowed more cost on us than others!

What is a man, that thou shouldest magnify him? and that thou shouldest set thy heart upon him? and that thou shouldest visit him every morning?" Man, in the pride of his heart, seeth no such great matter in it; but a humble soul is filled with astonishment. Isaiah 57:15 (KJV), "¹⁵ For thus saith the high and lofty One that inhabiteth eternity, whose name is Holy; I dwell in the high and holy place, with him also that is of a contrite and humble spirit, to revive the spirit of the humble, and to revive the heart of the contrite ones".

In Ezekiel 16:1-5 (KJV), "¹Again the word of the LORD came unto me, saying, ²Son of man, cause Jerusalem, to know her abominations, ³And say, Thus saith the Lord GOD unto Jerusalem; Thy birth and thy nativity is of the land of Canaan; thy father was an Amorite, and thy mother, a Hittite. ⁴And as for thy nativity, in the day thou wast born thy navel was not cut, neither wast thou washed in water to supple thee; thou wast not salted at all, nor swaddled at all. ⁵None eye pitied thee, to do any of these unto thee, to have compassion upon thee; but thou wast cast out in the open field, to the clothing of thy person, in the day that thou wast born".

We have a relation of the wonderful condescension of God to man, who is there resembled a wretched infant cast out in the day of its birth, in its blood and filthiness, no eye pitying it; such loathsome creatures are we before God; and yet when he passed by and saw us polluted in our blood, he said unto us, "Live." It is doubled because of the strength of its nature; it was "the time of love" Ezekiel 16:8 (KJV), "8 Now when I passed by thee, and looked upon thee, behold, thy time was the time of love; and I spread my skirt over thee, and covered thy nakedness: yea, I sware unto thee and entered into a covenant with thee, saith the Lord GOD, and thou becamest mine".

This was love indeed, that God should take a filthy, wretched thing, and spread his skirts over it, and cover its nakedness and swear unto it, and enter into a covenant with it, and make it His: that is, that he should espouse this loathsome thing to himself, that he would be a husband to it; this is love unfathomable, love inconceivable, self-principle love; this is the love of God to man, for God is love. Oh, the depth of the riches of the bounty and goodness of God! How is his love beautiful, and his grace past finding out! How do you find and feel your hearts affected upon the report of these things? Do you not see a matter of admiration and cause of wonder? Are you not as it was launched forth into an ocean of goodness, where you can see no shore, nor feel no bottom? Ye may make a judgment of yourselves by the motions and affections that ye feel in yourselves at the mention of this. For thus Christ judged of the faith of the centurion that said unto him, "Matthew 8:8-10 (KJV), "8 The centurion answered and said, Lord, I am not worthy that thou shouldest come under my roof: but speak the word only, and my servant shall be healed. 9 For I am a man under authority, having soldiers under me: and I say to this man, Go, and he goeth; and to another, Come, and he cometh; and to my servant, Do this, and he doeth it. 10 When Jesus heard it, he marveled, and said to them that followed, Verily I say unto you, I have not found so great faith, no, not in Israel".

Considering now that you know God is never far, He visits you when you call upon Him and gives you the desires of your heart, then why are you not seeing your blessings? James 1:17 (KJV), "¹⁷ Every good gift and every perfect gift is from above, and cometh down from the Father of lights, with whom is no variableness, neither shadow of turning."

God's blessings, started before you were born, continued with the cross, and the blood of Jesus that covers you and joins you to God, and proves the depths of love God has for you so that worries and such become trivial. Psalm 8 (KJV), "¹ O LORD, our Lord, how excellent is thy name in all the earth! whom hast set thy glory above the heavens. ² Out of the mouth of babes and sucklings, hast thou ordained strength because of thine enemies, that thou mightest still the enemy and the avenger. ³ When I consider thy heavens, the work of thy fingers, the moon, and the stars, which thou hast ordained; ⁴ What is a man, that thou art mindful of him? and the son of man, that thou visitest him? ⁵ For thou hast made him a little lower than the angels, and hast crowned him with glory and honor. ⁶ Thou madest him to have dominion over the works of thy hands; thou hast put all things under his feet: ⁷ All sheep and oxen, yea, and the beasts of the field; ⁸ The fowl of the air, and the fish of the sea, and whatsoever passeth through the paths of the seas. ⁹ O Lord our Lord, how excellent is thy name in all the earth!"

If you do not see your blessings, the likelihood is that you have not accepted all that God has offered you without your asking. Furthermore, you are missing your blessings perhaps because of the packaging. God does not send blessings wrapped up in neat, tidy bows. Therefore, the way you behave and treat others may be one of the sources of your blindness that is preventing you from seeing your blessings. Many times, God will send your blessings by using the least among you. 1 Corinthians 12:20-31 (KJV), "²⁰ But now are they many members, yet but one body. ²¹ And the eye cannot say unto the hand, I have no need of thee: nor again the head to the feet, I have no need of you. ^{22} Nay, much more those members of the body, which seem to be more feeble, are necessary: ^{23} And those members of the body, which we think to be less honorable, upon these we bestow more abundant honor; and our uncomely parts have more abundant comeliness. ^{24} For our comely parts have no need: but God hath tempered the body together, having given more abundant honor to that part which lacked. ^{25} That there should be no schism in the body; but that the members should have the same care one for another. ^{26} And whether one member suffers, all the members suffer with it, or one member is honored, all the members rejoice with it." So, how many times have you turned down God's offer and missed your blessings?

Likewise, the devil will use influential and well to do people who overload you with lustful desires, and greed that you cannot see your blessings through the plans God has set just for you. Therefore, do not spend your time focusing on people's achievements because they are blocking your sight of what God is trying to do for you or give you. Also, focusing your time on what other people have is consuming, and you are preventing God's plan for your growth and development through Christ; Stop it!

Additionally, you may not be seeing your blessings because of your lack of gratitude for the things that you take for granted. Sometimes the blessings you need the most is in the things that God gives you every day. Air to breathe, a sight to see, the ability to walk and talk, even your brokenness can be a blessing, but you will not see it if you cannot appreciate what God is doing in your life and through your life, how God is using you to fulfill His plan of salvation.

Your thoughts may be your blessing blocker. What do you think you need? Lots of money? A bigger house? A new top of the line car? Brand name clothes? You never seem to have enough or have the best; you want more. Your thinking can cause you to miss your blessing. But take a closer look. While God did not give you any of those things, instead God blessed you in other ways. You have a job you did not deserve, you can go home to your small house and turn a lock and go in, you flip a switch, and you have light, you turned on the thermostat, and you have heat, you turned on the pipe, and you have water, you looked in the refrigerator, and you have food. Also, while you did not get that top of the line car, you have a little hooptie that can get you from point A to point B and you have money for gas.

Oh! And yes, while you did not get the brand name clothes, you got clothes from the thrift store, or someone hands me down, but least you are not naked. So, if you do not see your blessing, you never gave thought to those who are less fortunate, the homeless that wish they have your small raggedy house, the people who loss everything in a fire and wish they had clothes for a week, and those who want to get around but can't afford to ride the bus because they do not have money to pay the fare. Your stinking thinking is blocking you from seeing how to bless you are and how valuable you are to God. You can turn to your Supplier, your Heavenly Father for your daily needs and God promised to supply all your needs. Philippians 4:19 (KJV), "19 But my God shall supply all your need according to his riches in glory by Christ Jesus". It may be food needed to sustain life, or spiritual food to strengthen you to deal with the chronic illnesses within the church.

The winds are blowing, and a fountain filled with blood is flowing. As you delight in the wonders of God and think on the treasures that await you up in Heaven, you can begin to appreciate your cupboard of food, whether a little or a lot, you can find pleasure at looking at the stars as you draw the curtain in your bedroom at night, and you can rejoice to the rising of the sun. Music from the birds chirping and welcoming in the morning becomes a delight. The waters are cascading over your hands and soothing your spirit, supplying a calmness for the day ahead.

Jesus teaches, look to God each day for God is who supplies all your needs. The Lord's is a loving God, aware of even the smallest needs of His children and eager to aid each one. God says in James 1:5 (KJV), "5 If any of you lack wisdom, let him ask of God, that giveth to all men liberally, and upbraideth not; and it shall be given him."

However, to see the blessings God had given you, spend your time in prayer. When you pray, contemplate your needs—both what you lack and what you need to protect.

Think about your successes and on what you can do to be better than the day before, never focus on your perceived failures of the day. Thank your Heavenly Father for the manna He has placed along the path that sustains your soul. These reflections will increase your faith in God, and you will begin to see His hands at work in your life and the blessings He has placed upon you. You will be able to rejoice one more day, as you make one more step toward eternal life.

Faith in God opens your eyes to your blessings. Psalm 138:7 (KJV) says, "7 Though I walk amid trouble, thou wilt revive me: thou shalt stretch forth thine hand against the wrath of mine enemies, and thy right hand shall save me."

That is, of course, tremendously reassuring, but still, some of you give more significance to those who shun and isolates you in the church. As you seek God, your only focus should be on growing your faith and trusting in God and His Son.

There is hope in Jesus, so do not get discouraged. Blessings are lying right around those mountains, and you must peak around to see all that awaits you. And so, it is. As you keep pressing to know God, who is real, who is Truth, and you set your minds on His Word, spending time, meditating on it, you will eventually become dependent on God. It is that dependence that opens your eyes to your blessings.

Well, now you question, "How can I see the blessings when there is always something blocking my view?" Simple, asking for and receiving God's grace plays a vital part in learning to trust Him and in enduring life's challenges. Ephesians 4:13-15 (KJV), " 13 Till you all come in the unity of the faith, and the knowledge of the Son of God, unto a perfect man, unto the measure of the stature of the fulness of Christ: 14 That you henceforth be no more children, tossed to and fro, and carried about with every wind of doctrine, by the sleight of men, and cunning craftiness, whereby they lie in wait to deceive; [15] But speaking the truth in love, may grow up into him in all things, which is the head, even Christ:"

As you reflect on resolving to be better, carefully select the resolutions, you make and why you are making them, and your obligations for keeping them. When you can be honest with yourselves, you can be honest with others, and the blessings will start to flow. God always blesses His children who work in harmony with each other.

Likewise, look at how you can use minister to others through your words and deeds. There are many blessings in being a servant that with even a little effort on your part, and with the workings of the Holy Spirit, can yield remarkable fruit.

However, when you have an attitude of, 'No, I am too busy,' The disdainful response can cause many souls to leave from the doorsteps of the church and never return. Therefore, when you can see how to bless you are so you can be a blessing to others, you can you cause a soul to be a loss.

Saying all this to say, you can see the benefits of your blessings when you take time out to be a blessing to others whether that is giving of yourself, your time, or providing an ear to the needs of your brethren. Sure, you get busy sometimes, but do not be so busy that you cannot help your brothers and sisters to unburden themselves. To do so may cause unrepairable damages.

Finding Peace In The Storm

If you have ever experienced the crushing weight of being not enough, struggled with extreme fears and insecurities, carried around the baggage of shame, or sunk into the pits of loneliness, God wants to set you free. Jesus can calm all storms in your life. Matthew 8: 23-27 (KJV), " 23 Then he got into the boat, and his disciples followed him. 24 Suddenly a furious storm came up on the lake so that the waves swept over the boat. But Jesus was sleeping. 25 The disciples went and woke him, saying, "Lord, save us! We're going to drown!" 26 He replied, "You of little faith, why are you so afraid?" Then he got up and rebuked the winds and the waves, and it was completely calm. 27 The men were amazed and asked, "What kind of man is this? Even the winds and the waves obey him!" He did it for them; He will do it for you."

You were repeatedly told that you would not amount to anything and have carried that hurt and pain throughout your life. You do not have to live in defeated – declare that it is over. Acts 27:23-24 (KJV), "23 For there stood by me this night the angel of God, whose I am, and whom I serve, 24 Saying, Fear not, …….." God's great restoration is on the way!

The Scripture of The Living God provides you the unshakable peace, well-being, and victory over all things through Christ that strengthens you. When you let Jesus into your heart, He will be you, anchor, when you feel tossed at sea. and the winds and the waves are crashing into you. You will remain steady and unshakeable in the harshest of winds that blow, and you will be able to withstand the storm and the rain. With Jesus as your anchor, nothing can move you until you feel so inclined to move. You become resilient.

You have lost someone near and dear to you. Or, you are living in regret over the years lost to arguments with family, anxiety, depression, sickness, or repeated failures. You are weighed down by your crushed dreams and your hopelessness. You are saying to yourself, "It's over for me!" You see no way out, and you even contemplate suicide. Life has nothing more to offer you.

If that is you, here is a powerful truth: The enemy is at the crooks of your despair, but God is waiting with loving arms for you to call out to Him. Repeat, "Jesus saves." Now cry out and ask Jesus to save you and trust Him by holding on. God can turn things around in your life, and He is willing and able to turn things around for you. God will restore you and set you higher than you have ever been.

Despite what has been taken from you, whether it was a promotion, a love, money, house, car, job, children, it does not matter, God got all your losses covered. No matter what you have lost, according to His Word, you can believe God to redeem all that has been stolen from you: Do you feel as if your health, your relationships, your peace of mind, or your hopes for the future have been "eaten up" by the enemy? God cares, and you have His promise that He will restore even the years you may have lost to addiction, sickness, depression, or financial lack and He will give you double. Zechariah 9:12 (KJV), "Turn you to the stronghold, ye prisoners of hope: even today do I declare [that] I will render double unto thee."

You can always expect God to work wonders in your life and restore you! Know beyond a shadow of a doubt that our Lord Jesus has bought every blessing, including restoration, for you at the cross.

So, do not be afraid if there is an area of your life that is under attack now. You do not have to accept defeat or live in despair. You do not have to be fearful of the future. Instead, you can say, "Lord, restore to me!", knowing that His sacrifice at the cross has qualified you to receive and enjoy His perfect restoration.

Even if you have made some poor decisions, do not feel condemned and lose hope. God not only cares that you have been robbed. He has the power to restore to you much more than what you have lost.

Just look at what Isaiah 61:7 (KJV), declares: [7] For your shame ye shall have double, and for confusion, they shall rejoice in their portion:

therefore in their land, they shall possess the double: everlasting joy shall be unto them."

Doesn't this word just bring so much comfort and hope to your heart? When you put your trust in Him, not only is there no area in your life beyond restoration, but you can trust Him to give to you a restoration greater than what you have lost. Because of His restoration, you can come out of your trial a gainer! Experiencing God's much-more restoration is your blood-bought right in Christ

The scriptural foundation will help set up you in all your rights to restoration and show you how to activate His much-more restoration in your very area of need.

Who Then Can Be Saved?

To be saved means deliverance from the righteous judgment of God through no act of your own but by His unmerited favor. Revelation 7:9 (KJV), "⁹ After this I beheld, and, lo, a great multitude, which no man could number, of all nations, and kindreds, and people, and tongues, stood before the throne, and before the Lamb, clothed with white robes, and palms in their hands."

Fear not, however, Isaiah 11:6 (KJV), "¹ And there shall come forth a rod out of the stem of Jesse, and a Branch shall grow out of his roots: ² And the spirit of the LORD shall rest upon him, the spirit of wisdom and understanding, the spirit of counsel and might, the spirit of knowledge and of the fear of the LORD; ³ And shall make him of quick understanding in the fear of the LORD: and he shall not judge after the sight of his eyes, neither reprove after the hearing of his ears: ⁴ But with righteousness shall he judge the poor, and reprove with equity for the meek of the earth: and he shall smite the earth: with the rod of his mouth, and with the breath of his lips shall he slay the wicked. ⁵ And righteousness shall be the girdle of his loins, and faithfulness the girdle of his reins. ⁶ The wolf also shall dwell with the lamb, and the leopard shall lie down with the kid; and the calf and the young lion and the fatling together, and a little child shall lead them." The Tree of Jesse is describing the descent of Jesus or the depicted in the lineage of Jesus

The Bible says knowledge will increase Daniel 12:4 (KJV), "⁴ But thou, O Daniel, shut up the words, and seal the book, even to the time of the end: many shall run to and fro, and knowledge shall be increased."

The Throne of God is seen in Revelation 4:2-11 (KJV), "² And immediately I was in the spirit: and, behold, a throne was set in heaven, and one sat on the throne. ³ And he that sat was to look upon like a jasper and a sardine stone: and there was a rainbow round about the throne, in sight like unto an emerald." What an amazing vision of God!

Verse "⁴ And round about the throne were four and twenty seats: and upon the seats, I saw four and twenty elders sitting, clothed in white raiment; and they had on their heads crowns of gold." The twenty-four elders surrounding God are Christians from the New Testament church. We do not know who they are, but we do know that they are saints or "holy ones" because they are clothed in white garments. God had promised those who attended two of the seven churches (Sardius and Laodicea) that if they responded to His warnings, they would be clothed in white (Rev. 3:5, 18). The crowns show that God has given these twenty-four elders authority. These elders appear in the book of Revelation throughout the Tribulation.

When the Tribulation ends, they disappear from the heavenly scene because Jesus' kingdom is set up on earth. When the earthly kingdom is established, all Christians will reign with Christ Revelation 20:6 (KJV). "⁶ Blessed and holy is he that hath part in the first resurrection: on such the second death hath no power, but they shall be priests of God and of Christ, and shall reign with him a thousand years." This is the promise that Jesus has given to us (2 Tim. 2:12). This is a wonderful reminder that we are joint-heirs or fellow heirs with Christ (Rom. 8:17). We will share in Jesus' inheritance. Verse "⁵ And out of the throne proceeded lightnings and thunderings and voices: and there were seven lamps of fire burning before the throne, which are the seven Spirits of God." Before God are seven lamps. These lamps stand for the Holy Spirit. Verses 6-8, "⁶ And before the throne there was a sea of glass like unto crystal: and in the midst of the throne, and round about the throne, were four beasts full of eyes before and behind. ⁷ And the first beast was like a lion, and the second beast like a calf and the third beast had a face as a man, and the fourth beast was like a flying eagle. ⁸ And the four beasts had each of them six wings about him, and they were full of eyes within: and they rest not day and night, saying, Holy, holy, holy, LORD God Almighty, which was, and is, and is to come." We know very little about these four living creatures – angels. Cherubim are described in Ezekiel 1:5-25 and in Ezekiel 10:1-22. Cherubim have four wings (Ezekiel 10:8, 20-21) and seraphim have six wings (Isa. 6:2-3). The faces of the four creatures are like the faces of the cherubim, and their wings are like the wings of the seraphim. This is the only place in scripture where the four living creatures appear to be described. Verses 9-11, "⁹ And when those beasts give glory and honor and thanks to him that sat on the throne, who liveth for ever and ever, ¹⁰ The four and twenty elders fall down before him that sat on the throne, and worship him that liveth for ever and ever, and cast their crowns before the throne, saying, ¹¹ Thou art worthy, O Lord, to receive glory and honour and power: for thou hast created all things, and for thy pleasure they are and were created."

John 1: 7-20 (KJV), "⁷ Behold, he cometh with clouds; and every eye shall see him, and they also which pierced him: and all kindreds of the earth shall wail because of him. Even so, Amen. ⁸ I am Alpha and Omega, the beginning, and the ending, saith the Lord, which is, and which was, and which is to come, the Almighty. ⁹ I John, who also am your brother, and companion in tribulation, and in the kingdom and patience of Jesus Christ, was in the isle that is called Patmos, for the word of God, and for the testimony of Jesus Christ. ¹⁰ I was in the Spirit on the Lord's day, and heard behind me a great voice, as of a trumpet, ¹¹ Saying, I am Alpha and Omega, the first and the last: and, What thou seest, write in a book, and send it unto the seven churches which are in Asia; unto Ephesus, and unto Smyrna, and unto Pergamos, and unto Thyatira, and unto Sardis, and unto Philadelphia, and unto Laodicea. ¹² And I turned to see the voice that spake with me. And being turned, I saw seven golden candlesticks; ¹³ And in the midst of the seven candlesticks one like unto the Son of man, clothed with a garment down to the foot, and girt about the paps with a golden girdle. ¹⁴ His head and his hairs were white like wool, as white as snow; and his eyes were as a flame of fire; ¹⁵ And his feet like unto fine brass, as if they burned in a furnace; and his voice as the sound of many waters. ¹⁶ And he had in his right hand seven stars: and out of his mouth went a sharp two-edged sword: and his countenance was as the sun shineth in his strength. ¹⁷ And when I saw him, I fell at his feet as dead. And he laid his right hand upon me, saying unto me, Fear not; I am the first and the last: [18] I am he that liveth, and was dead; and, behold, I am alive for evermore, Amen; and have the keys of hell and of death. [19] Write the things which thou hast seen, and the things which are, and the things which shall be hereafter; [20] The mystery of the seven stars which thou sawest in my right hand, and the seven golden candlesticks. The seven stars are the angels of the seven churches: and the seven candlesticks which thou sawest are the seven churches."

Conclusion

Someday when we come before God, we will finally understand that God loves us.

In bringing a spiritual perspective to issues of the world events and daily life, relying on the word of God is the only reliable source and authority on how to live right, and just, and healthy. Of course, there will always be those who do not believe. And therefore, God provides His position statement in 2 Corinthians 6:14 (KJV), "[14] Be ye not unequally yoked together with unbelievers: for what fellowship hath righteousness with unrighteousness? and what communion hath light with darkness?"

Let us not forget that Satan, the prince of darkness, is at the heart of all your biases and burdens and He blocks your blessings. Satan is not that repulsive red creature many of you imagine with horns, tail, and carrying a pitchfork - the typical image of Satan that many people have. In fact, this is a very dangerous misrepresentation and can prevent people from seeing the roaring lion at work. The Bible paints an image of Satan for you in Ezekiel 28:12-19 (KJV) "[12] Son of man, take up a lamentation upon the king of Tyrus and say unto him, Thus saith the Lord GOD; Thou sealest up the sum, full of wisdom, and perfect in beauty. [13] Thou hast been in Eden the garden of God; every precious stone was thy covering, the sardius, topaz, and the diamond, the beryl, the onyx, and the jasper, the sapphire, the emerald, and the carbuncle, and gold: the workmanship of thy tabrets and of thy pipes was prepared in thee in the day that thou wast created. [14] Thou art the anointed cherub that covereth; and I have set thee so: thou wast upon the holy mountain of God; thou hast walked up and down in the midst of the stones of fire. [15] Thou wast perfect in thy ways from the day that thou wast created, till iniquity was found in thee. [16] By the multitude of thy merchandise, they have filled the midst of thee with violence, and thou hast sinned: therefore I will cast thee as profane out of the mountain of God: and I will destroy thee, O covering cherub, from the midst of the stones of fire. [17] Thine heart was lifted up because of thy beauty; thou hast corrupted thy wisdom by reason of thy brightness: I will cast thee to the ground, I will lay thee before kings, that they may behold thee. [18] Thou hast defiled thy sanctuaries by the multitude of thine iniquities, by the iniquity of thy traffick; therefore will I bring forth a fire from the midst of thee, it shall devour thee, and I will bring thee to ashes upon the earth in the sight of all them that behold thee. [19] All they that know thee among the people shall be astonished at thee: thou shalt be a terror, and never shalt thou be any more." After reading this, you see man's image of Satan is further from the truth of God's painted image of him. Satan was, in fact, an anointed cherub who sat in heaven in an exalted position. God created him, and he was a "seal of perfection."

When we can see Satan for who he is, we can see him in the new technology which has become part of our daily lives. You can see him in the technology in our vehicles, our homes, on our clothes, built into our travel bags. Once Christians use to faithfully drive in their cars and listen to Christian music on their radios, now they are checking social media to see what is happening and where they can go to have fun. Technology is replaced their cares to be holy to be happy. Also, these days techs that have become part of Christians personal relationship with God. Satan has infiltrated churches and replaced the traditional Bible book with technology. Christians have taken technology from being at arm's length on the home computer and bring it into church using tablets and smartphones. This may seem convenient, but it is how Satan has control over how much time you spend listening to God as he distracts and detracts from God's words. Technology consumes Christians, they are spending less time paying attention to the sermon that is being preached, and to hear God's words, more spending more time on the technology being mesmerized by what is happening out in the world. Satan has even cleverly designed a "memory mirror" that remembers everything you do when you stand in front of it, gone are the days of just seeing just your reflection in the old mirror that has existed for thousands of years. But to God, you are the same person he knew before you were born, that will never change.

However, the shame of your biases burdens you and causes you to attempt often to go it alone. You overestimate your ability, and even when you recognize you need God, you continue to underestimate the weight of your struggles and are determined to carry your burdens by yourself.

Pride does go before the fall, and soon you find that you are adding insult to injury when you forget Christ's willingness to carry you on His shoulders. Instead, many people are choosing the world which is under the direct control of Satan, instead of the Word and submitting to the will of God.

Still, it is God who has given Satan free reign over the earth to do as he pleases. Jesus calls Satan, *"the ruler of this world."* John 12:31 (KJV) *"31 Now is the judgment of this world: now shall the prince of this world be cast out."* The Apostle Paul calls him *"the god of this world."* 2 Corinthians 4:4. However, this is God's plan to provide proof of the deceitfulness of sin, and that following Satan's way will lead to death and destruction.

Therefore, despite your biases and your burdens, your blessings far outweigh anything negative that may deter you in your Christian journey. Arguing from the standpoint that Christ bore your most significant responsibility and pressing priority (your sin and its penalty) and continues to bear every other burden you have. There are many burdens you are not meant to bear alone. You cannot. The cross, the crown, and the drops of blood at Gethsemane serve as a reminder to you of this. Christ continues to hold the weight of the world upon His shoulders and carries all of your worries. Lamentations 3:19–24 (KJV), *"19 Remembering mine affliction and my misery, the wormwood, and the gall. 20 My soul hath them still in remembrance and is humbled in me. 21 This I recall to my mind; therefore, have I hope. 22 It is of the LORD's mercies that you are not consumed because his compassions fail not.*

[23] They are new every morning: great is thy faithfulness. [4] The LORD is my portion, saith my soul; therefore, will I hope in him."

Take up the whole armor of God, that you may be able to withstand Satan. Ephesians 6:10-17 (KJV), "[10] Finally, my brethren, be strong in the Lord, and in the power of his might. [11] Put on the whole armor of God, that ye may be able to stand against the wiles of the devil. [12] For we wrestle not against flesh and blood, but against principalities, against powers, against the rulers of the darkness of this world, against spiritual wickedness in high places. [13] Wherefore take unto you the whole armor of God, that ye may be able to withstand in the evil day, and having done all, to stand. [14] Stand therefore, having your loins girt about with truth, and having on the breastplate of righteousness; [15] And your feet shod with the preparation of the gospel of peace; [16] Above all, taking the shield of faith, wherewith ye shall be able to quench all the fiery darts of the wicked. [17] And take the helmet of salvation, and the sword of the Spirit, which is the word of God."

Turn to the back of your Bible, and you will see that all your bias and burdens, your trial and tribulation ends with your final blessing, the joy of knowing that in the end, "God wins."

References

Unless otherwise indicated, All Scripture quotations are from the King James Version®. KJV® Bible, Public Domain.

For more information about Bev Gilliard,
please visit www.bevgilliard.com

58028112R00146

Made in the USA
Columbia, SC
18 May 2019